# Ashland Huntington, Ironton and Portsmouth

## THROUGH TIME

TERRY L. BALDRIDGE

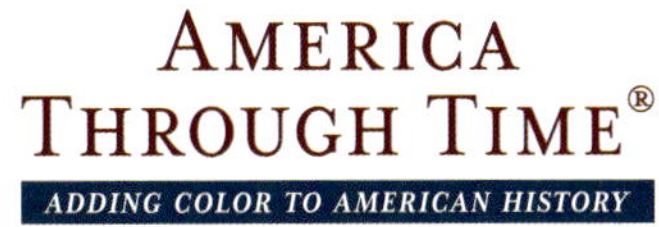

# Dedication

I would like to thank my many friends and family that have assisted me so kindly as I worked on this project. I would like to thank the cities of Ashland, Catlettsburg, Greenup, Huntington, Ironton, Portsmouth, and Russell. I would also like to thank James Powers, the Boyd County Public Library, the Greenup County Public Library, Portsmouth Library, and the Greenup County Kentucky History Site on Facebook for their help with researching information contained herein. No project is ever possible without my wife, Heather, and son, Keenan's help.

America Through Time is an imprint of Fonthill Media LLC

First published 2016



ISBN 978-1-62545-043-2



Typeset in Mrs Eaves XL Serif Narrow

Published by Arcadia Publishing by arrangement with Fonthill Media LLC
For all general information, please contact Arcadia Publishing:
Telephone: 843-853-2070
Fax: 843-853-0044
E-mail: sales@arcadiapublishing.com
For customer service and orders:
Toll-Free 1-888-313-2665

Visit us on the internet at www.arcadiapublishing.com

Printed and bound by CPI Group (UK) Ltd, Croydon, CR0 4YY

# Introduction

From the Guyandotte River Valley in western West Virginia to the Scioto River Valley in south central Ohio, the people share common denominators; the Ohio River, railroads, iron, and blood lines. In many instances the people of the area look at the river cities of Kentucky, Ohio, and West Virginia as not belonging to a particular state as much as belonging to the beautiful Ohio Valley. During the morning rush hours, commuters will pass on their way from their homes to their job in a different city, county, and/or state.

Huntington, West Virginia is the largest city in the Kentucky, Ohio, and West Virginia metropolitan area. As of the writing of this book the population hovered around 50,000.

For many decades in its early history travelers simply knew the city as a layover during their journey westward by river or rail. From those humble beginnings until today, the people that stay are rewarded with a mixture of Appalachian foothills and the twists and turns of the Ohio River.

The tri-state area was first explored by Captain Celeron de Bienvillea and his group in 1749. Several decades later the area was granted as payment to veterans of the French and Indian War. George Washington owned thousands of acres near the area.

Around 1869, railroad entrepreneur Collis P. Huntington envisioned his Chesapeake and Ohio Railway coming to the area. This would intertwine his railway holding with his river barge holding. Two years later in honor of the railroader, the name Huntington was born.

Ashland, the largest city in eastern Kentucky, is located in Boyd County. It was first incorporated by an act of the legislature in 1856. At that time it was located in Greenup County.

Before taking the Ashland name from the estate of famed Kentucky Congressman, Henry Clay, the area was known as Poage Settlement. The Poage family patriarch, George Poage purchased 5,000 acres of land from Gen. James Wilkinson.

The area was rich in iron and coal, therefore drawing various industries to this part of Kentucky. Transporting the iron and coal was big business and Ashland served as a center point of river and rail transportation. The Lexington and Big Sandy Railroad was one of the first railroads to make a hub in Ashland. The railroad sold all of its holdings in the 1920s to the C&O Railway where it continues under the CSX name in the area as of the writing of this book.

The lumber industry flourished in the Ashland area until the early 1900s. It was at this time that many of these northern foothills of the Appalachia were completely stripped of their tree growth.

In 1981 it became legal to sell liquor in downtown Ashland. The Simeon Willis Memorial Bridge opened in May 1985, followed by the Ashland Plaza Hotel in September 1985. The business district extended west to the $42 million Ashland Town Center shopping mall in 1989.

As of the writing of this book, Ironton Ohio's population is at the 11,000 mark. This is just under 1 percent decline from 10 years earlier. Even though the iron jobs have left the city, what hasn't exited is the extreme pride the peoples have of their Ironton heritage.

The city was founded was founded by iron entrepreneur, John Campbell in 1849. It was Campbell and his associates that labored and spent great sums of money to have the Lawrence county seat moved from Burlington (several miles east) to Ironton. Thus Ironton became the center of the Hanging Rock Iron Region of northeast Kentucky and south-central Ohio.

Ironton was one of the northern Underground Railroad, safe havens for enslaved African Americans. Many city notables, including John Campbell, hid these men, women, and children in their homes and in secret hidden places throughout the area.

Ironton was home to one of the very first semi-professional football teams in the world. They were called the Ironton Tanks. They began play in 1919 and disbanded in 1930 with impressive records over several NFL teams including the Chicago Bears and New York Giants.

The oldest city in the area is Portsmouth Ohio. The old Indian village known as Shannoah Town or Shawnee Town was located where western Portsmouth meets the Scioto River. By the late 1790s, the area was called Alexandria, after the holder of the patent Alexander Parker.

Because of the numerous floods that plagued the area yearly the town was moved out of the flood plain by Henry Massie. It was there in 1803 that he began to map out streets and selling off plots of land to homesteaders and businesses. It was at this time the city began to be called Portsmouth.

As is the case with the other river cities, Portsmouth has seen a decline in industry and population. But the past is ever present in the dreams that once again the city can attract both small and large businesses.

Portsmouth also hosted a professional football team; the Portsmouth Spartans played in the semi-pro and NFL ranks. Drawing such notable alumni as Jim Thorpe. The team moved to Detroit in 1934 and was renamed, the Detroit Lions.

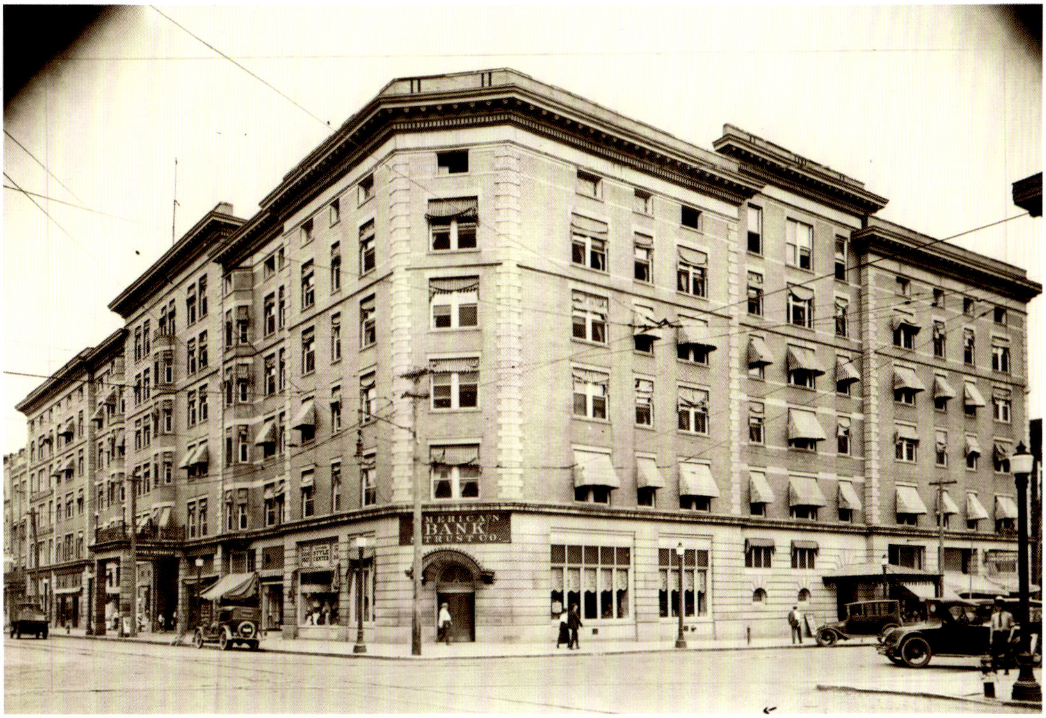

DOWNTOWN HOTEL: The Frederick Hotel Building, photographed in the early 1930s from the northeast corner of Forth Avenue and Eleventh Street has changed very little when compared to the modern color photograph. Many businesses have made the lower floors home over the years.

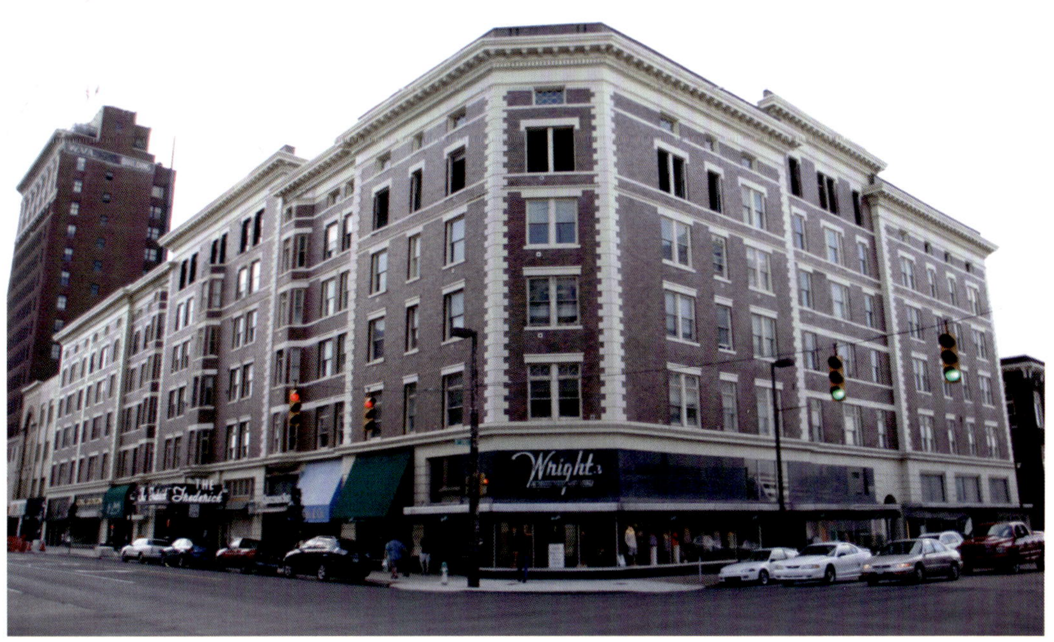

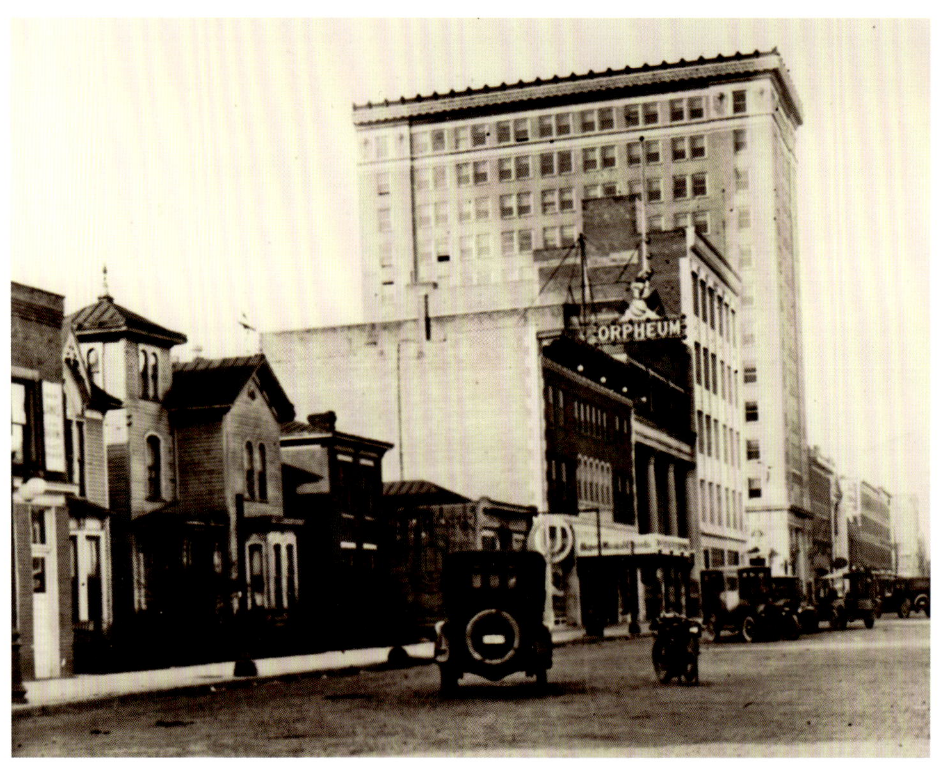


THE ORPHEUM THEATER: this theater hosted many vaudeville acts and silent pictures in its early days. The older photograph from around 1920 shows the Orpheum Theater during its heyday with the original St. James building in the background.

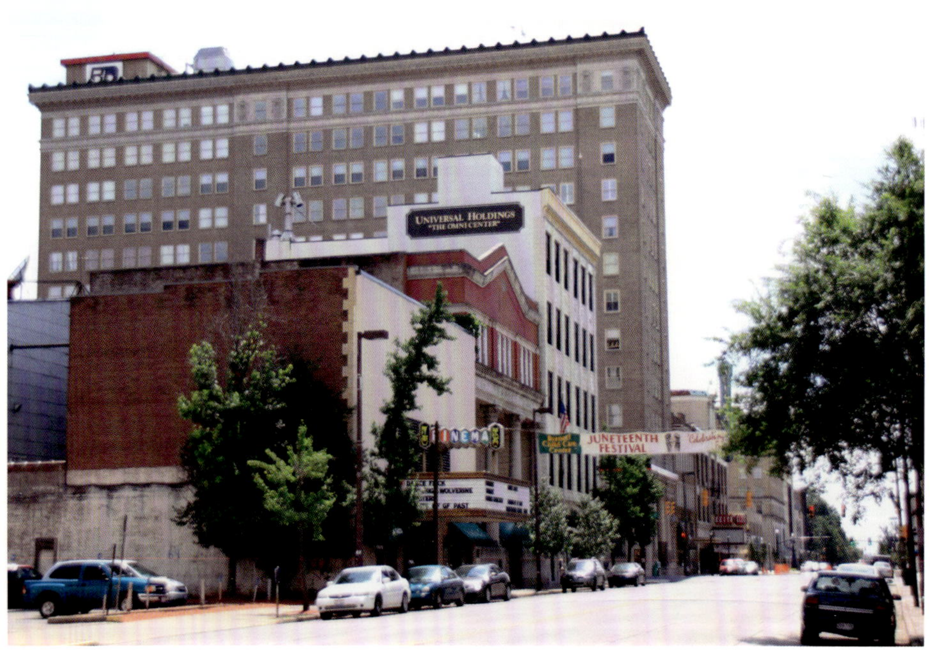

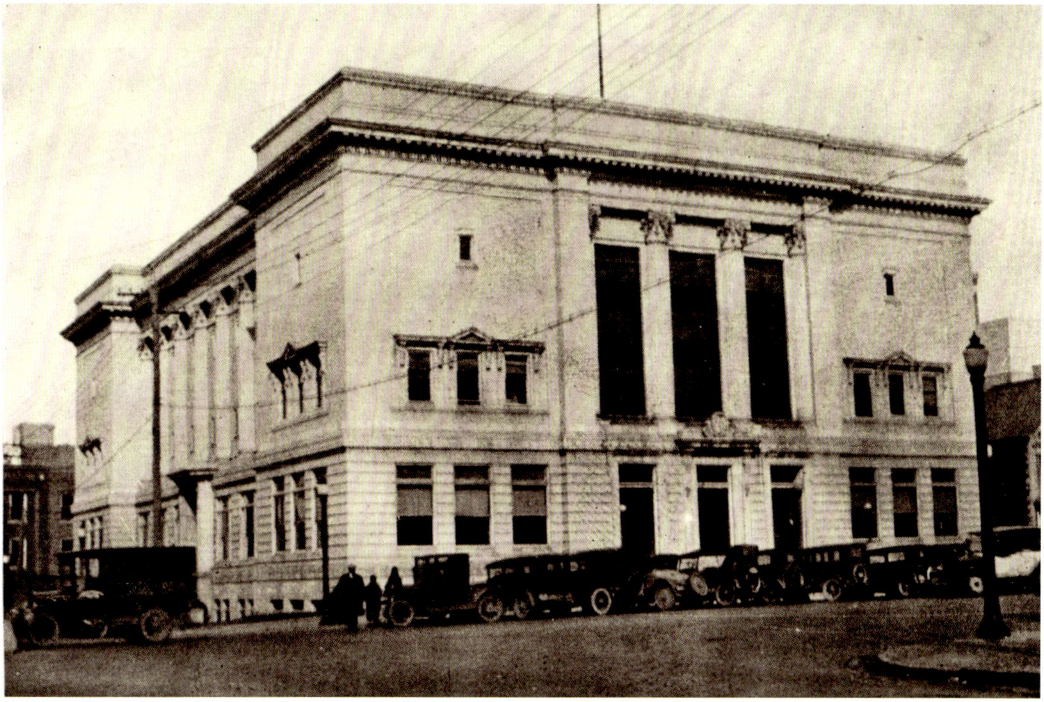

HUNTINGTON CITY HALL: The hall stands unmovable like the Parthenon. The older photograph is from around 1930 and shows that the classical structure has undergone very few external changes over the years. The entrances are reminiscent of structures designed by classical student and third president, Thomas Jefferson.

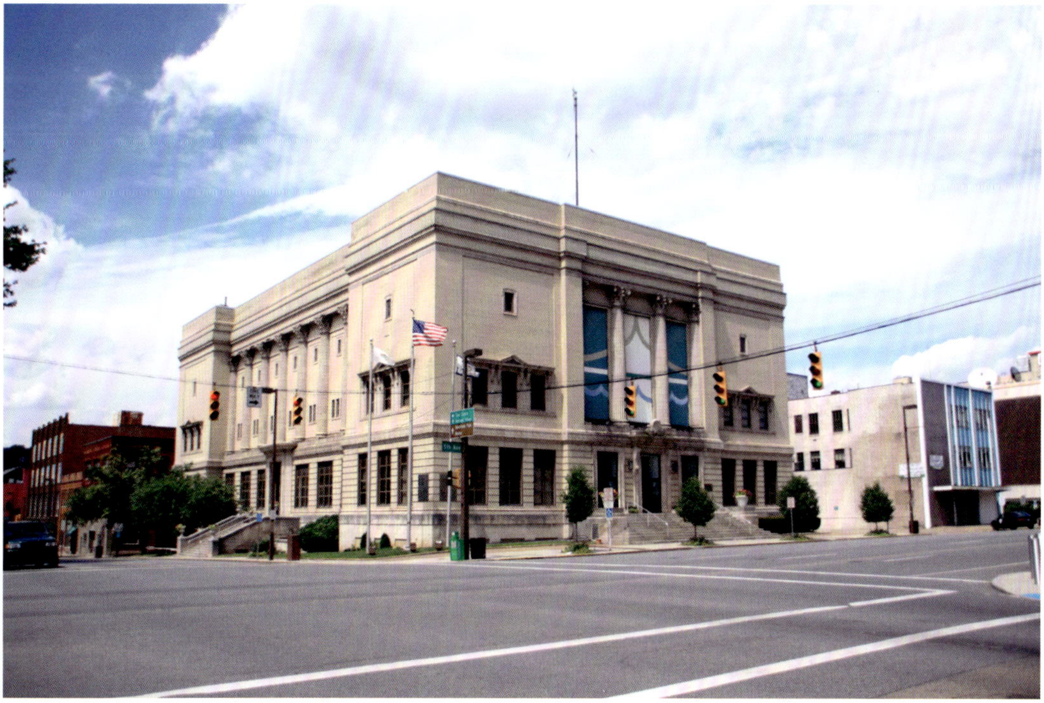

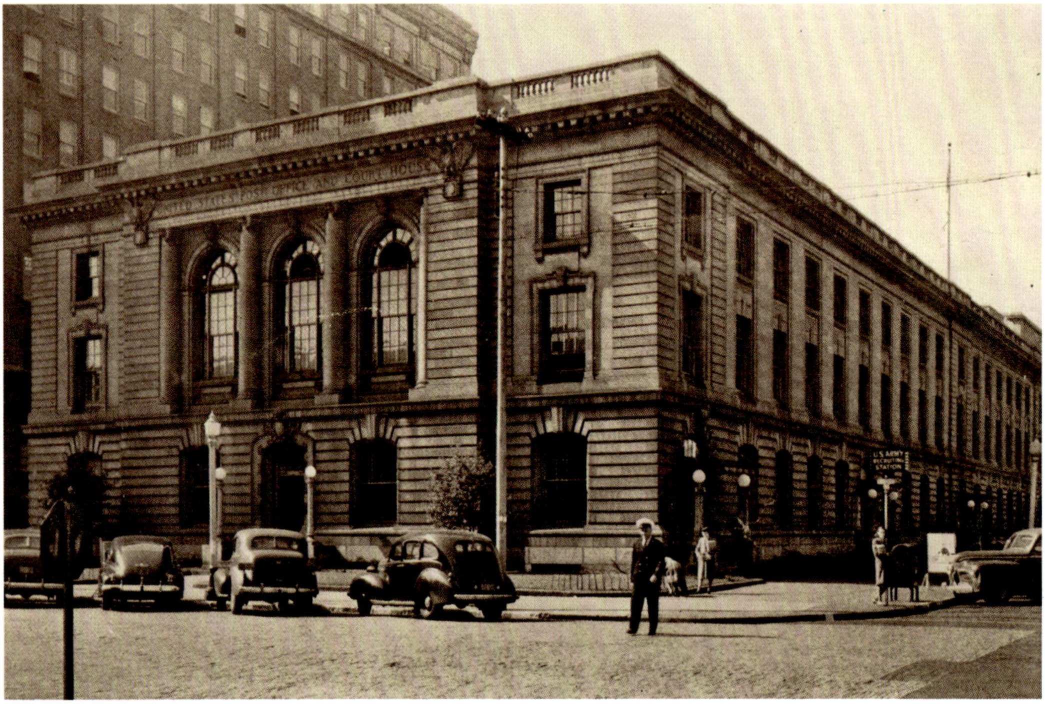

**THE POST OFFICE:** These photographs of the old U.S. Post Office and courthouse dates from the 1940s and the year before publication of this book. The only discernable changes in the photographs are of the vehicles. Notice the Guaranty Bank and Trust building in the background. The two structures have been decades long companions.

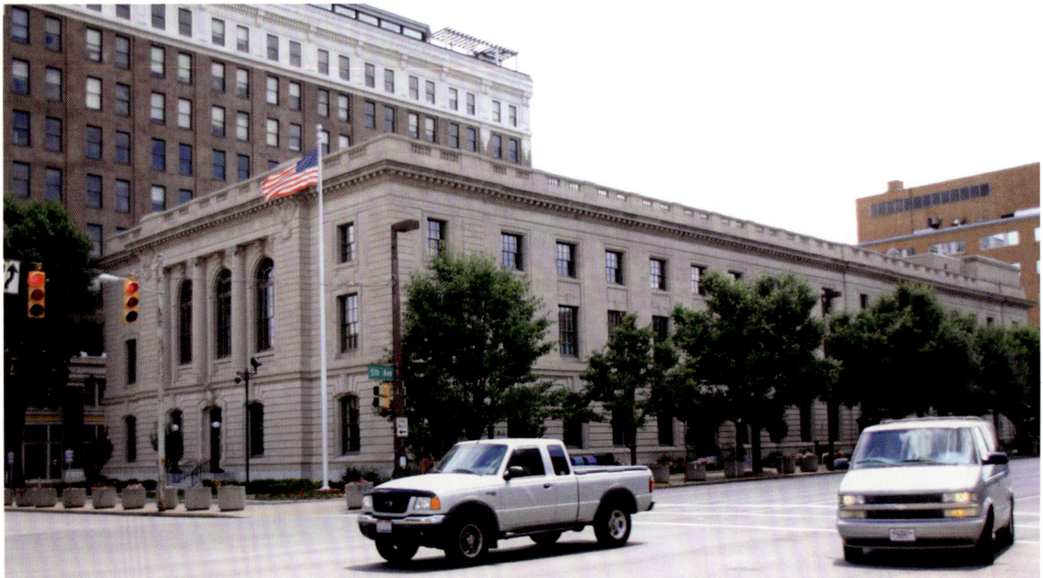

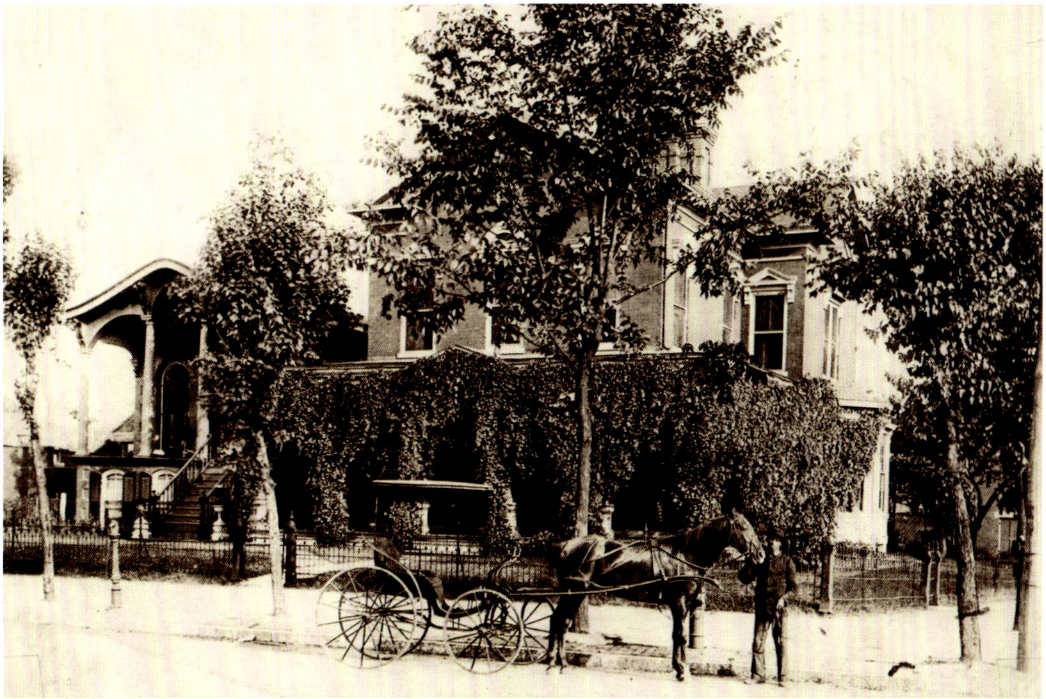

THE HARVEY AND ENSLOW HOMES: Built in 1874 and occupied for a time by economist and 1932 presidential candidate William "Coin" Harvey, this beautiful home of Third Avenue is a window to Huntington's post-Civil War past. The Enslow home is to the right of the "Coin" Harvey home in the older photograph dating from 1892.

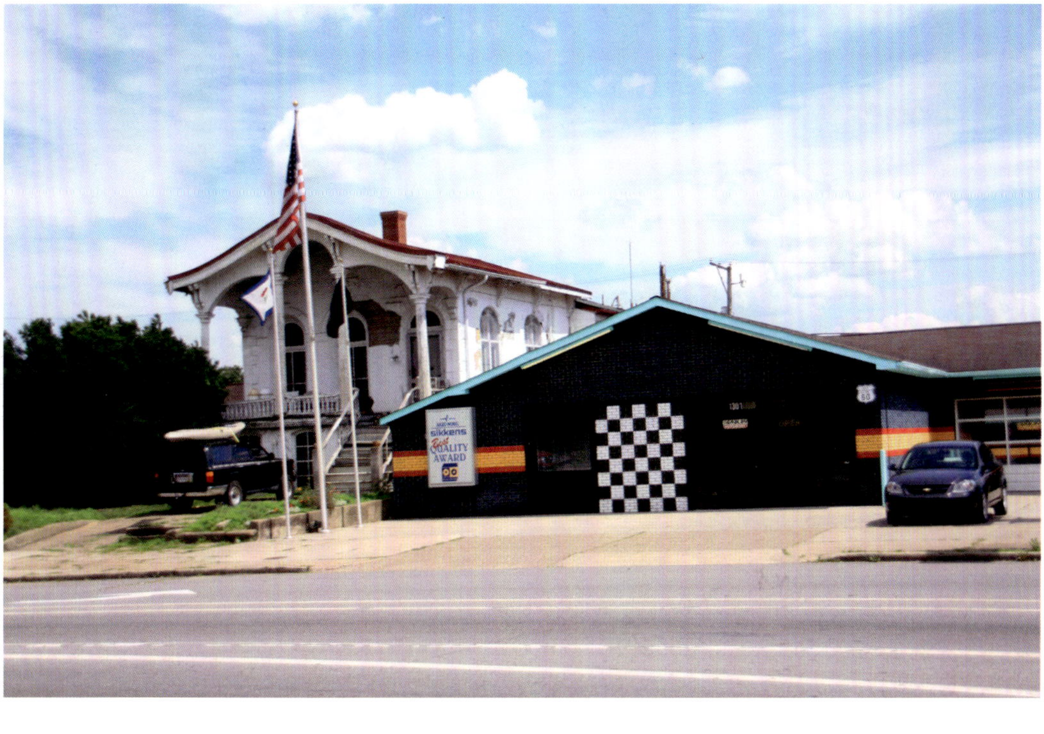

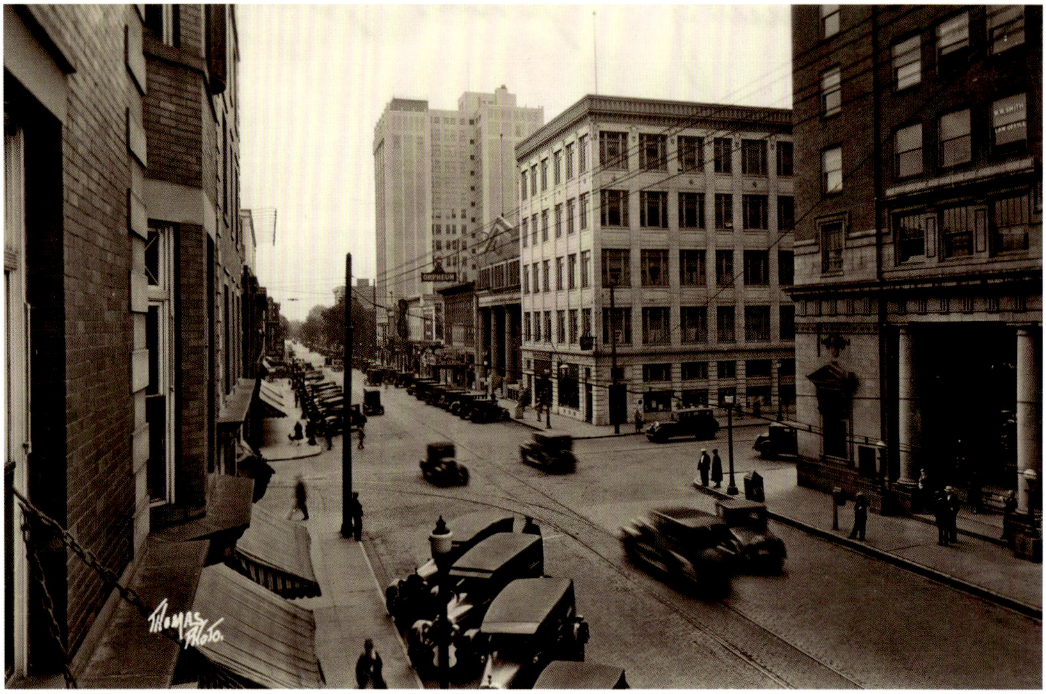

THE KEITH ALBEE THEATER: The older photograph taken in 1932 by Thomas Studios from the second floor of the Frederick Building just across Fourth Avenue from the Keith Albee Theater. The photographer was looking east at the intersection of Forth Avenue and Tenth Street at the base of the St. James Building to the right.

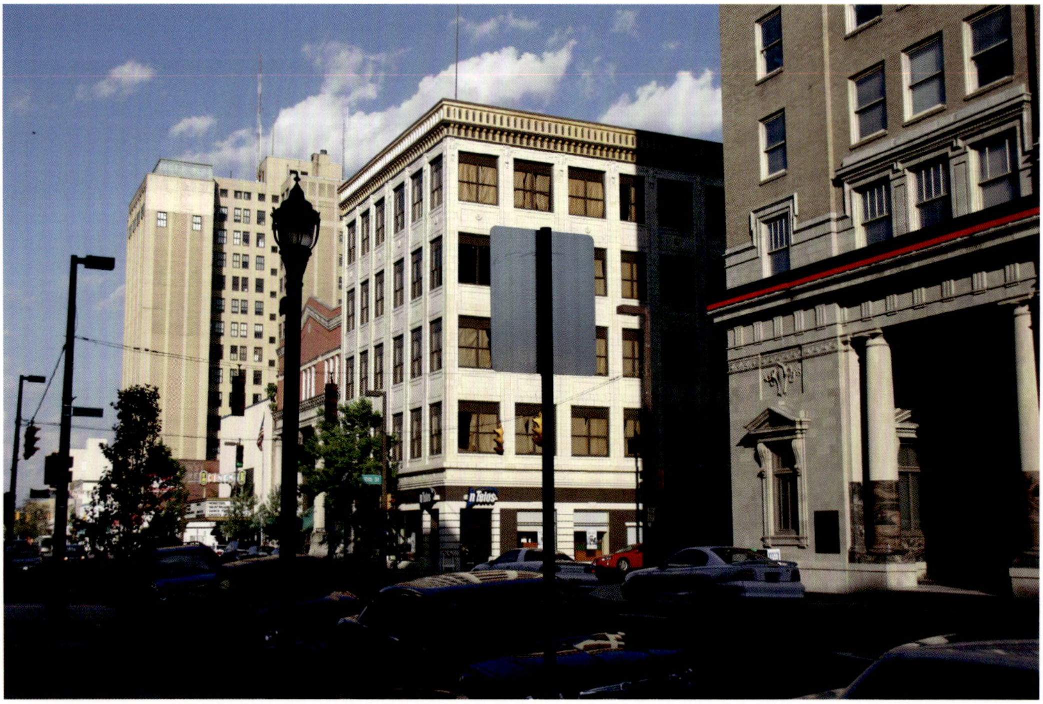

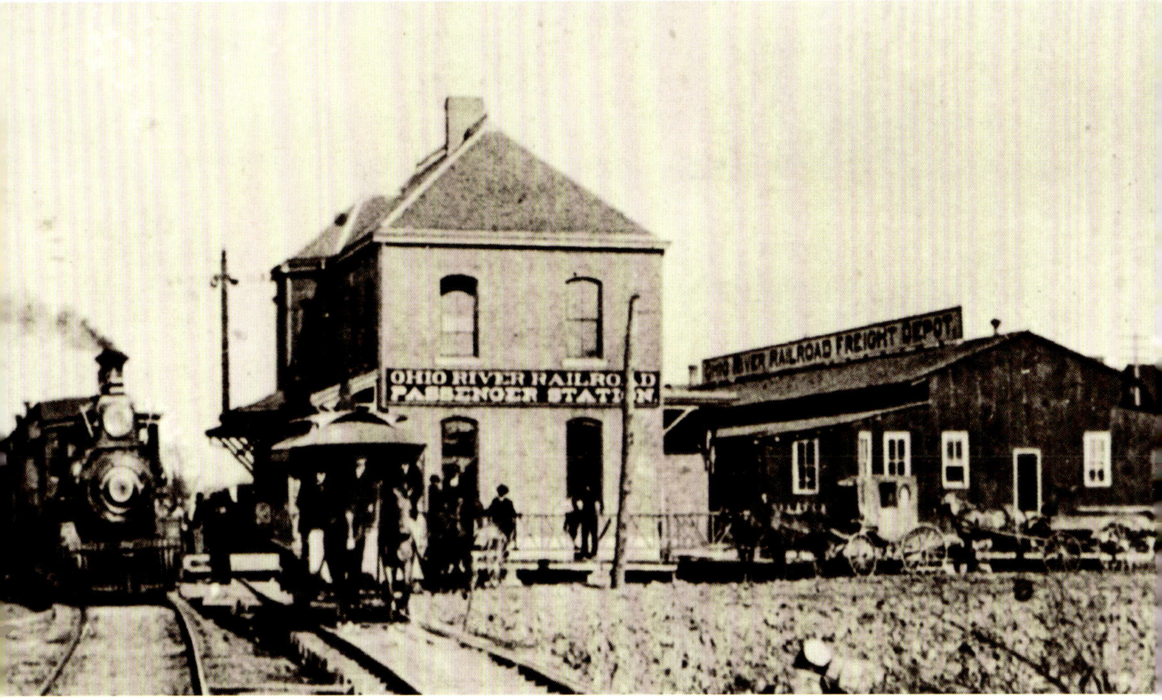

THE BALTIMORE AND OHIO: Photographed from around 1895 is the Baltimore and Ohio (B&O) passenger station, which was built in 1892 by the Ohio River Railroad. Today known locally as Heritage Station, which includes the Huntington National Bank, possibly robbed by famed criminal, Jesse James. Also on the property are several specialty shops as well as a fine dining establishment.

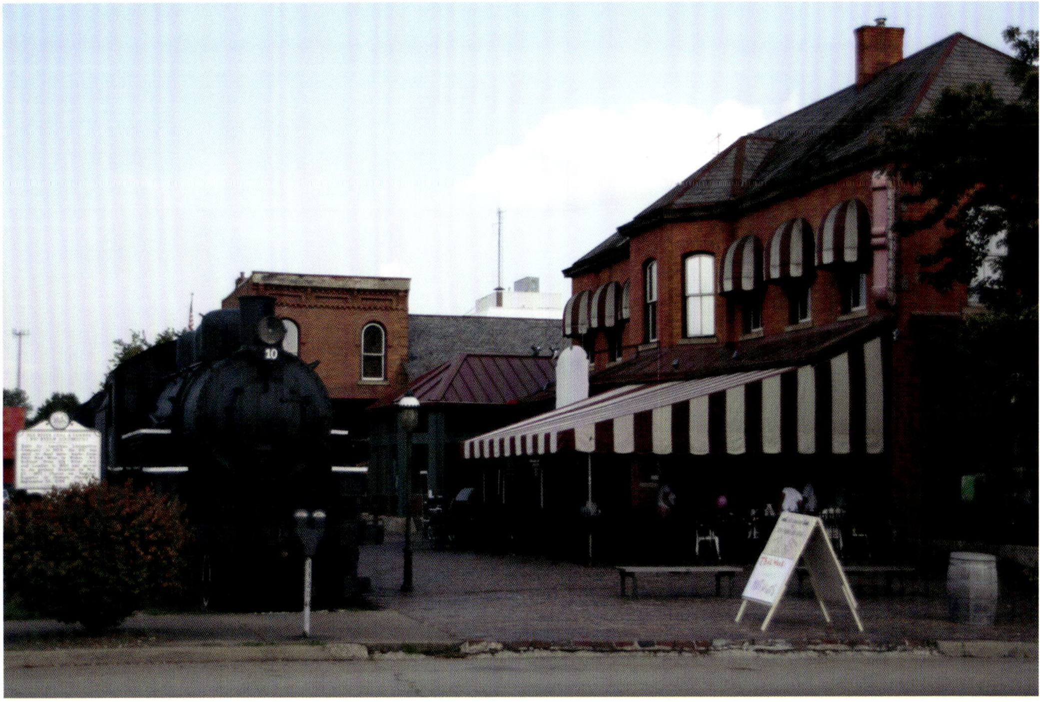

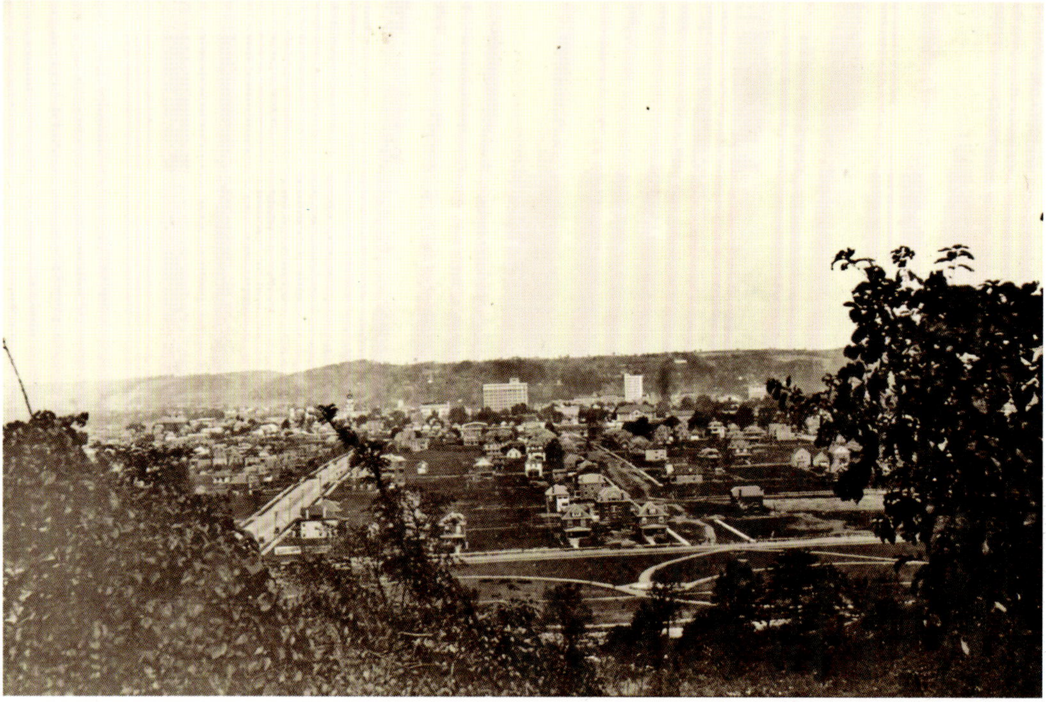

**HUNTINGTON FROM THE HILLS:** The older photograph shows Huntington from the hills above Ritter Park around 1920. Note how sparse the neighborhood is between Eighth Street and Ninth Street and how small the trees are around the park. Much has changed throughout the years when viewing Huntington from above.

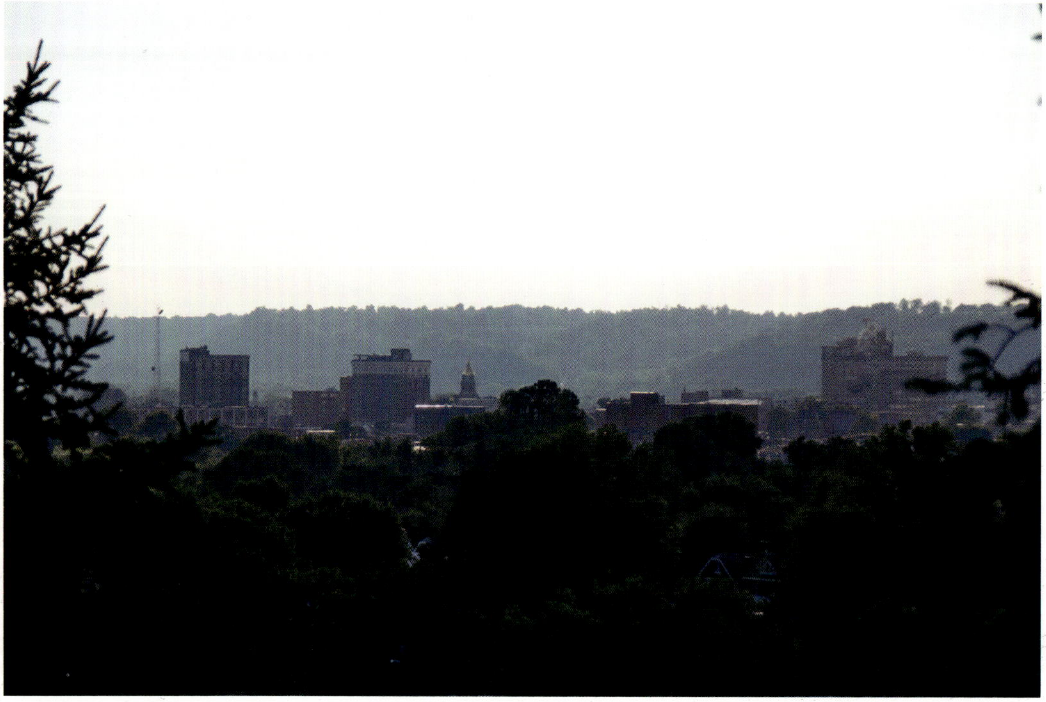

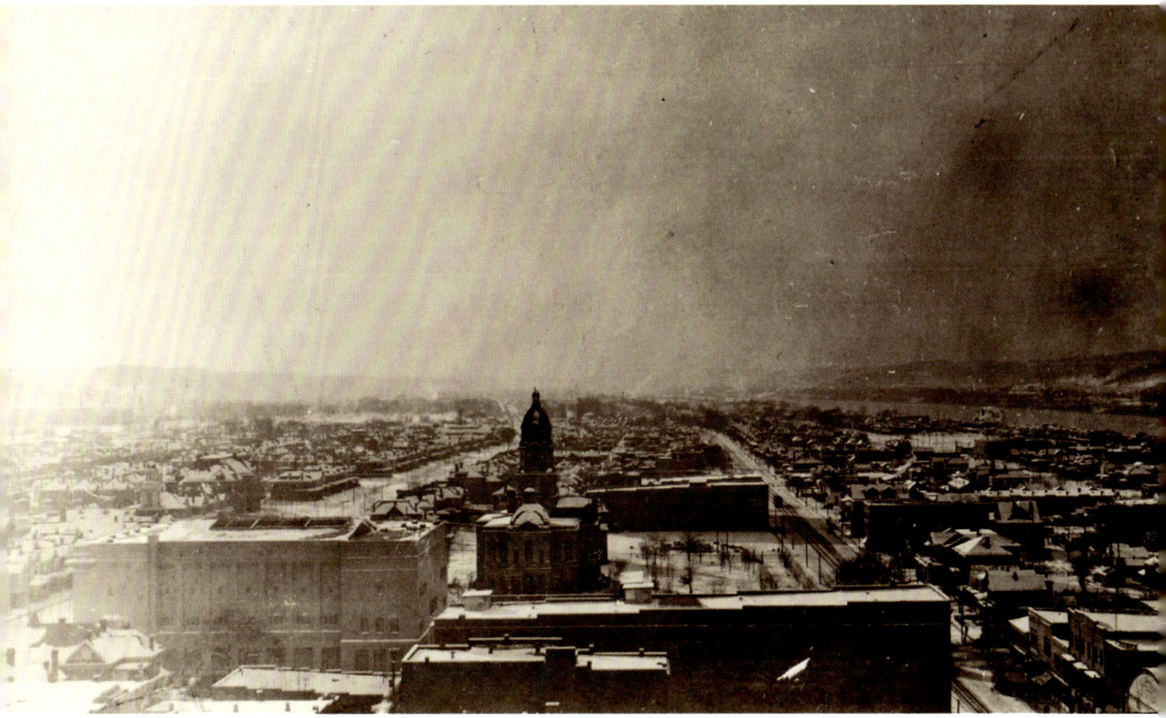

LOOKING EASTWARDS BETWEEN FOURTH AVENUE AND FIFTH AVENUES: The older photograph dates from 1915 and shows a lone streetcar running between Seventh and Sixth Streets. Located in the same area today on Fourth Avenue and Sixth Street is the Department of Veterans Affairs Regional Office.

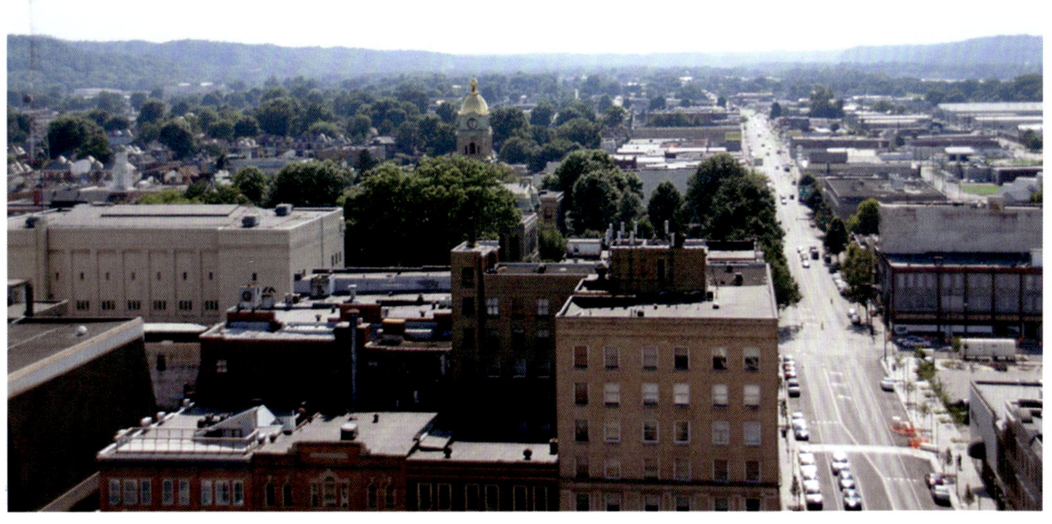

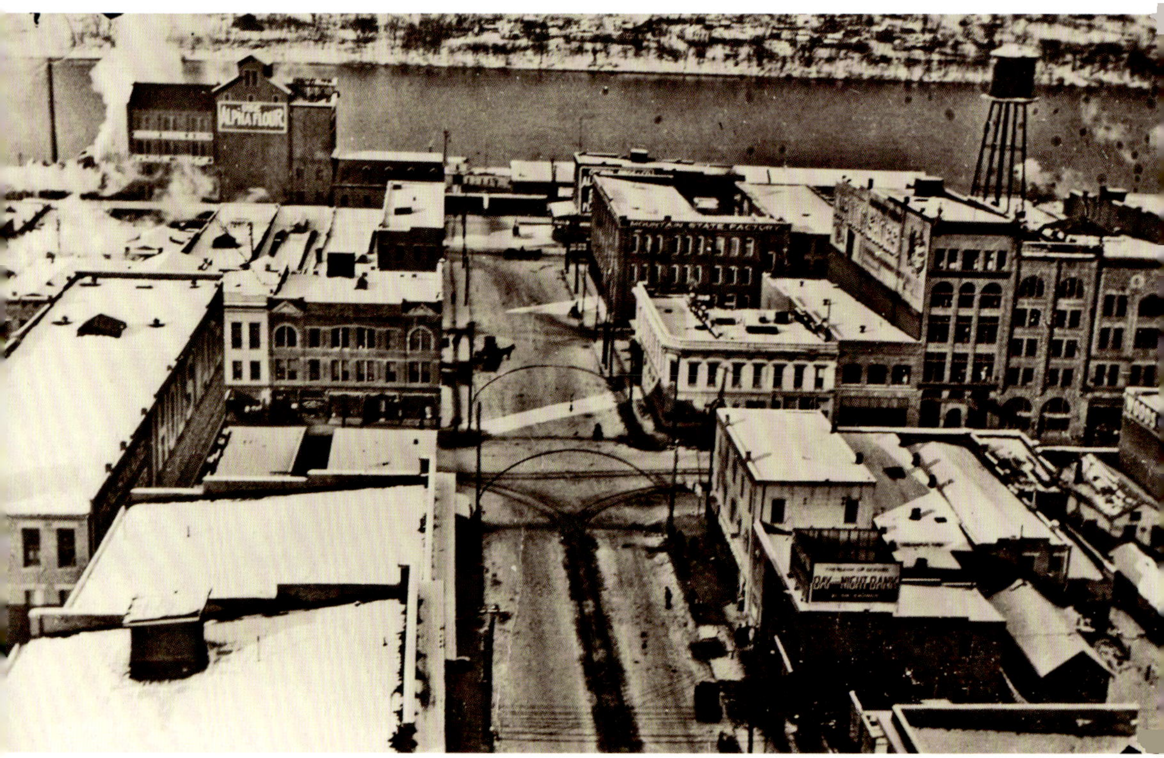

HUNTINGTON HORSE POWER: A couple of horse-drawn wagons move along snow covered Tenth Street around 1915. A large 'Use Alpha Four" advertisement is on the south side of the old six-story mill. To the right, where Red Lobster is located as of the writing of this book, is the three-story Mountain State Factory building.

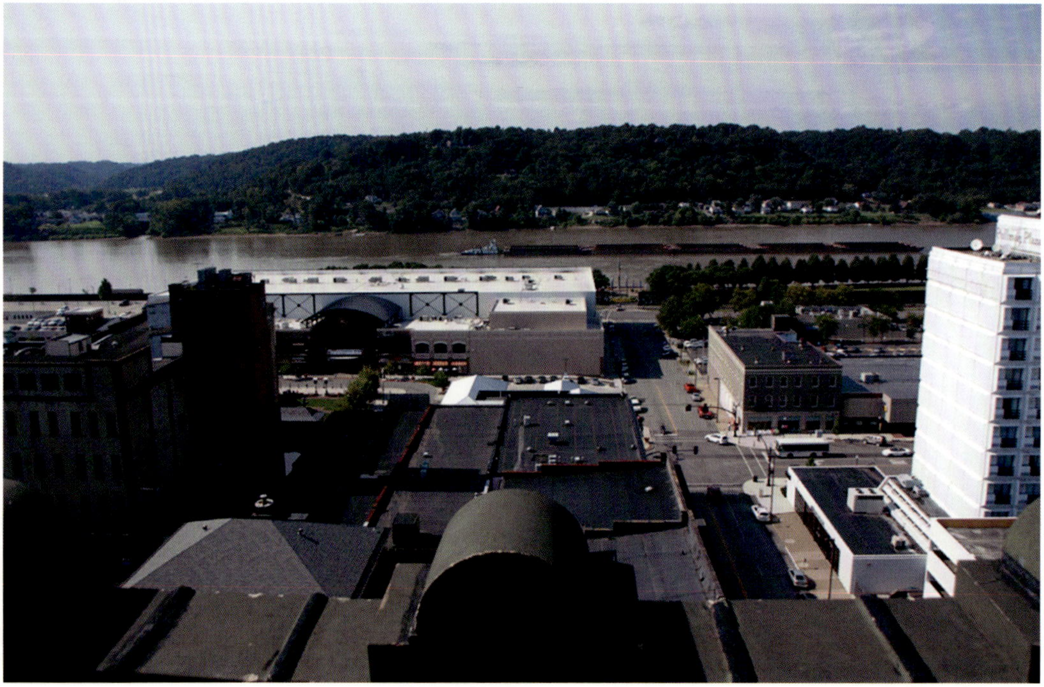

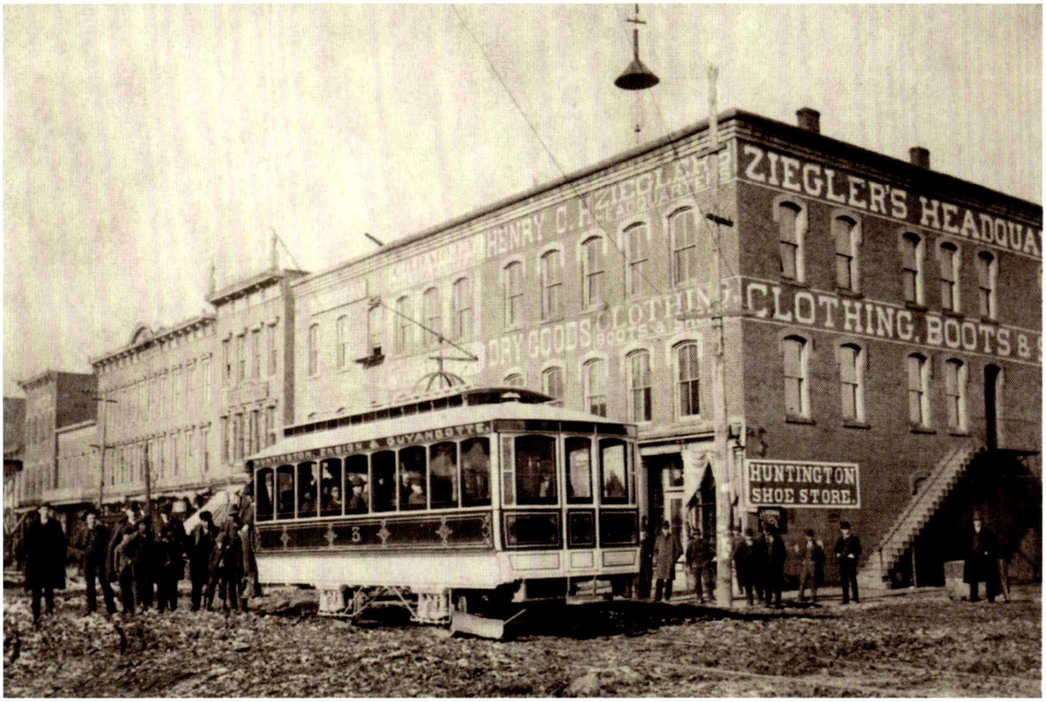

THE FIRST ELECTRIC TROLLEY: Pictured is Huntington's first electric trolley, which ran through town to Guyandotte and back several times a day. It was able to remain on schedule, whereas the road conditions made other methods of travel laborious and slow. Notice the terrible condition of the streets in the 1880s in downtown Huntington.

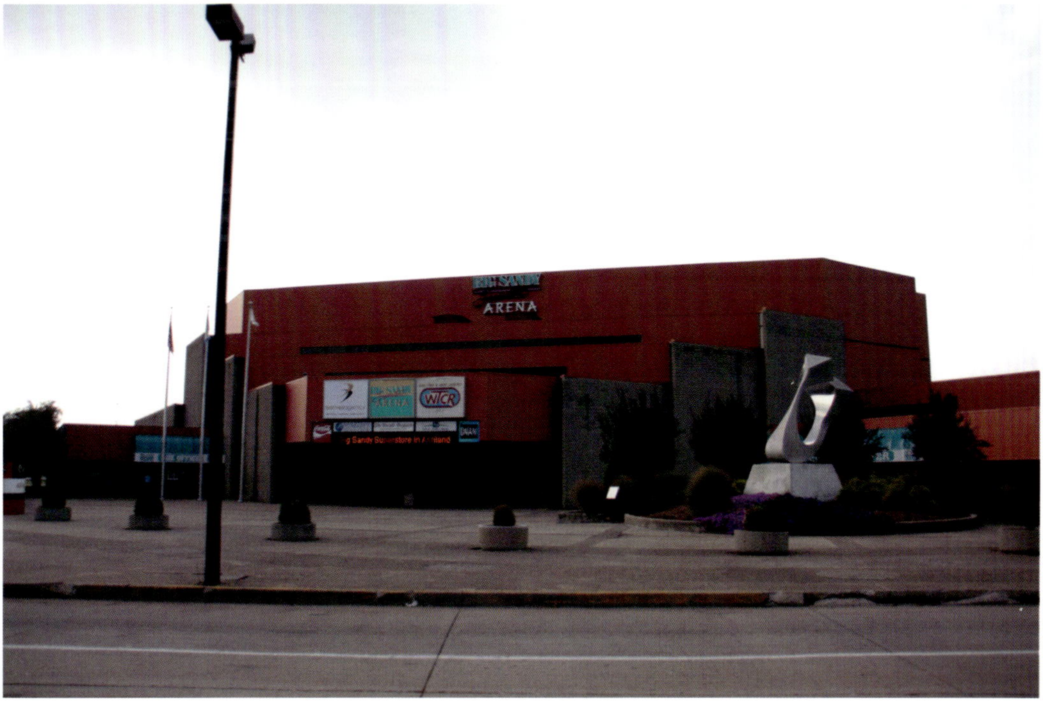

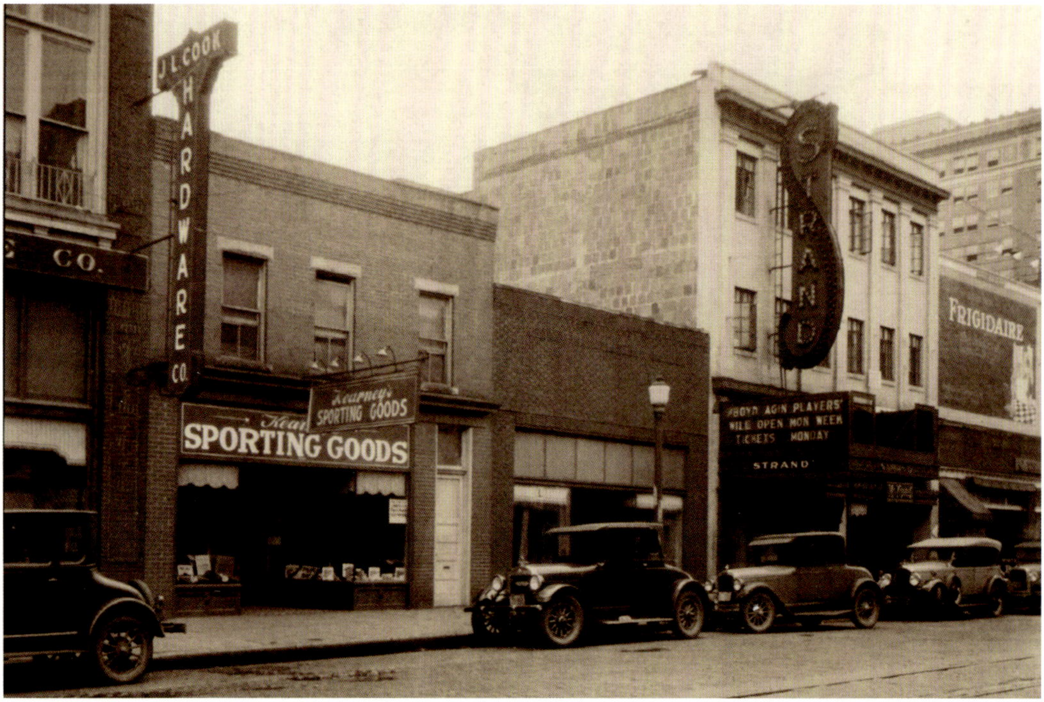

BUSINESSES BETWEEN TENTH AND ELEVENTH: Shown in this image from 1931 are several businesses between Tenth and Eleventh Streets on Fourth Avenue; J. L. Cook Hardware Company, Kearney's Sporting Goods, and the Strand. Today, looking west from near the same location, several Huntington landmarks can be viewed.

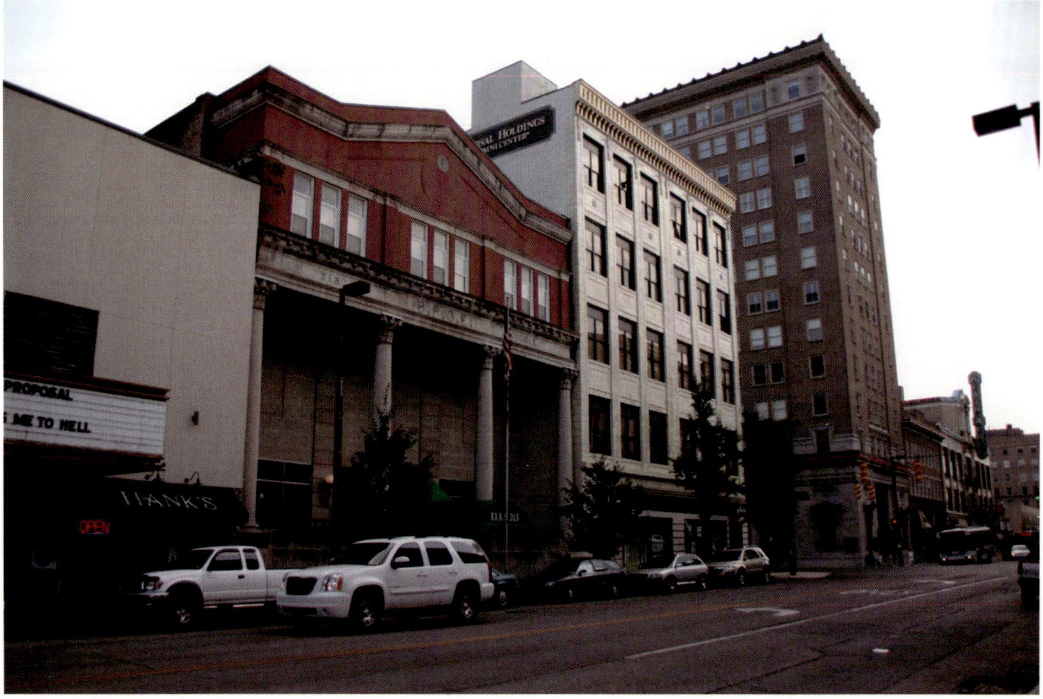

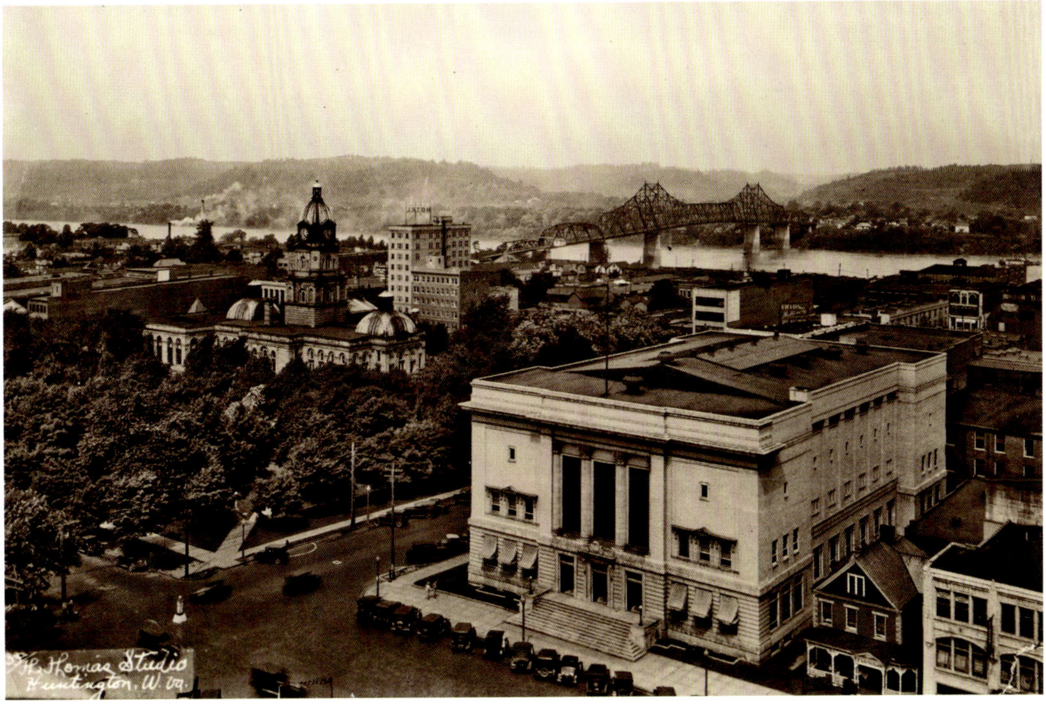

THE COURTHOUSE CLOCK TOWER: The older photograph dating from the early 1930s was taken from the rooftop of the Chaffin Building. The familiar Cabell County Courthouse Clock Tower and Huntington City Hall have changed very little. The courthouse has been extended and a gold covering added to the dome of the clock tower.

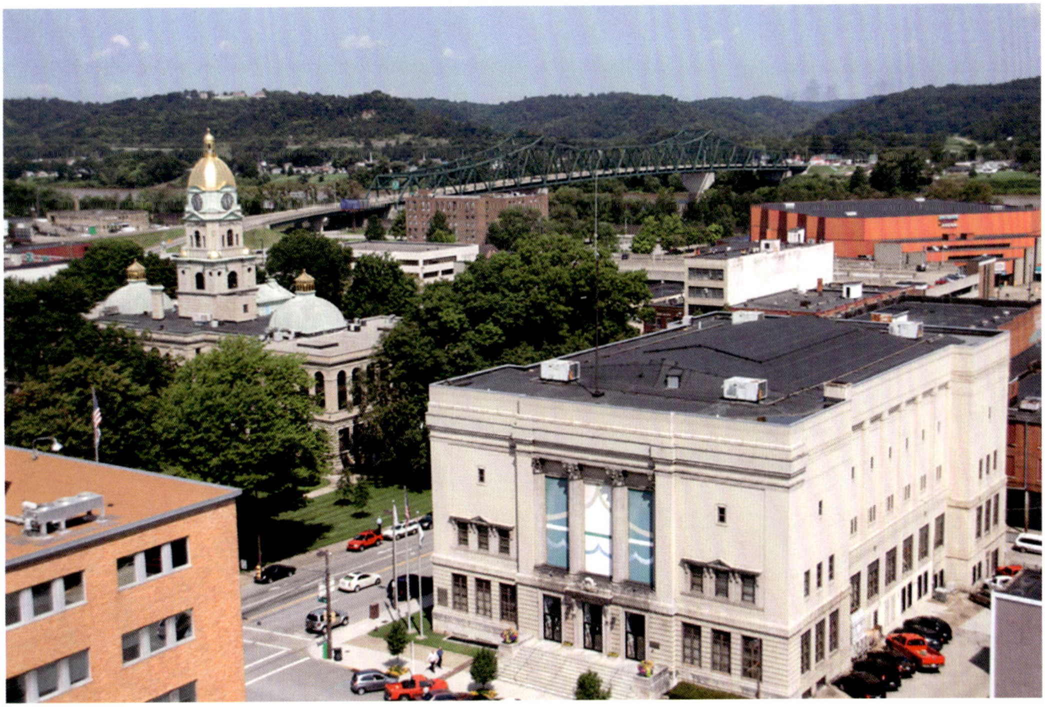

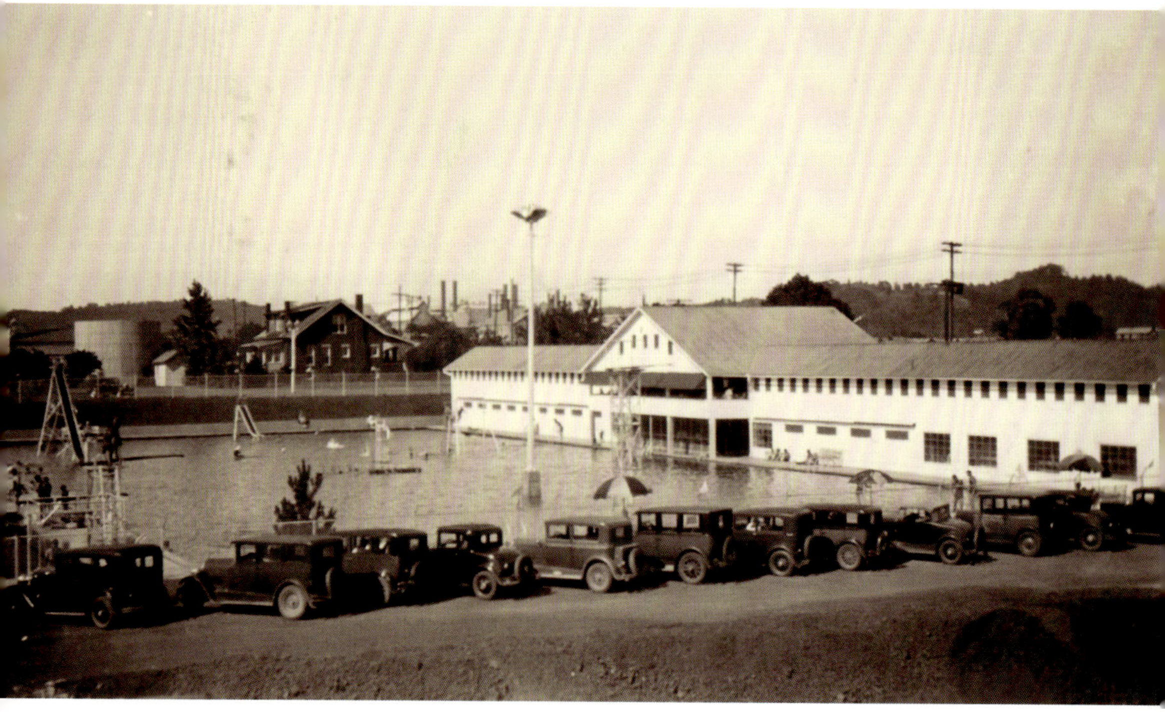

DREAMLAND: For many decades since the 1930s the locals have taken advantage of one of the largest pools in the area, Dreamland. During the pool's heyday, many big band acts would perform for swimmers and for couples picnicking on the surrounding grassy areas. The pool continues to cool the throngs who visit every summer.

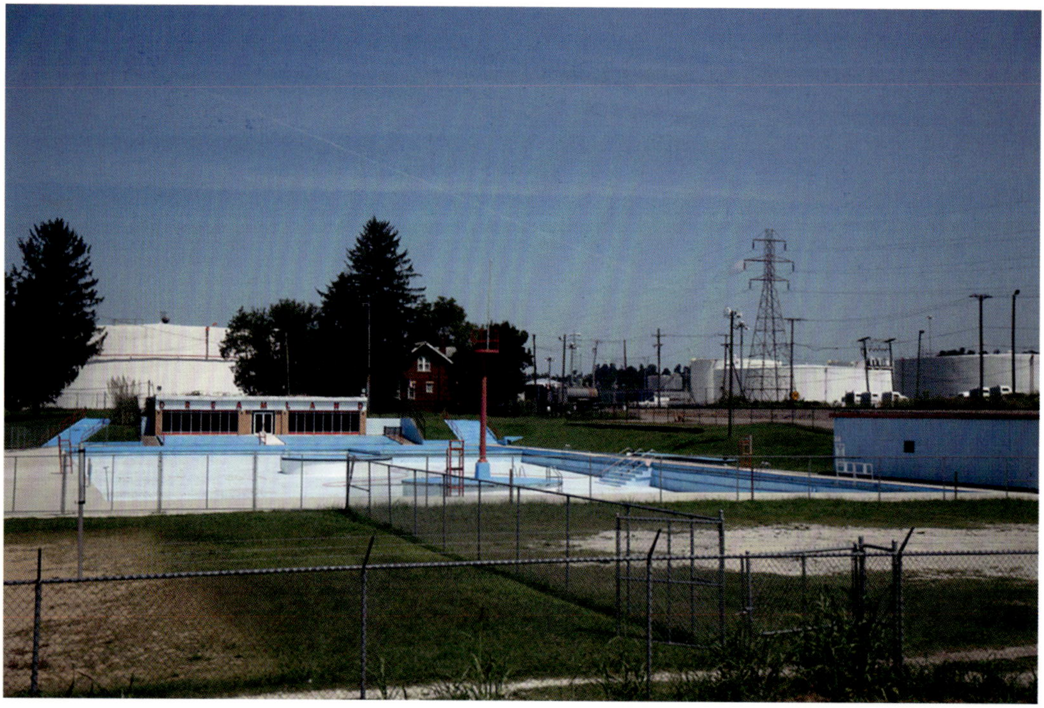

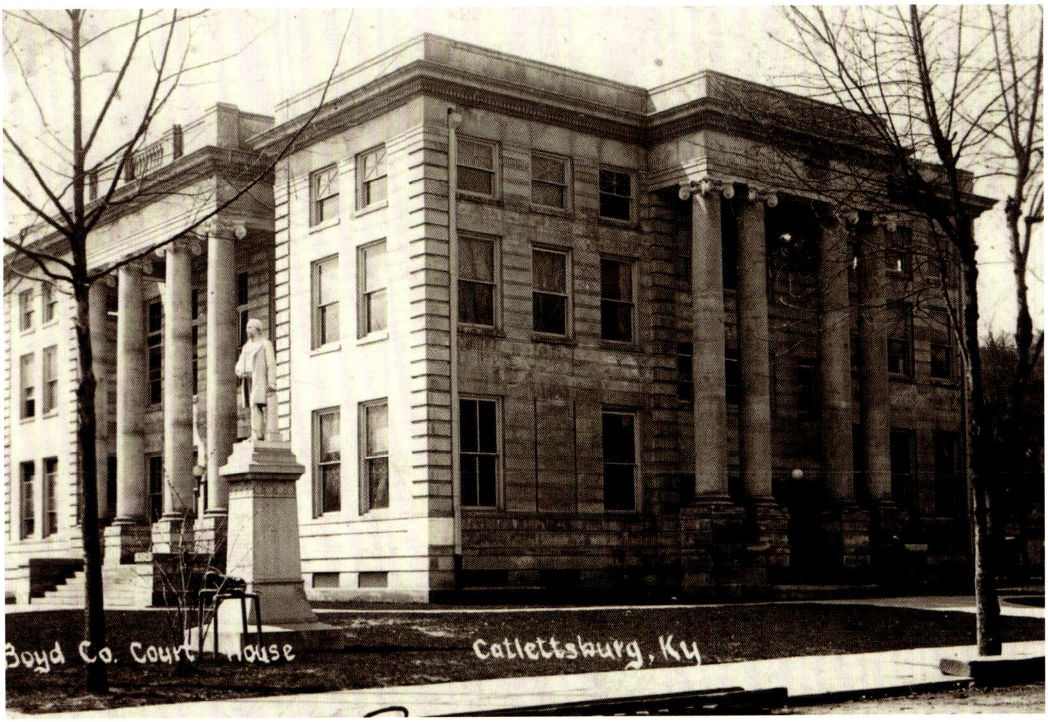

JOHN MILTON ELLIOTT: The statue of John Milton Elliott has stood as a memory of the murdered Kentucky lawyer and politician for well over a century. He looks over dirt and brick-covered Louisa Street in 1910 and continues his oversight of the city's progress today.

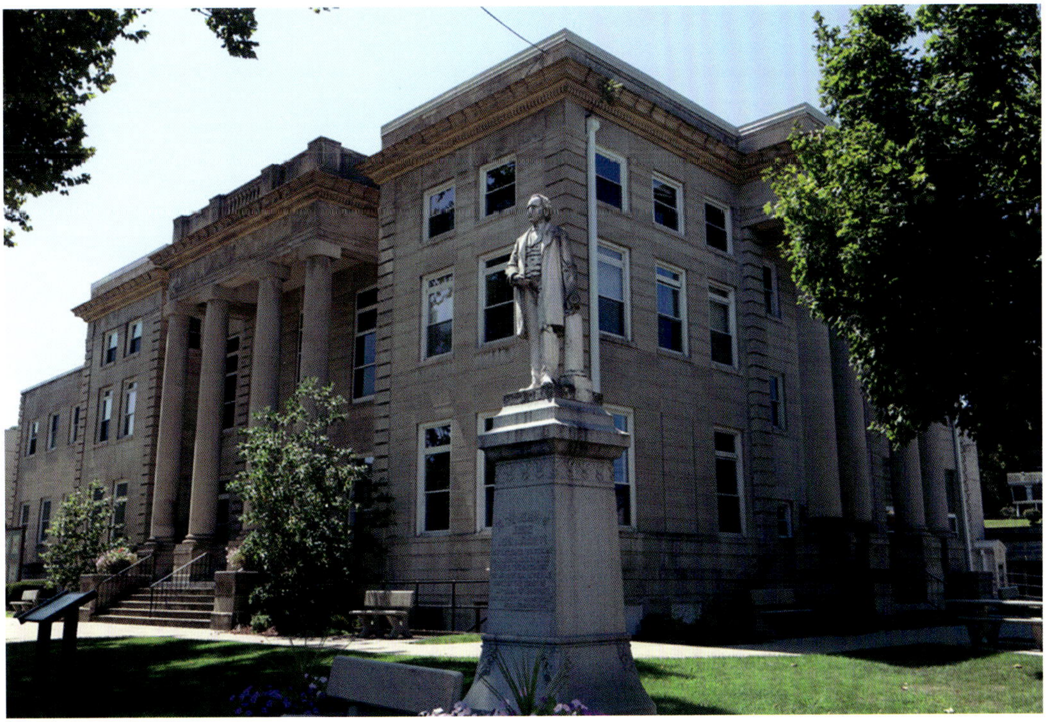

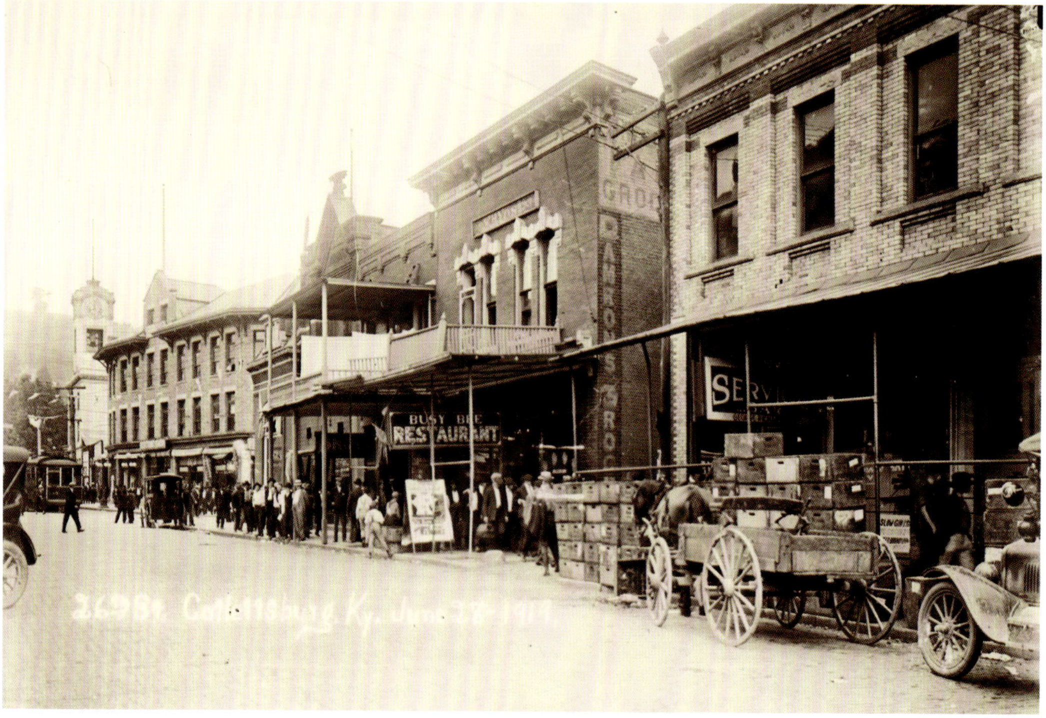

THE BUSY BEE RESTAURANT: Patrons of the Busy Bee Restaurant look on as the photographer captures their 1919 gazes along with early automobiles and wagons. Today the crowds, restaurant, and wagons are long gone, replaced by apartments, small businesses, and modern vehicles.

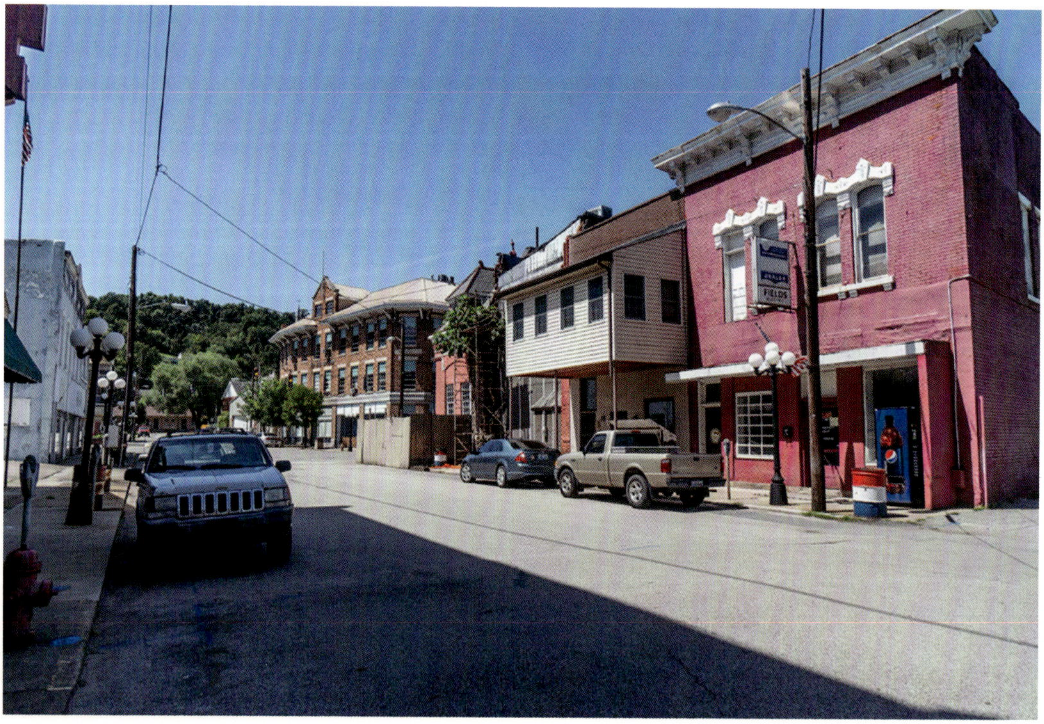

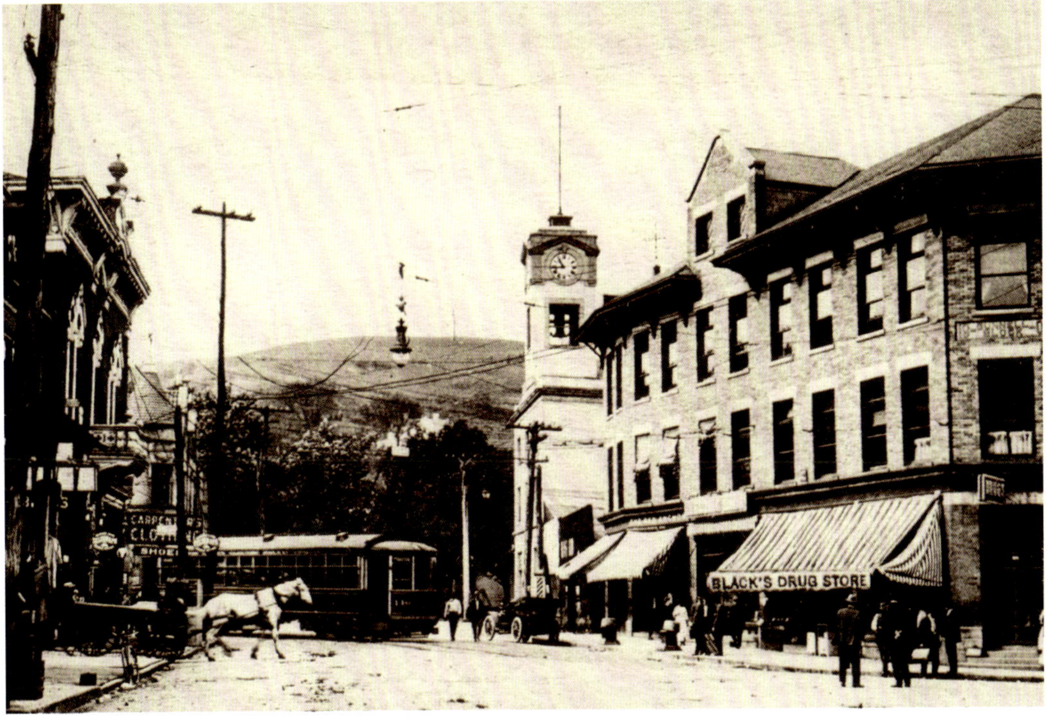

THE COUNTY SEAT: Catlettsburg became the seat of Boyd County just two years after the county was incorporated in 1858. Up until that time the city was part of Greenup County. Pictured her is 26th Street's Black's Corner *c.* 1910 and the same corner as it appears today.

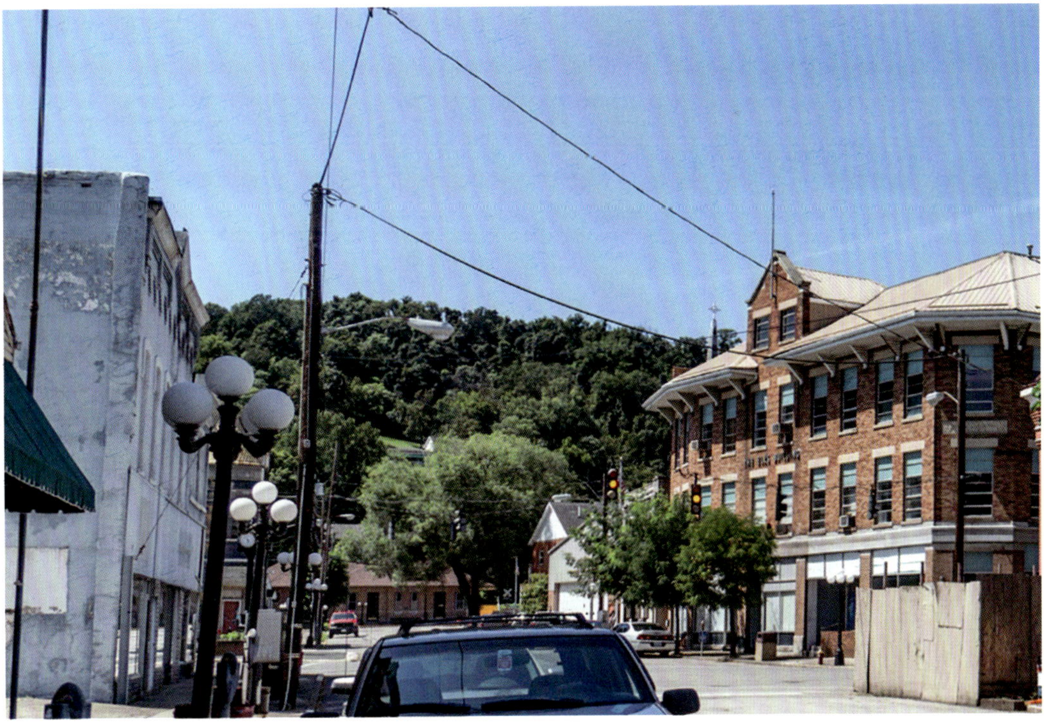

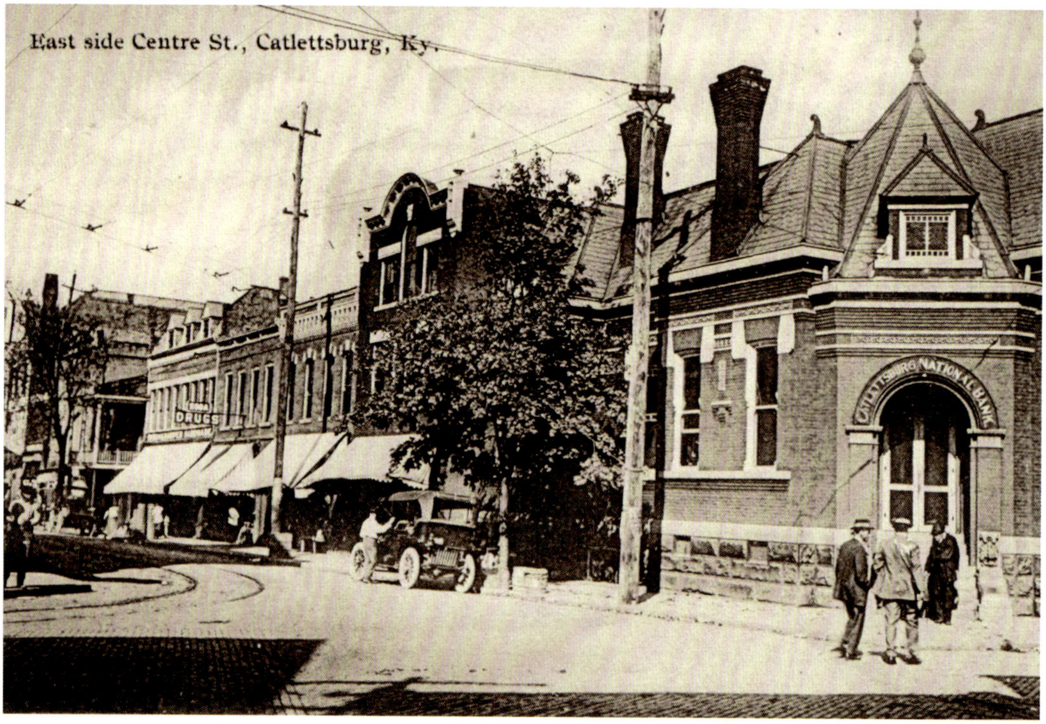

LOST VICTORIAN GRANDEUR: The modern photograph of the old Catlettsburg National Bank shows an abandoned building that was once a stately Victorian-style structure that stood near the center of town. The building has since been demolished due to structural concerns.

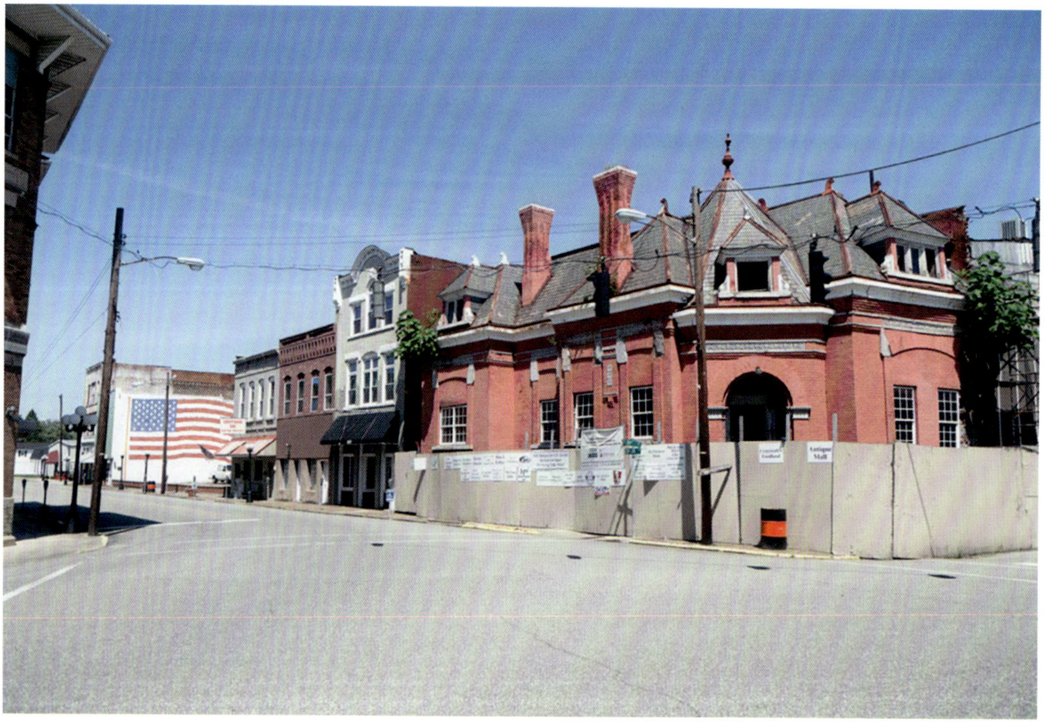

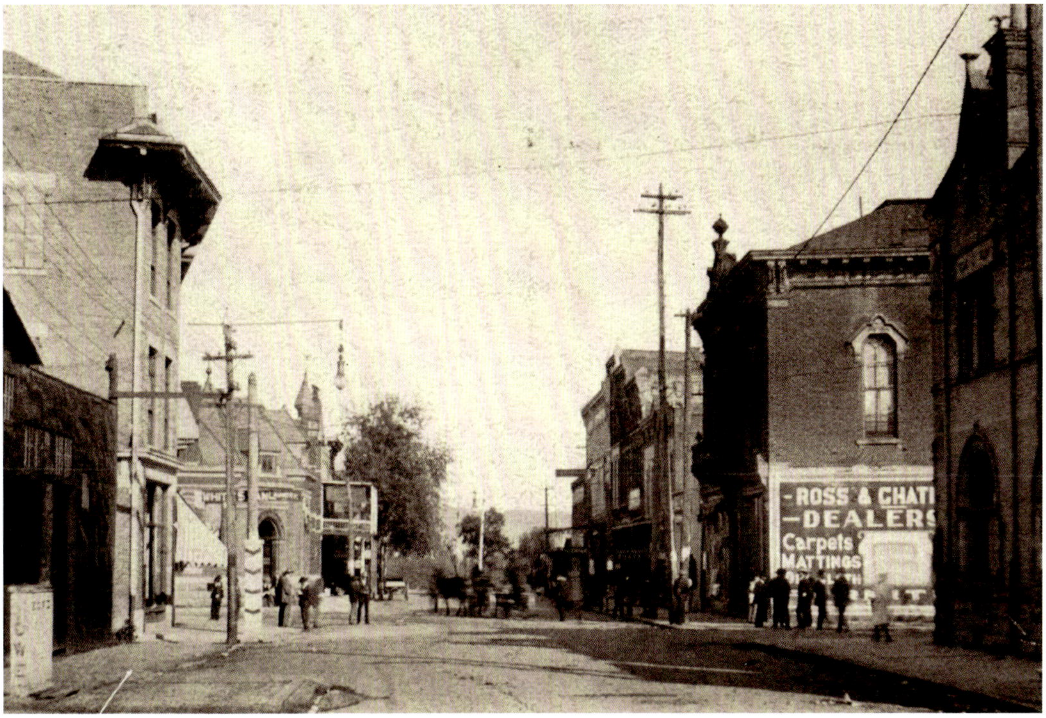

RIVER TOWN CHARM: Division or 26th Street looking west toward the Ohio River and busy Front Street in 1911. Though many structures from the early century have been replaced, the city still retains its small river town charm and innocence.

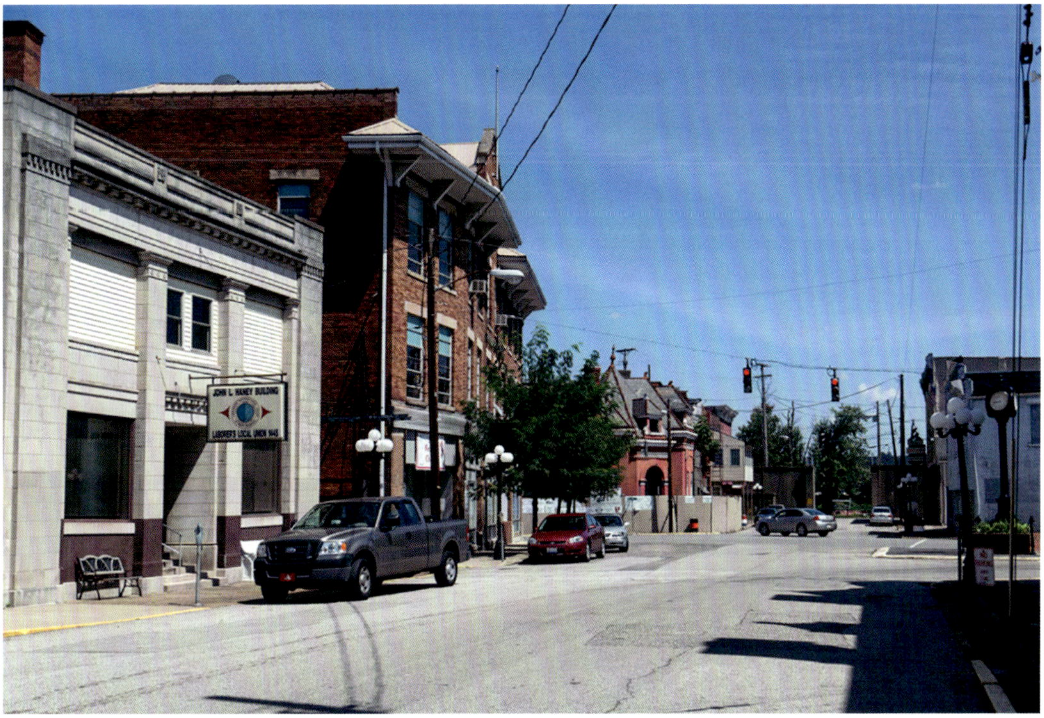

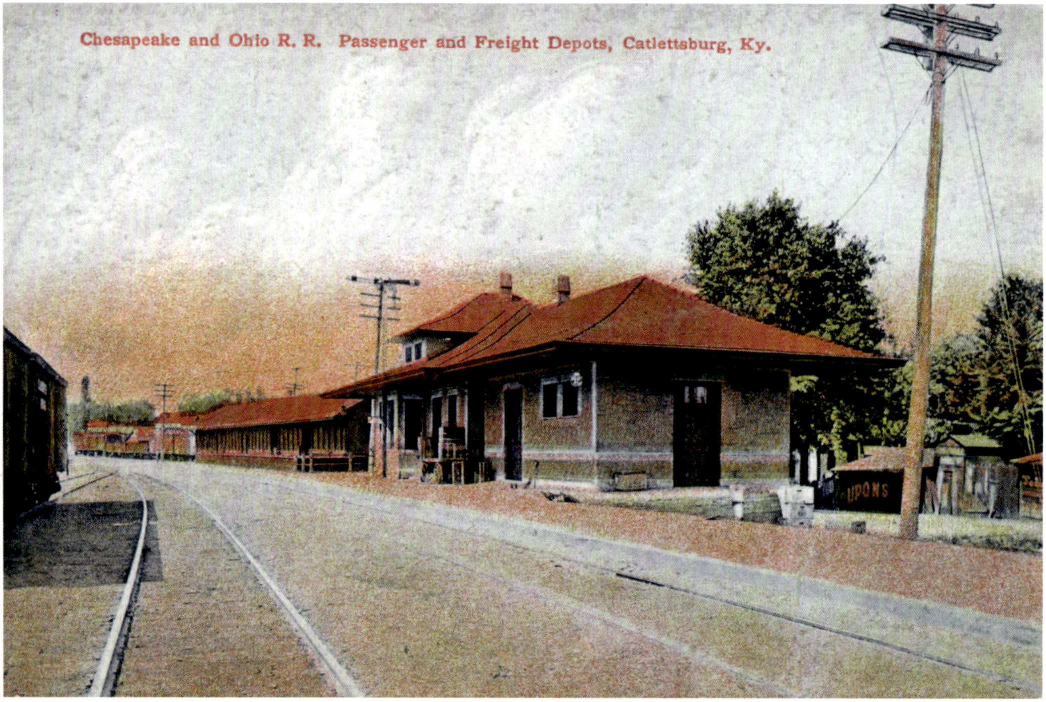

THE CATLETTSBURG DEPOT: The Chesapeake and Ohio Railroad came to Catlettsburg around 1911. The postcard view of the Catlettsburg depot dates from around 1920 and is quite comparable to the present day view. The depot has since discontinued being at the service of the railroad, but is happily used as a local history and railroad museum.

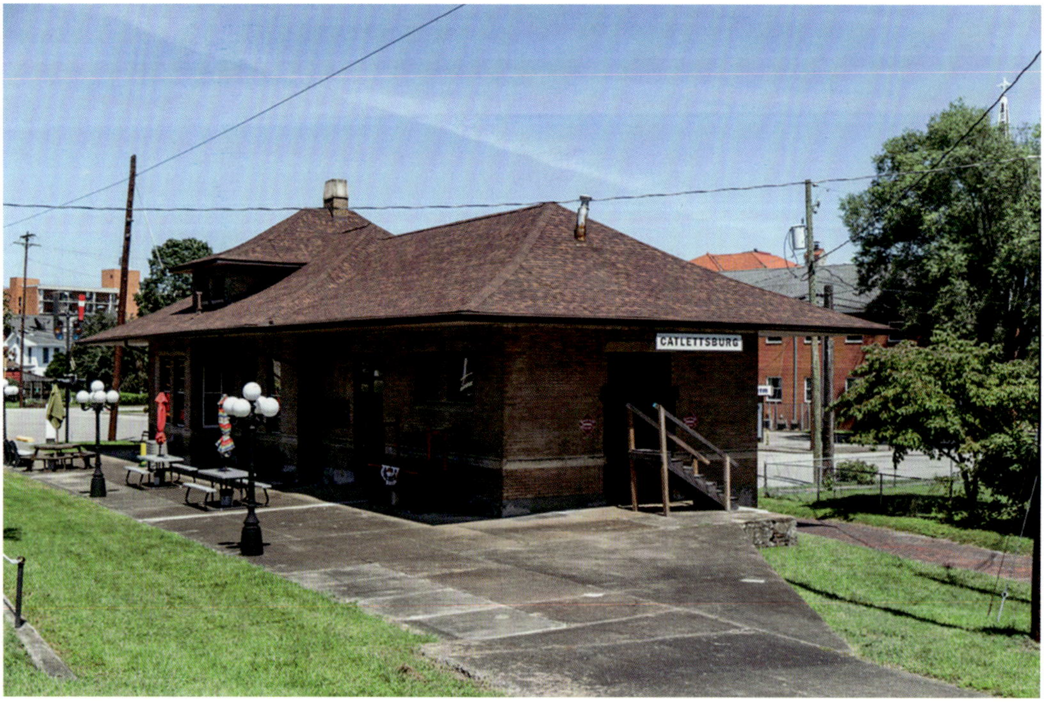

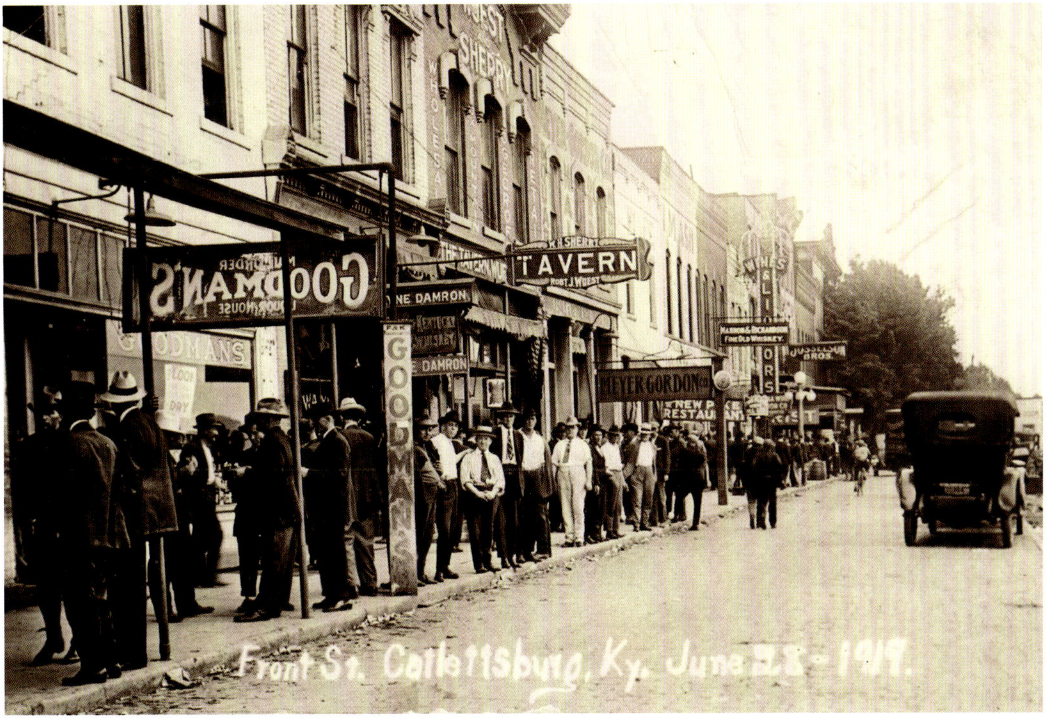

**River Traveler Hostelries:** Front Street ran parallel to the Ohio River. Many river travelers and workers frequented Catlettsburg's taverns to drink, gamble, and spin their stories of life along the river. Today a floodwall stands where the hotels and bars of Front Street stood a century ago.

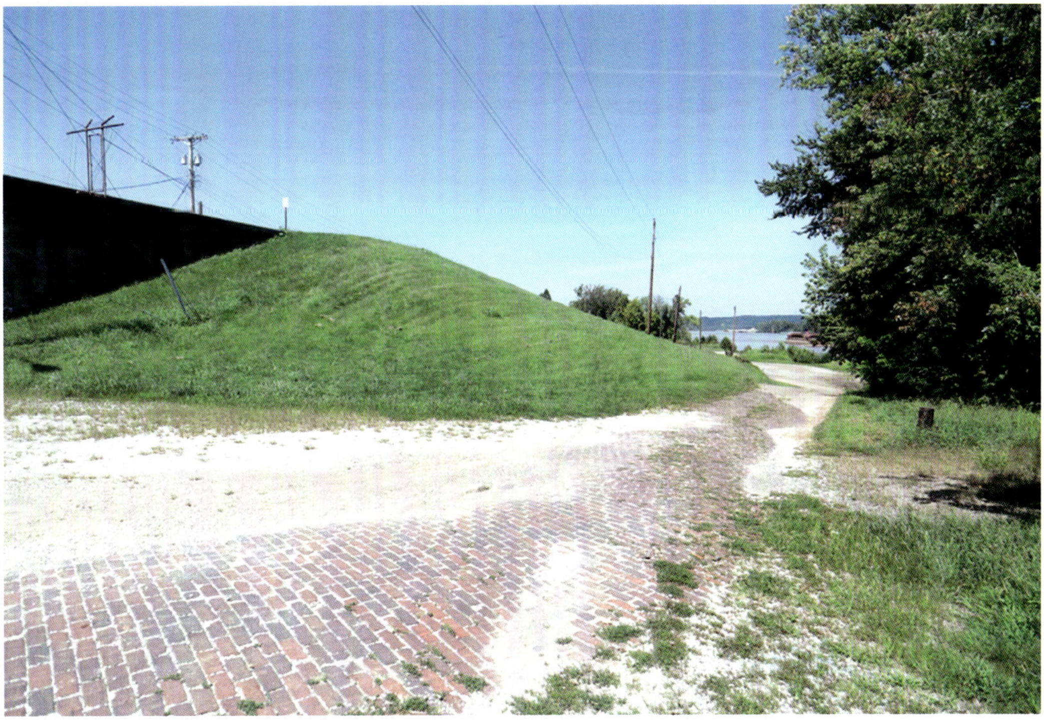

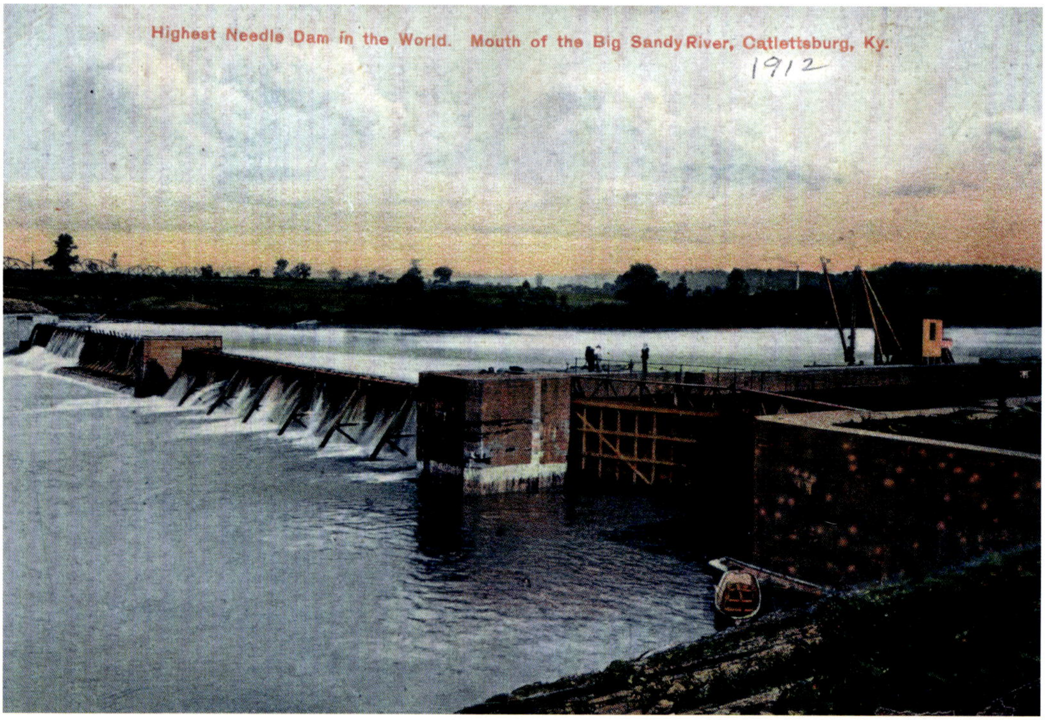

THE LOST DAM: Not many know that the world's highest needle dam sat between Catlettsburg Kentucky and Kenova West Virginia at the mouth of the Big Sandy River. The postcards dates from around 1912 and the new photograph shows no sign of the dam today.

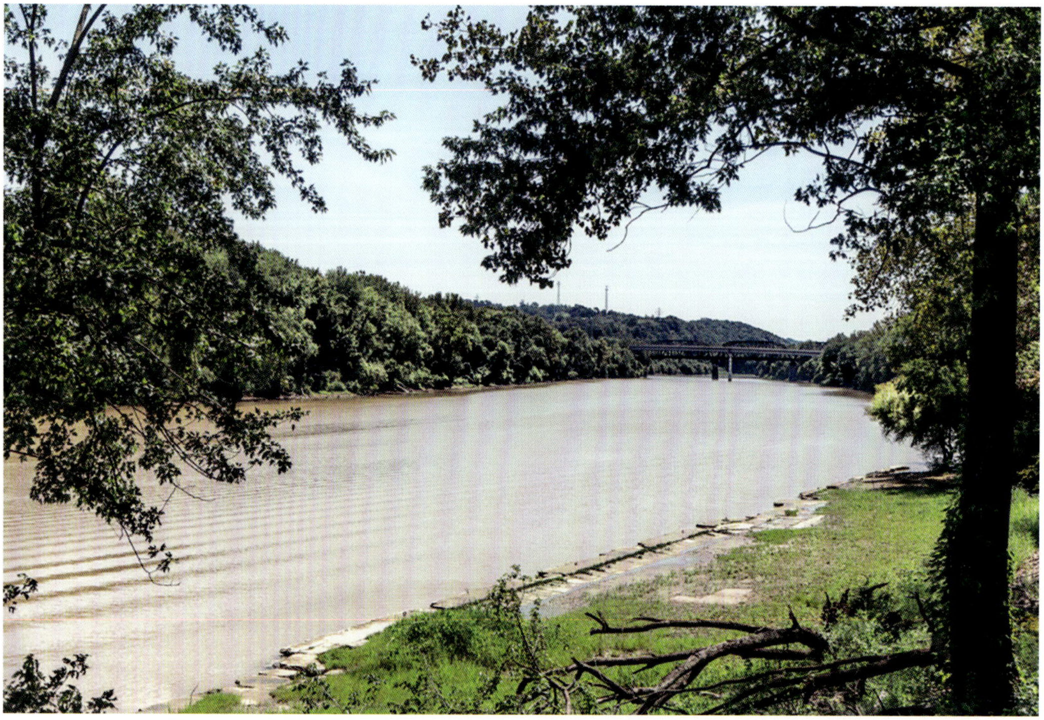

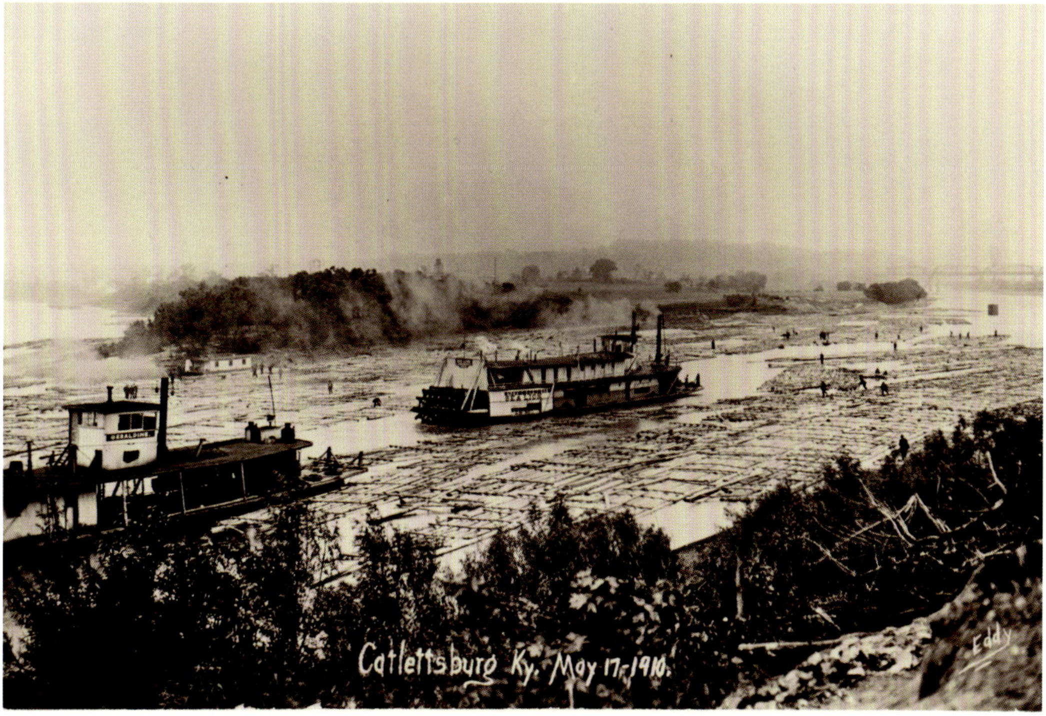

FLOATING DOWN THE LUMBER ON THE RIVER: Logs traveling down the Little Sandy River found their way to the Ohio River via paddleboats and strong oarsmen. The older photograph dates from 1910 in Catlettsburg and shows lumber buyers walking and inspecting prospective purchases for their companies.

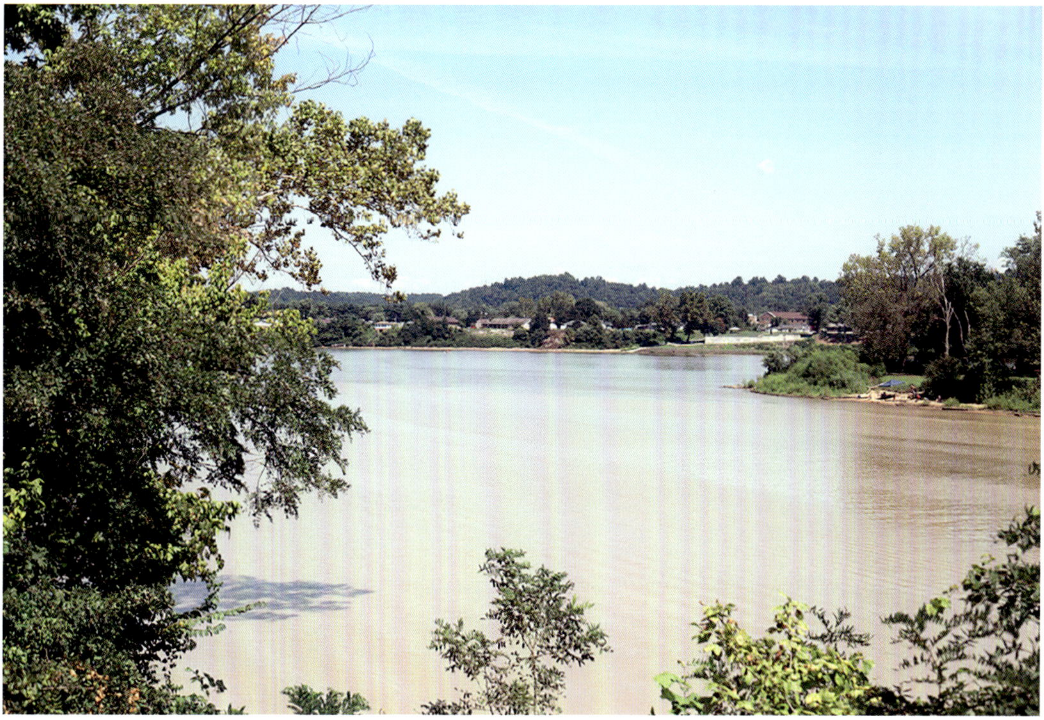

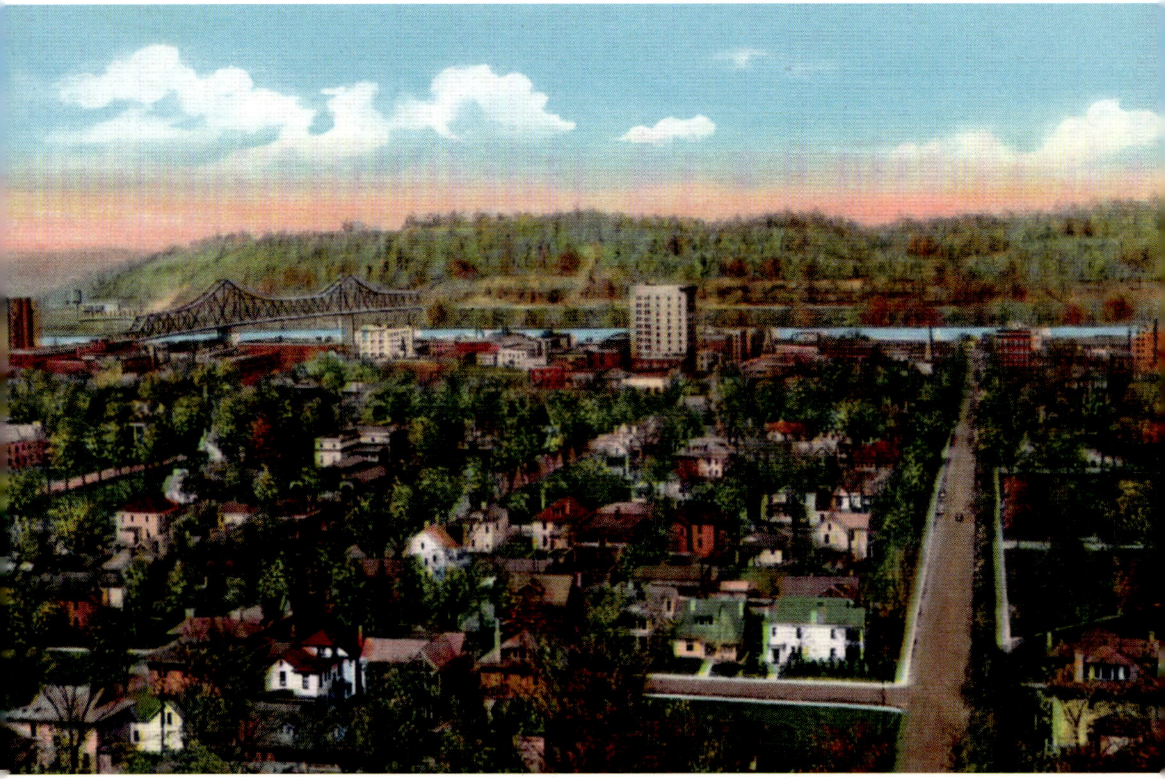

A BIRD'S EYE VIEW OF ASHLAND: This postcard from *c.* 1940 show a city with very little change when compared to the cityscape today. The National Bank Building is nearly at the center of the city and apart from a slight change to the upper façade looks much as it was when completed in the late 1920s.

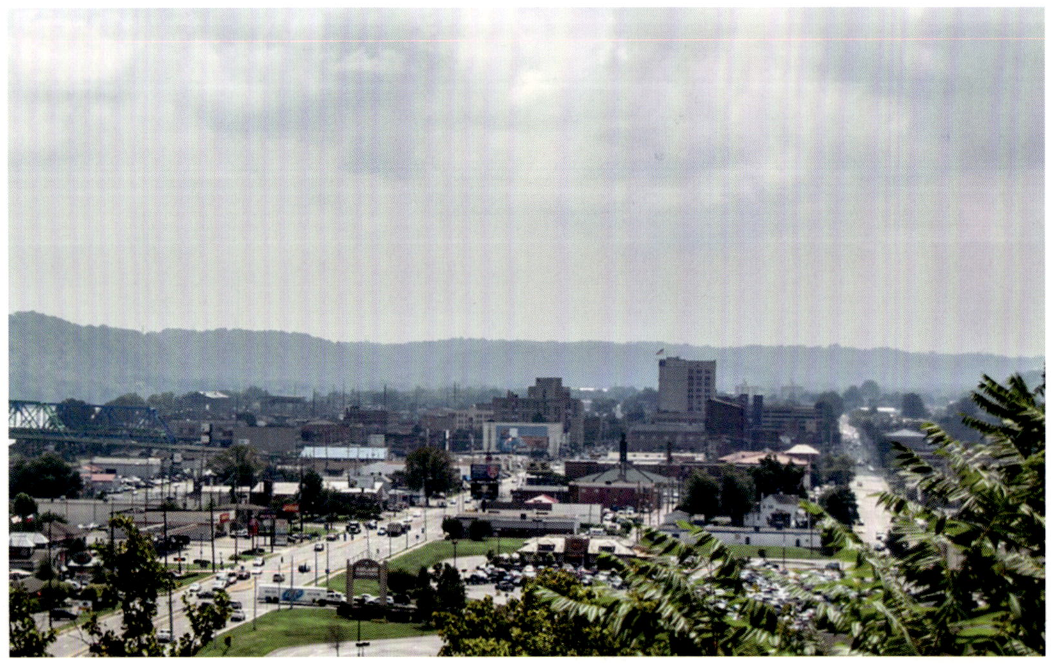

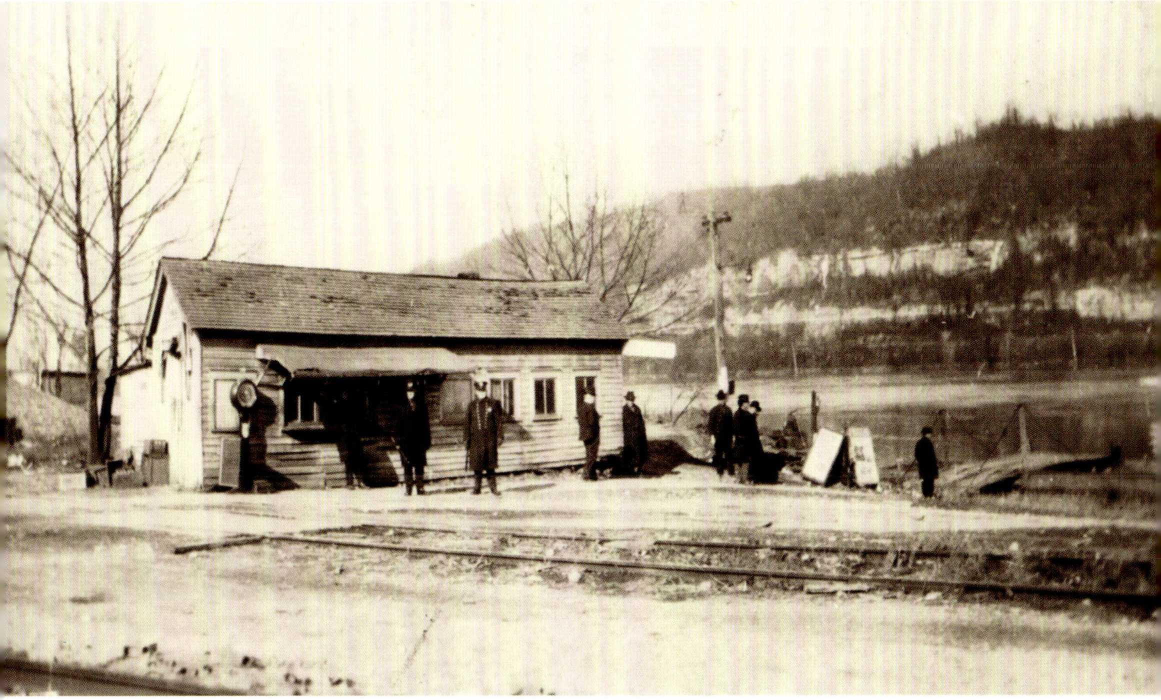

STEAM FERRY ACROSS THE MIGHTY OHIO: Before the construction of the Ben Williamson Memorial Bridge in 1932, taking the steam ferry across the mighty Ohio River was the only connection between Ohio and Kentucky at this point. In 1985 the blue Simeon Willis Memorial Bridge joined the Ben Williamson in spanning the river.

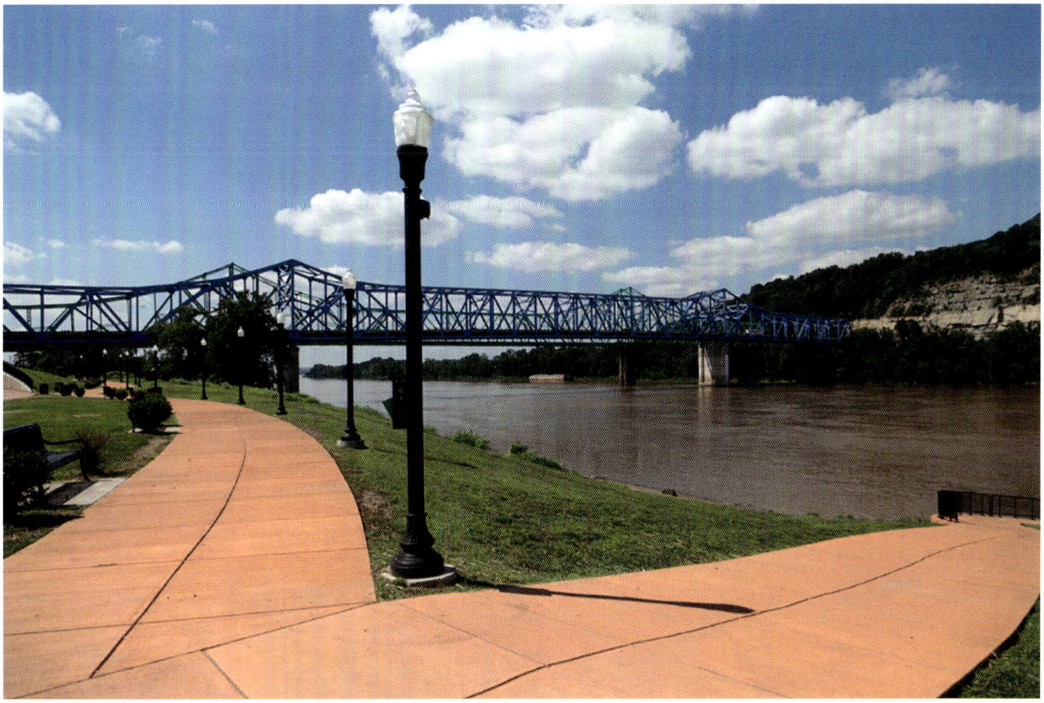

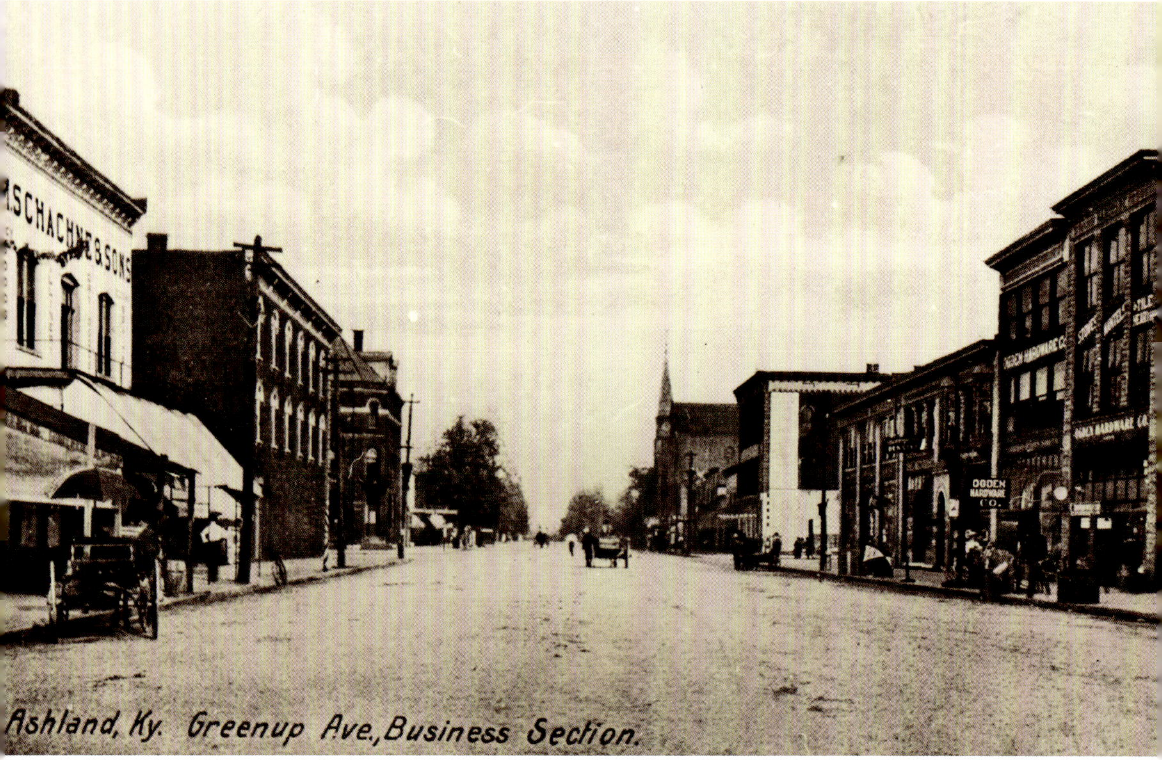

Ashland, Ky. Greenup Ave., Business Section.

GREENUP AVENUE: Many of the businesses that sprang up in Ashland began along Greenup Avenue as rental properties were less than nearby Winchester Avenue. Presently there are many empty storefronts on both Greenup and Winchester Avenue.

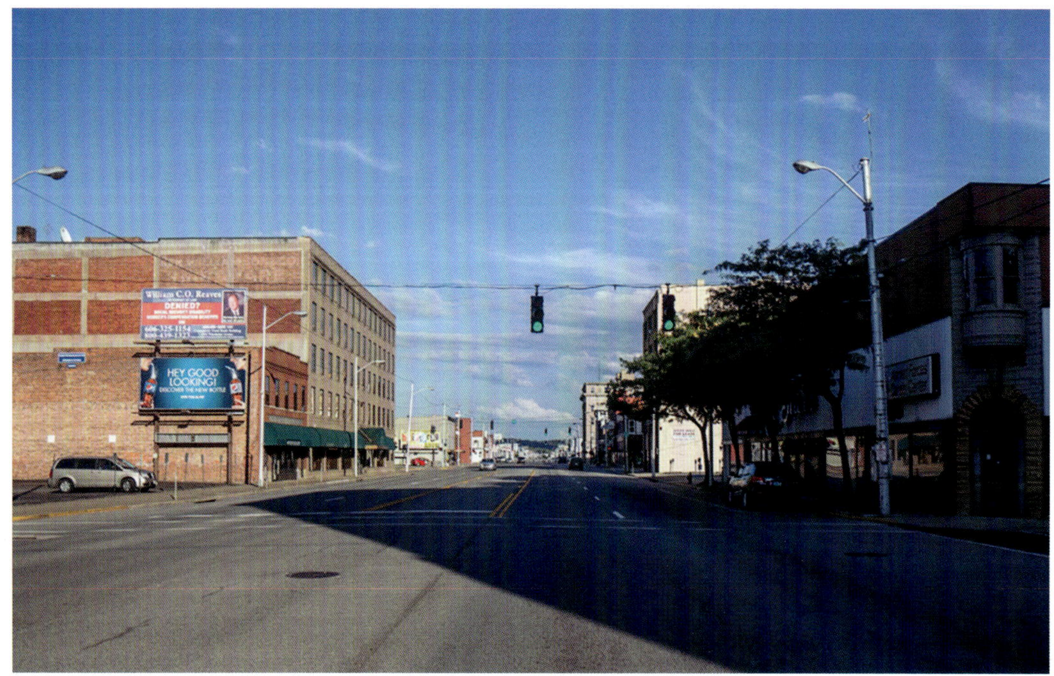

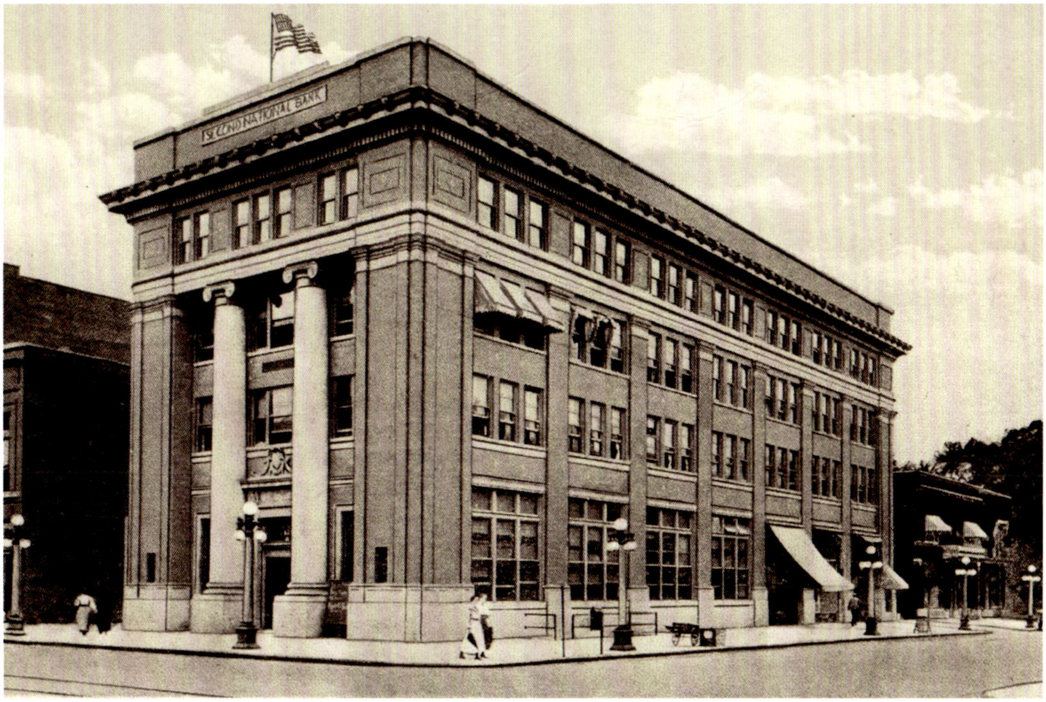

THE SECOND NATIONAL BANK: Two Ionic columns greet customers at the entrance of the Second National Bank building's Winchester Avenue doors. Presently the beautiful structure is being renovated inside with an eye on future use. Across Fifteenth Street side of the building stands the popular restaurant "Fat Pattys".

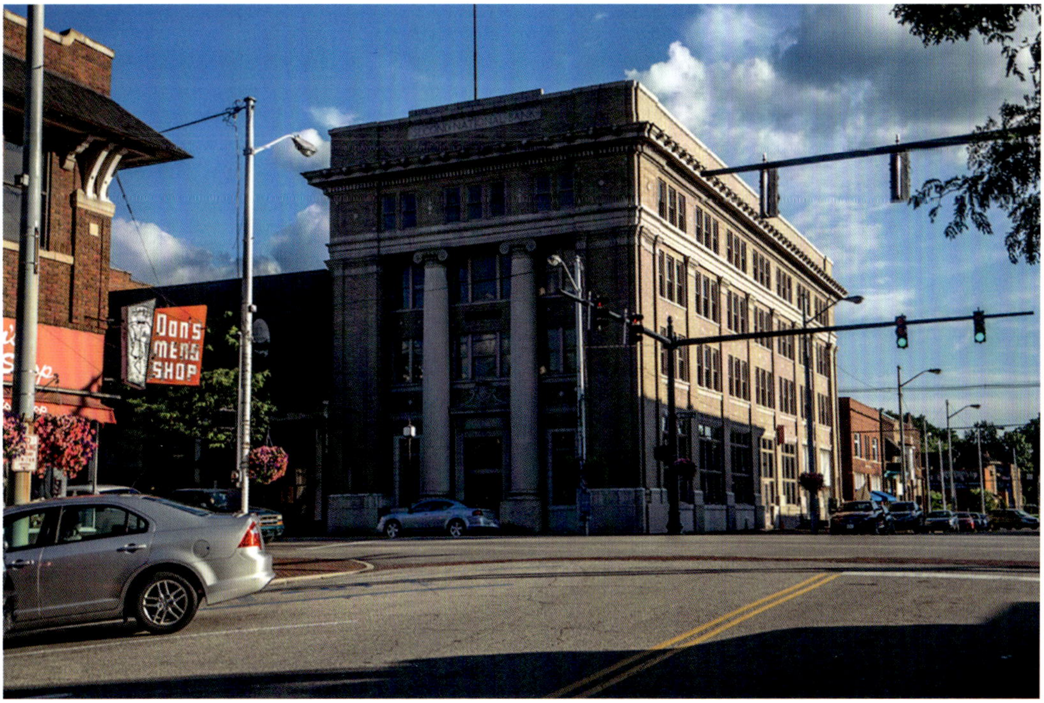

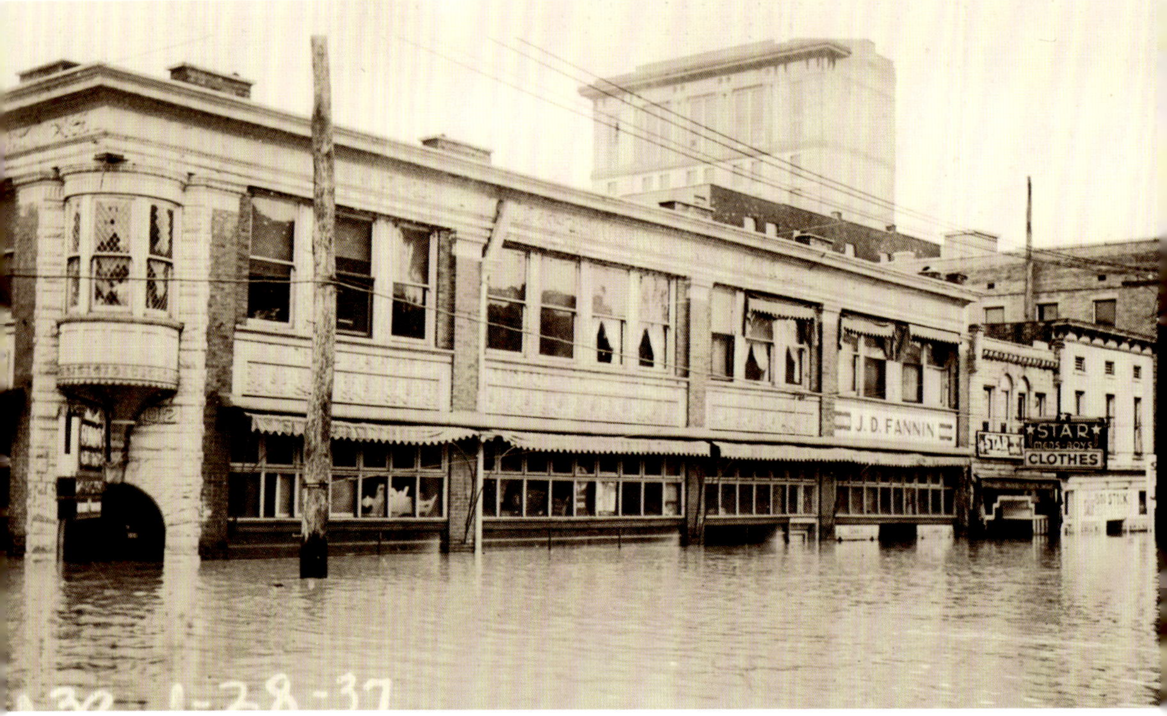

A FLOOD ON GREENUP AVENUE: The old Stars Fashion World and Armed Forces Career Center building was completed in 1903 as listed on its Greenup Avenue entrance. During the flood of 1937 the entrance just below the arch became a measuring point of just how devastating the flood had been.

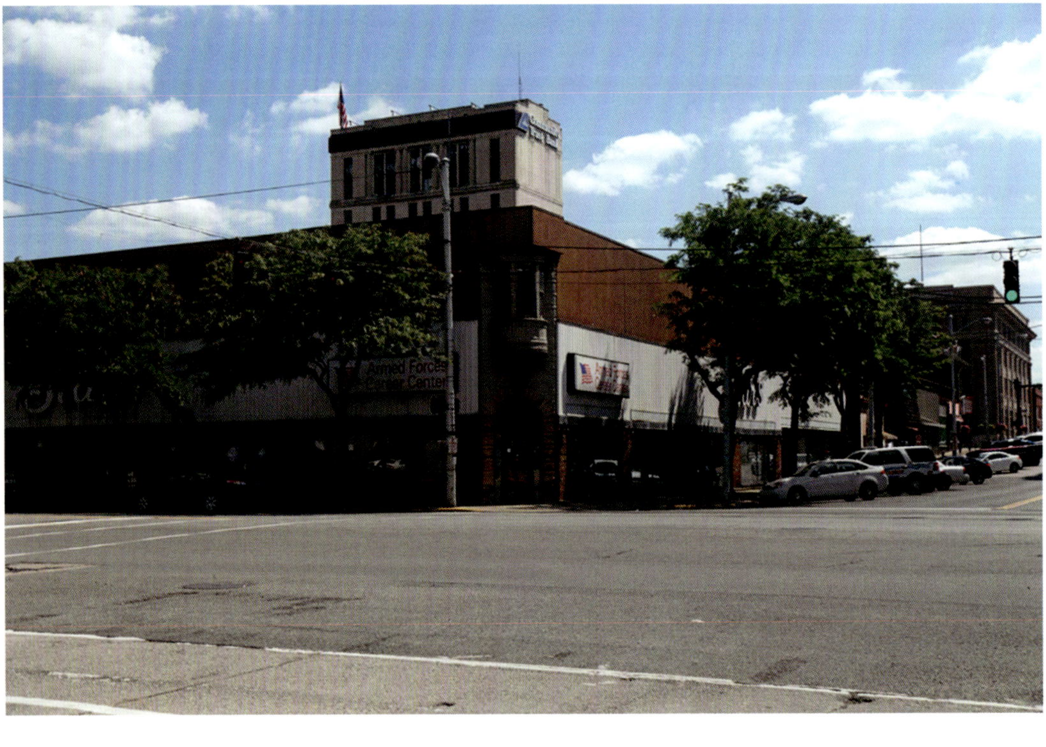

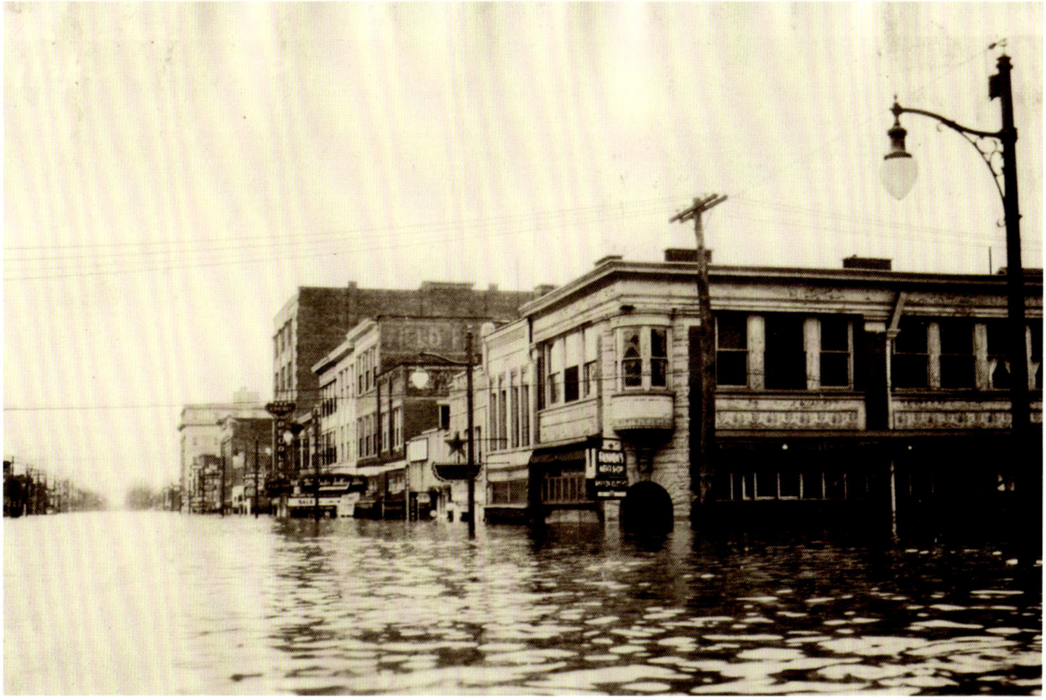

THE FLOOD OF A CENTURY: It was thought that the great flood of 1913 was one of those once-in-a-century floods however the flood of 1937 surpassed that. The Ohio Valley from Pittsburg to the Mississippi River felt the heaviness of this natural disaster. Many river communities including Ashland, constructed flood walls after that terrible event.

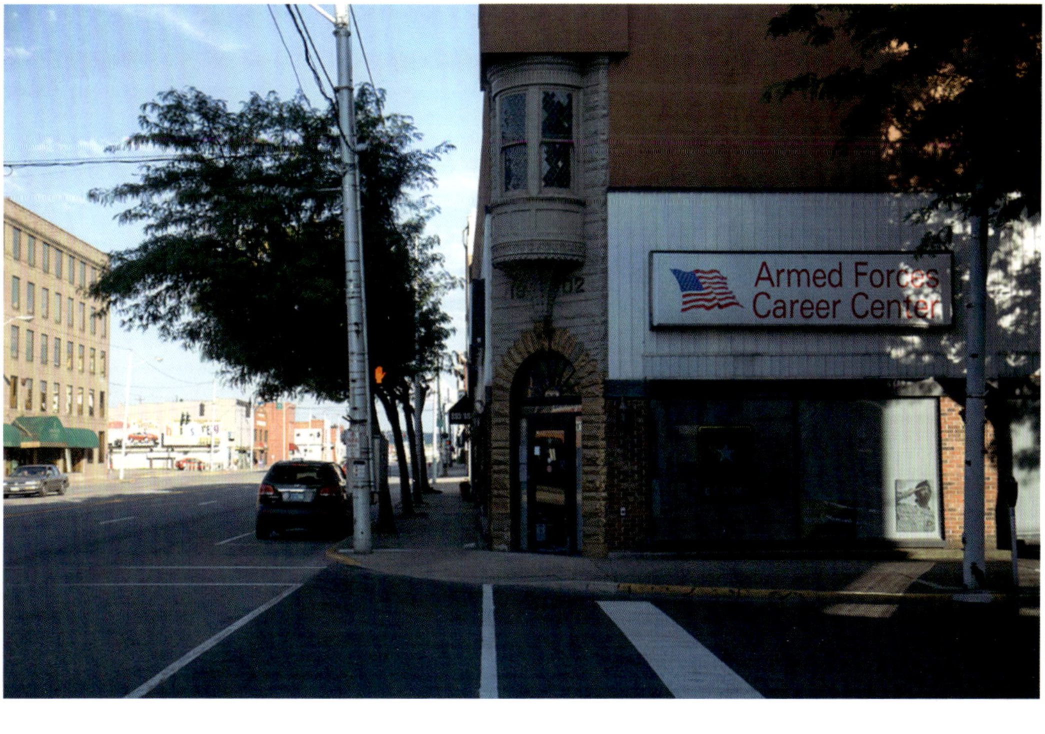

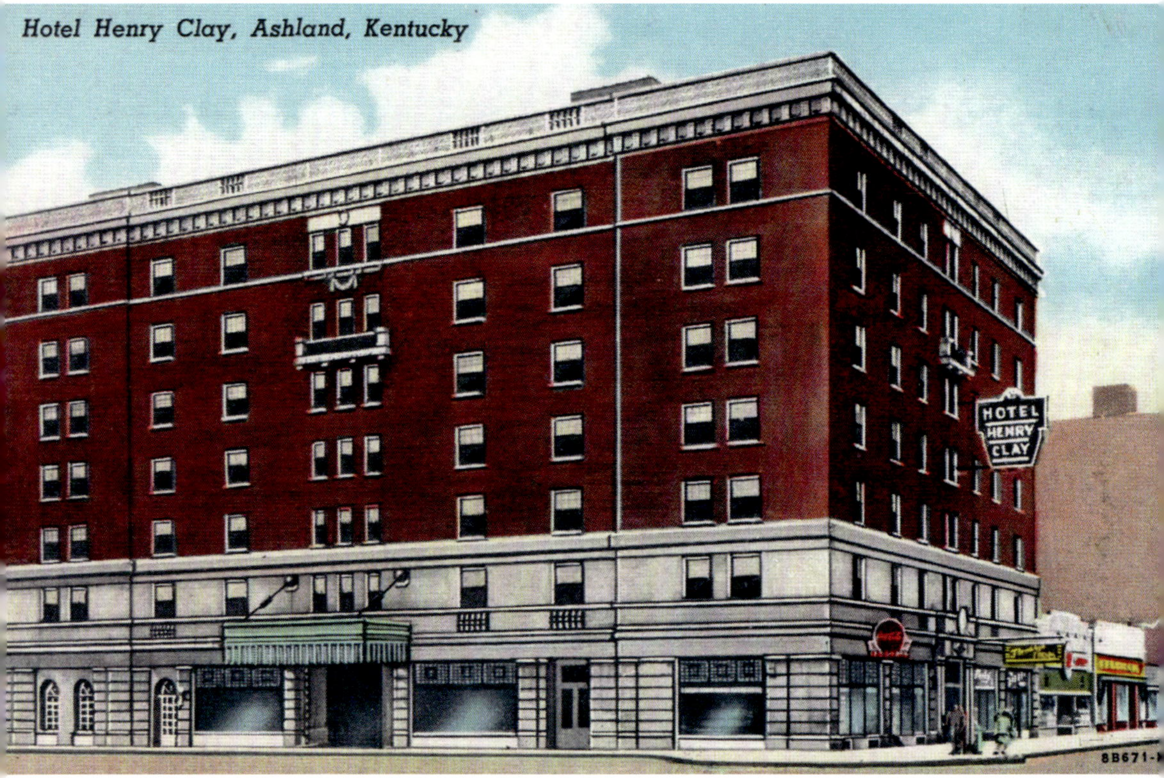

*Hotel Henry Clay, Ashland, Kentucky*

HOTEL HENRY CLAY: No longer a large hotel, the former Hotel Henry Clay was named after the famed Kentucky statesman, Henry Clay. The city of Ashland was named in honor of Clay's estate in Lexington, which in turn was named after the group of Ash Trees on his property.

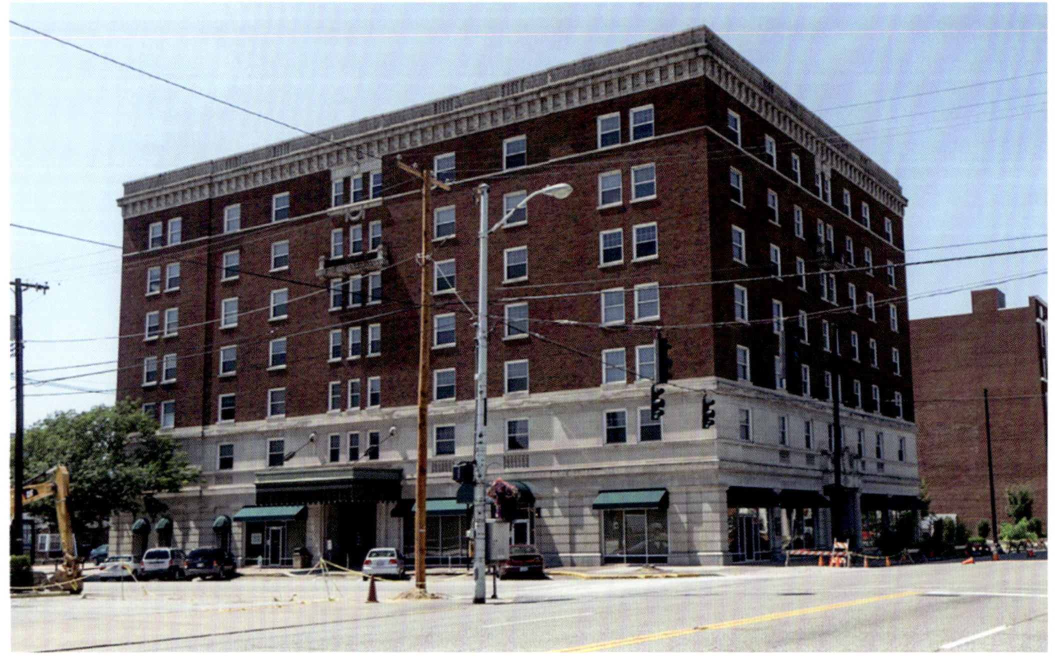

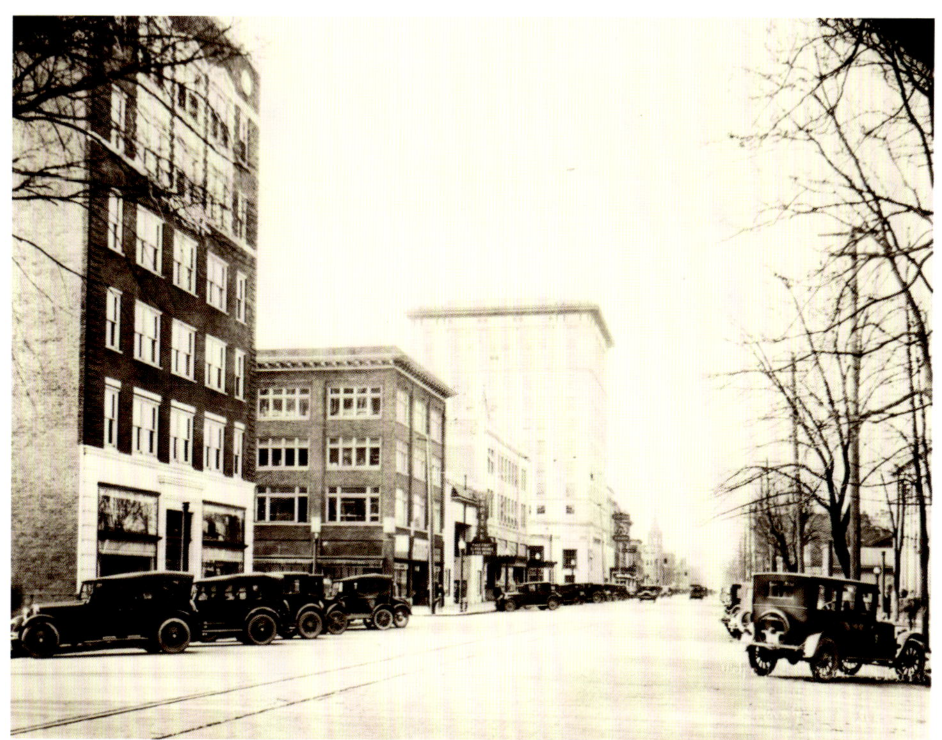

WINCHESTER AVENUE LOOKING WEST: A view toward the largest building in Ashland; the 116 feet tall Community Trust Bank. It was in this area that people flocked to stores such as: J. C. Penney, Sears, F. W. Woolworth, and many other businesses. Currently many small businesses are located here in the heart of Ashland.

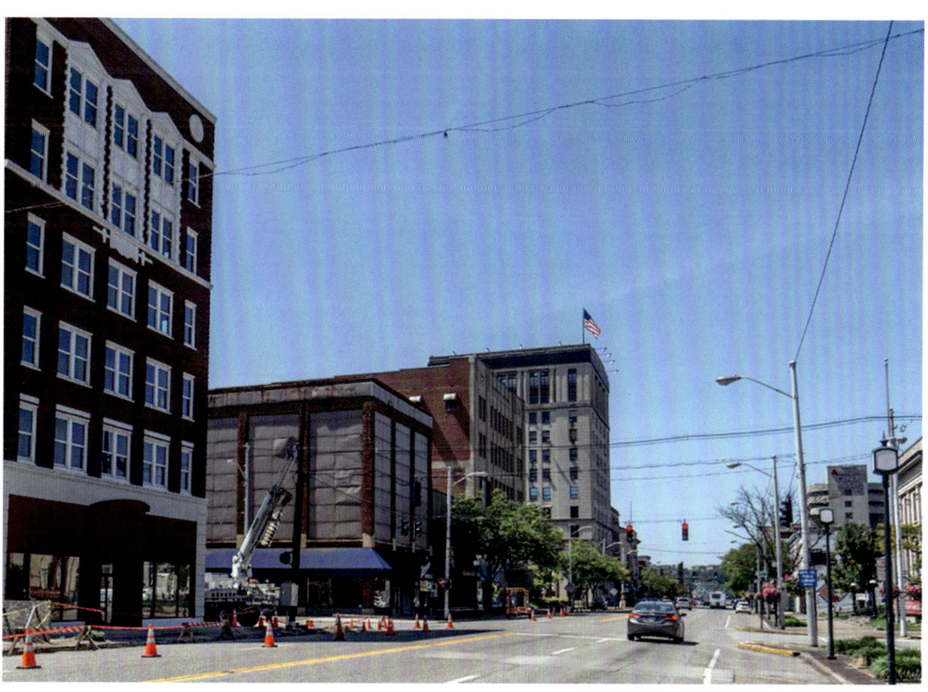

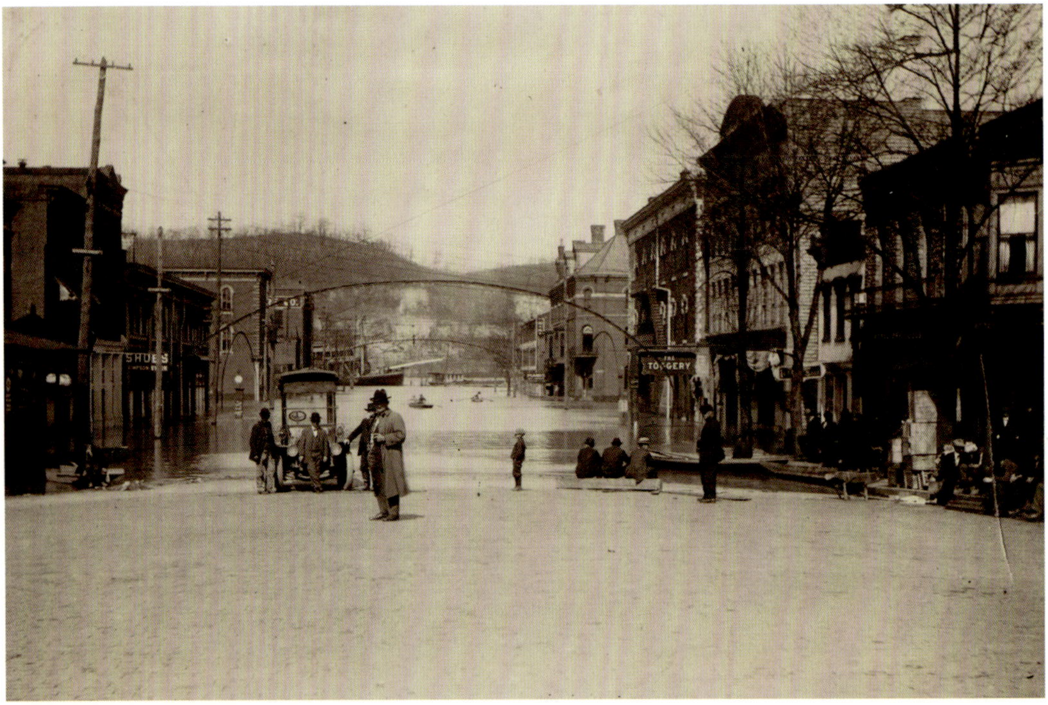

**Waiting for the Floodwater Peak:** The flood of 1913 was devastating along the mighty Ohio River and her tributaries. Pictured on Ashland's 16th Street are the river waters slowing creeping south from midway between Greenup Avenue and Winchester Avenue. A group slowly watches anxiously to see where the crest will stop.

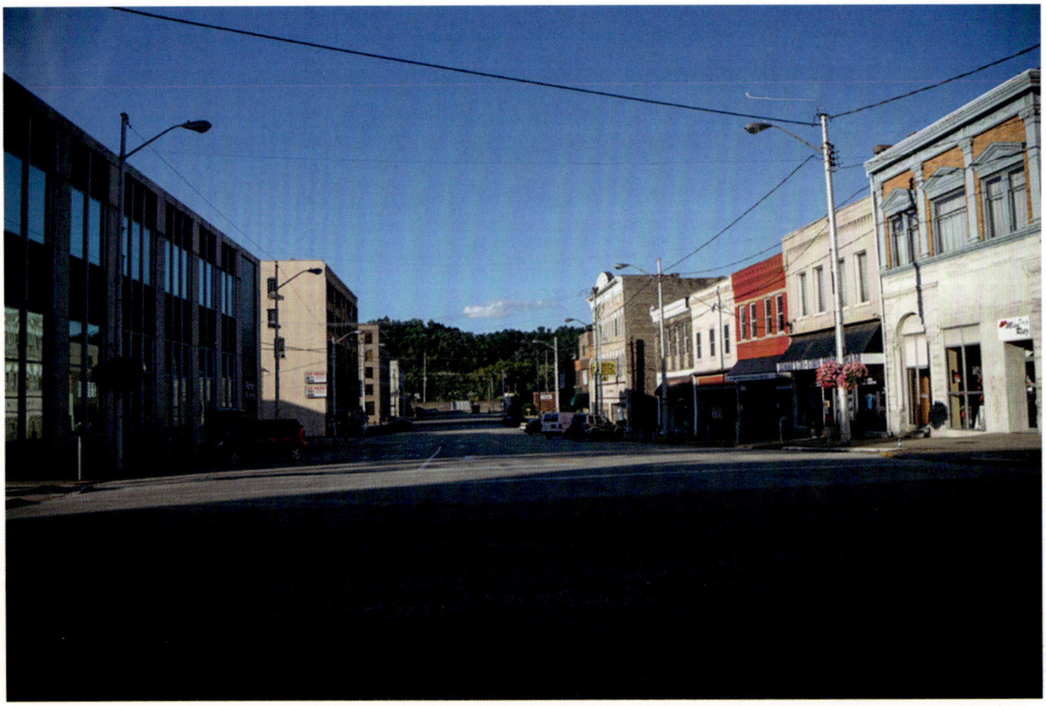

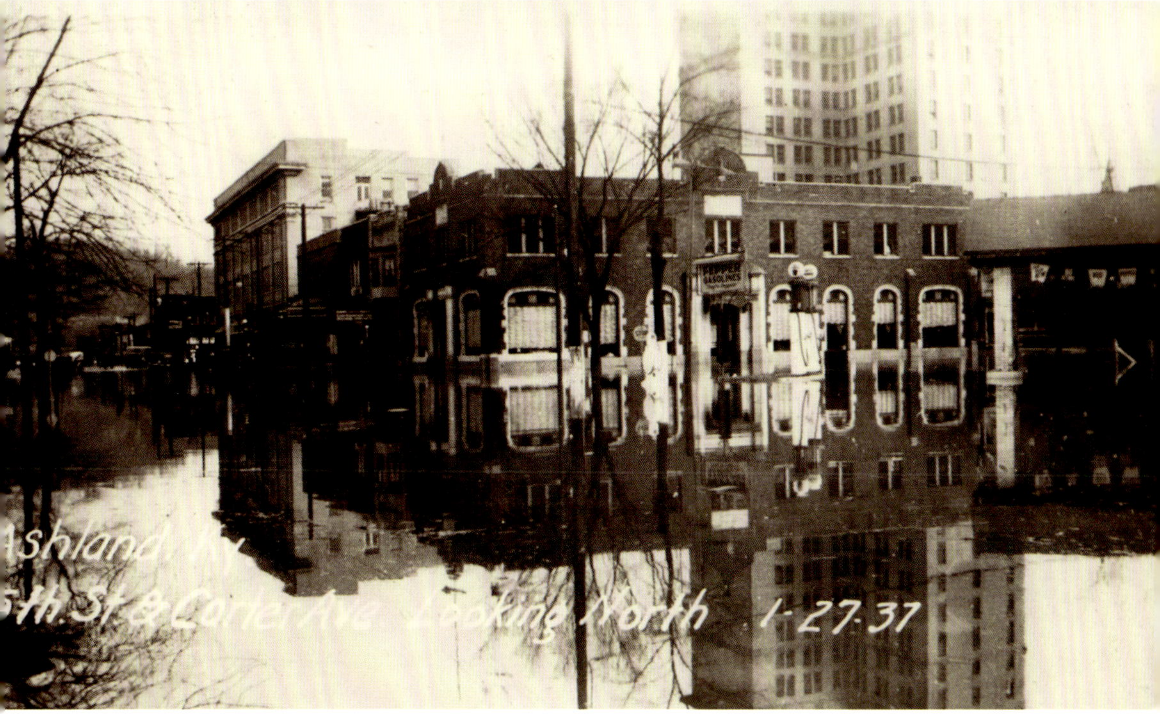

THE OHIO VALLEY FLOOD OF 1937: This was the worst flood in the area in recorded history. Photographed is the old Pepper Gasoline station on 15th Street and Carter Avenue as the river overtook the pumps. Today, it would seem, the Ohio River has been tamed by a dam system and floodwalls.

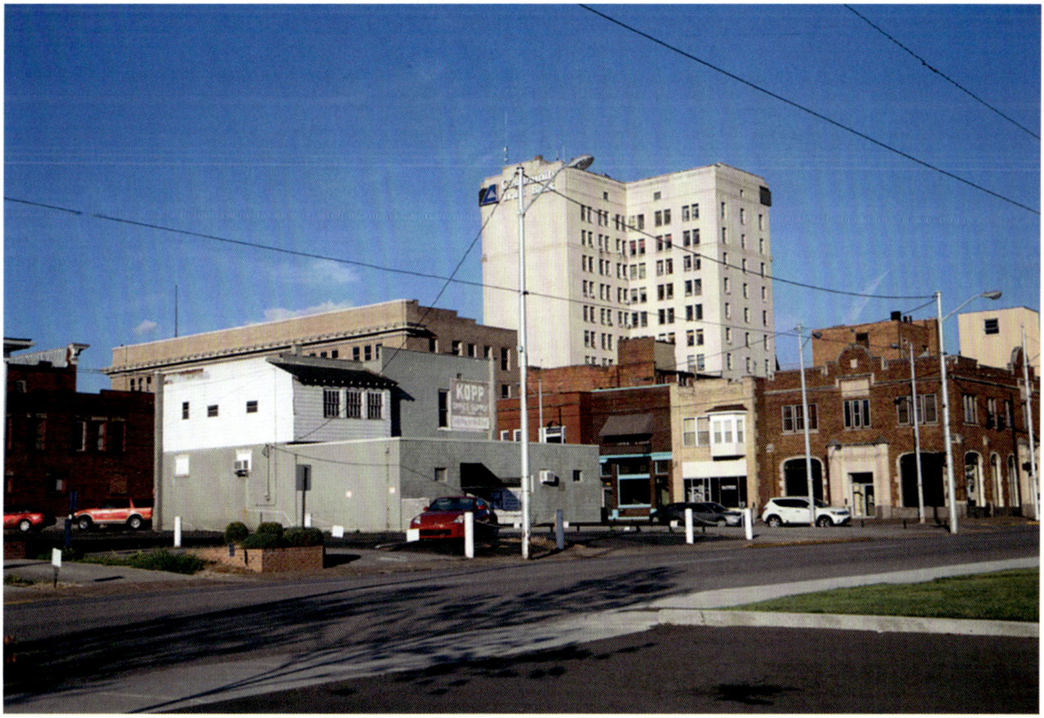

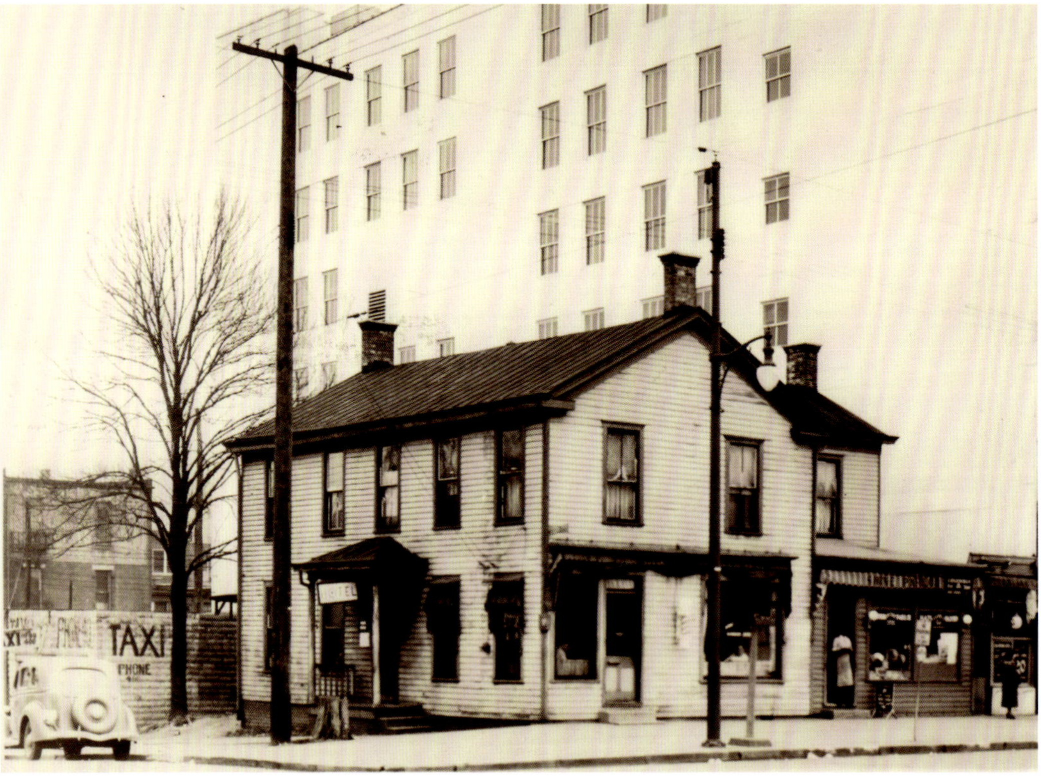

THE JOSEPH BURDETT HOME: The home was built in 1863 on the corner of 16th Street and Winchester Avenue. It was torn down in the early 1950s to make room for the Johnson Center Building, which housed Ashland Oil's Headquarters for many years. At the time of the printing of this book, the radio station WLGC is located here.

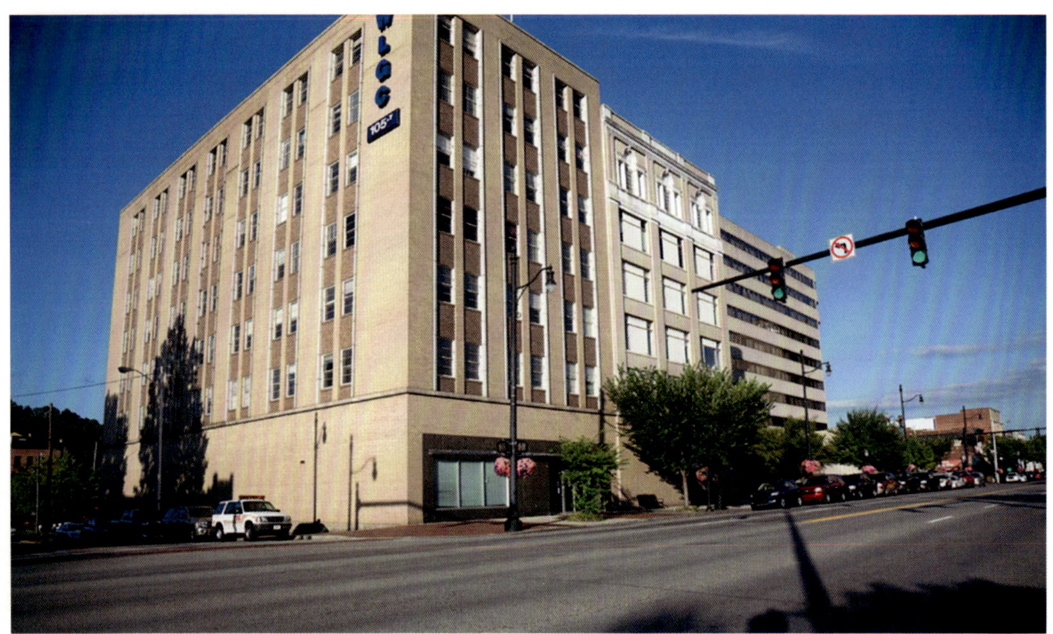

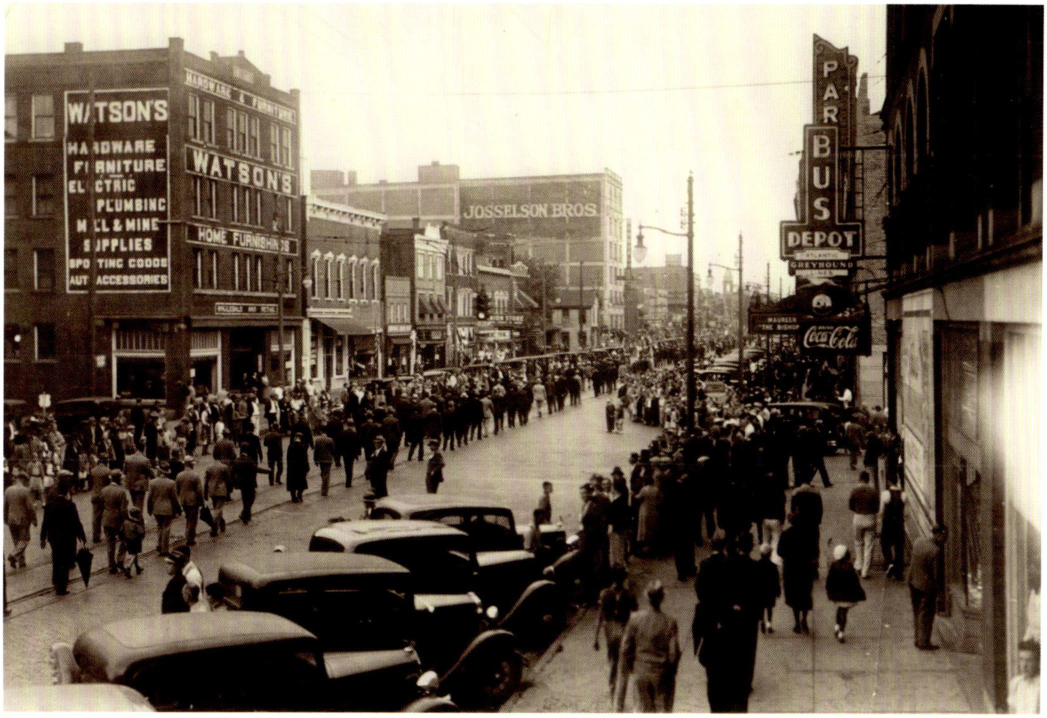

IRONWORKERS PARADE EAST ALONG WINCHESTER AVENUE: Crowds line the sidewalks in front of the old Watson's Hardware and Furniture on the north side and the Paramount Theater and its popular marquee on the south side in this 1935 photo. Both buildings stand as of the printing of this book.

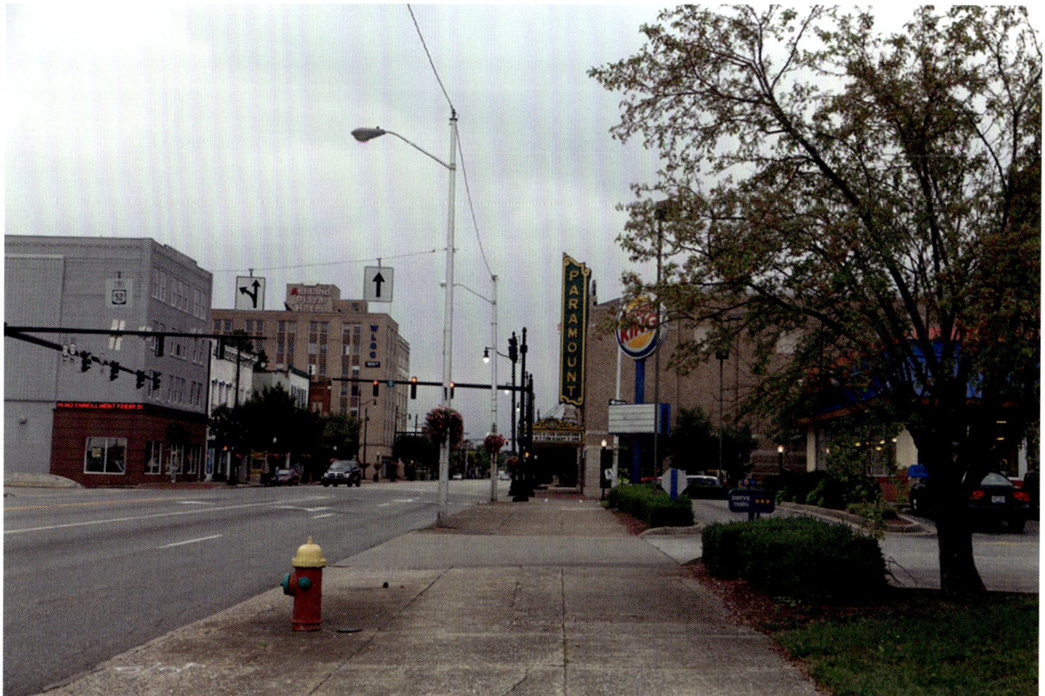

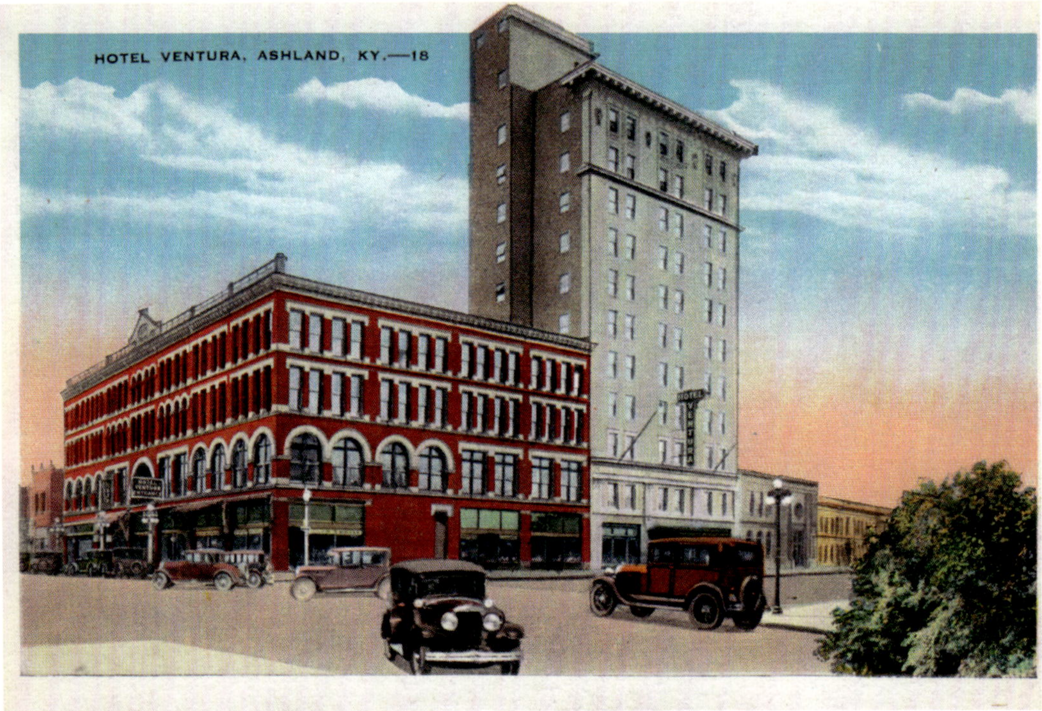

**HOTEL VENTURA:** In this postcard view of the Hotel Ventura in 1934, the 11-story addition just east stands out compared to the old red brick structure. The Hotel Ventura is long gone and a Burger King and Starbucks coffee shop occupy the same location.

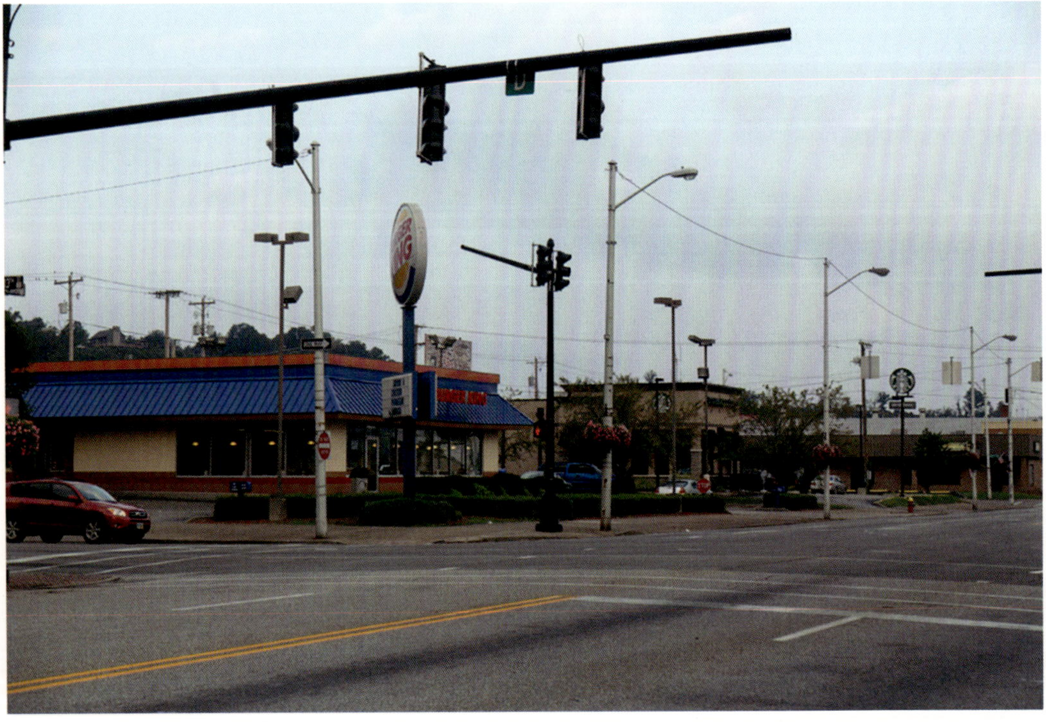

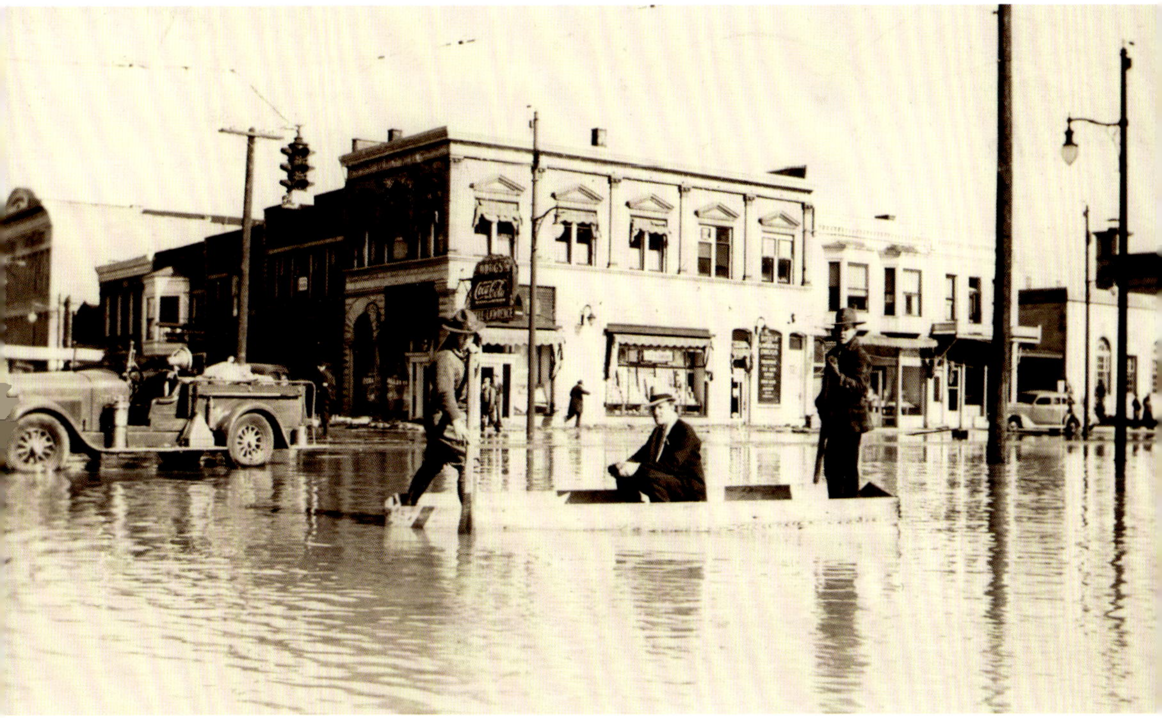

**BOATING ON WINCHESTER AVENUE:** Three young men pose for the camera in their homemade boat on Winchester Avenue in front of Steele and Lawrence Drug Store. The 1937 flood introduced the Ohio River to many streets in Ashland that had never experience the muddy waters.

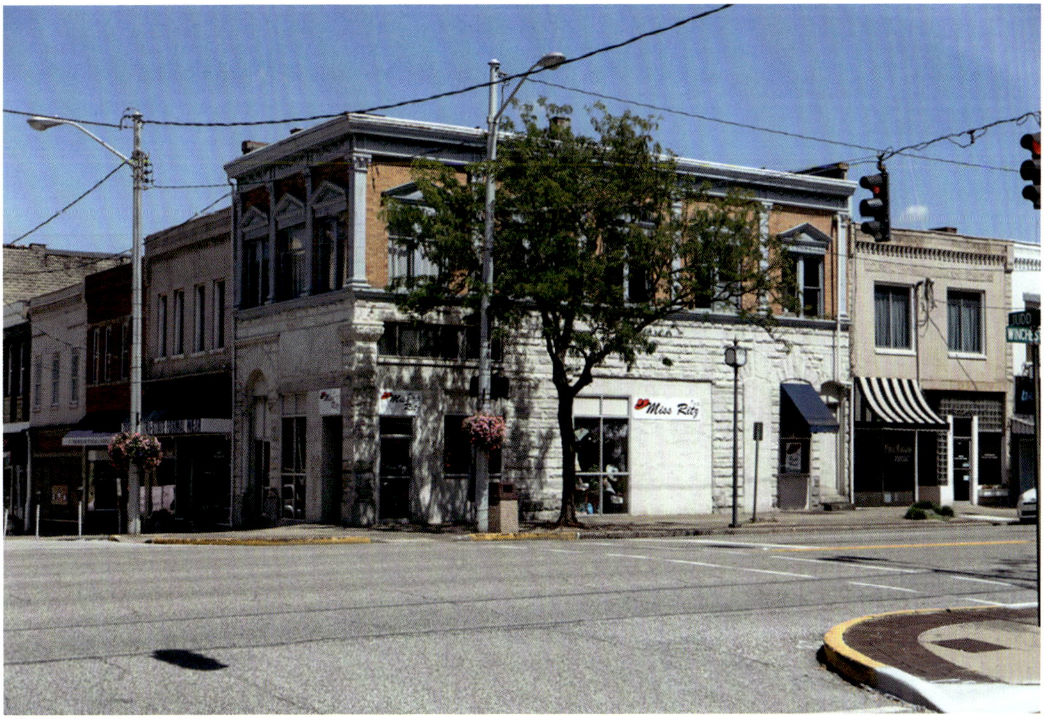

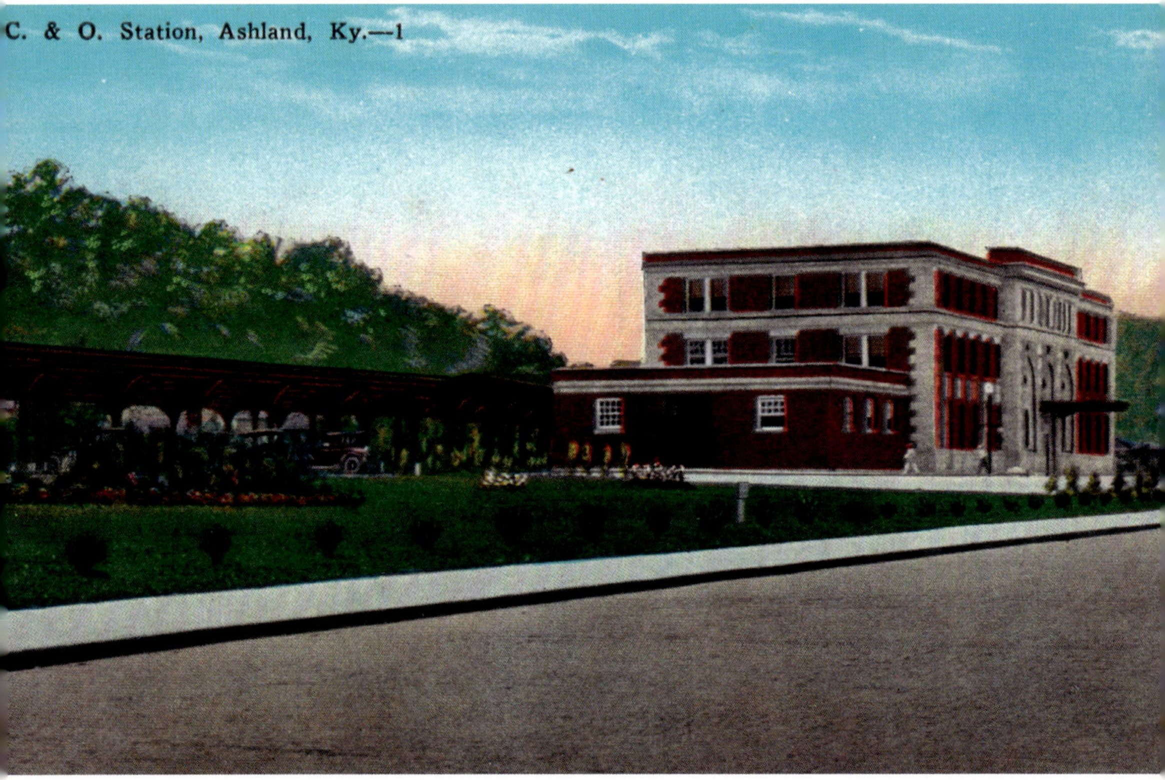

C. & O. Station, Ashland, Ky.—1

THE C&O RAILWAY DEPOT: The depot was built in the 1920s and continued as such until the late 1970s or so. As of the printing of this book the building is owned and operates as the National City Bank. A rail passenger car is parked behind the building where some rails have been left in place.

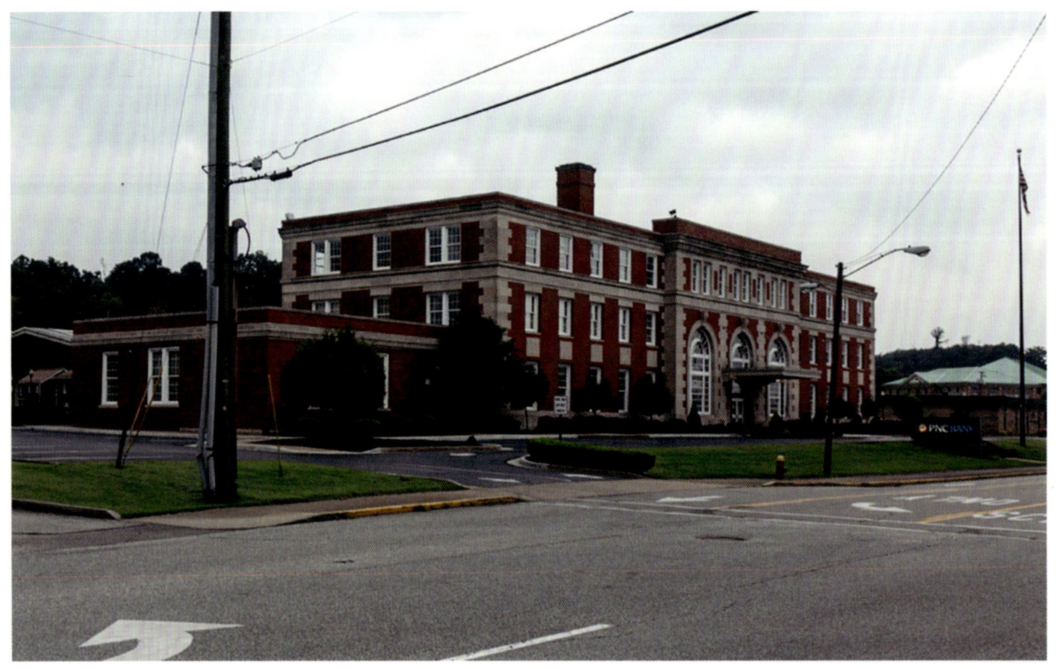

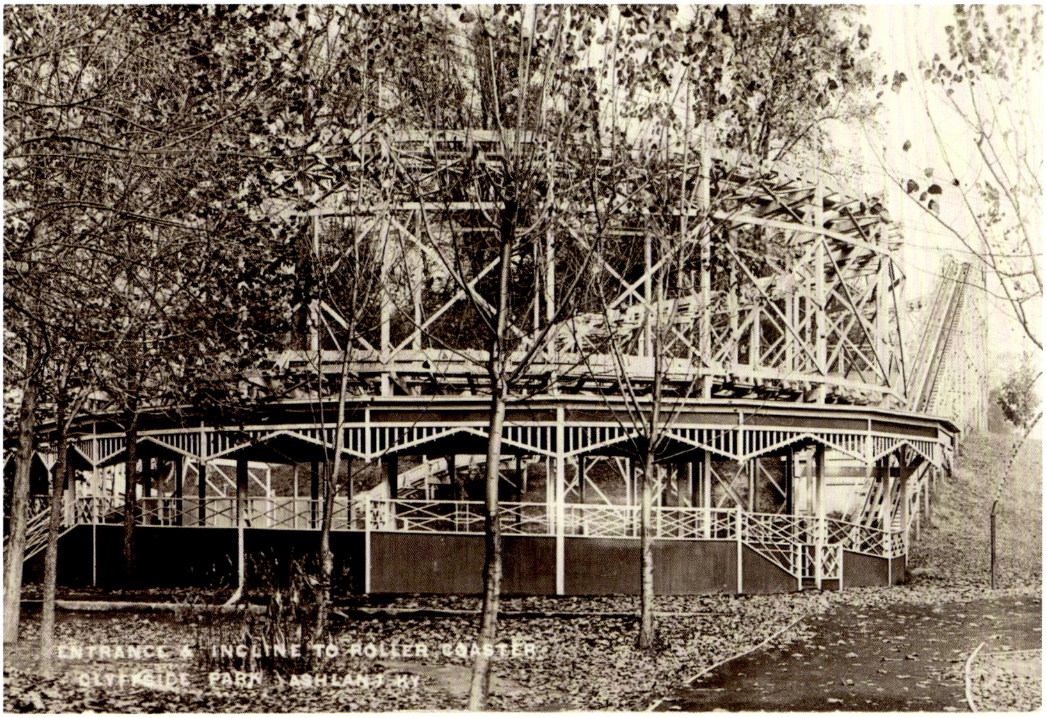

THE ROLLERCOASTER: This rare postcard photograph from *c.* 1900 shows the area's first rollercoaster. Located at Clyffside Park, it drew thrill-seekers from hundreds of miles away. Currently there are several ballparks located on the same property.

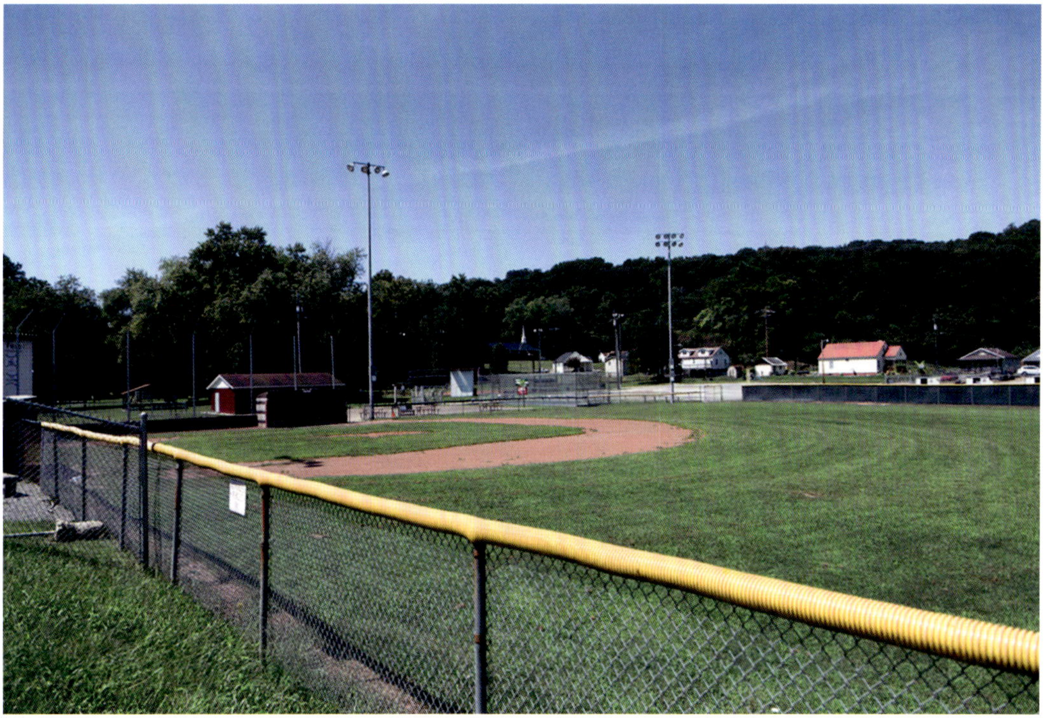

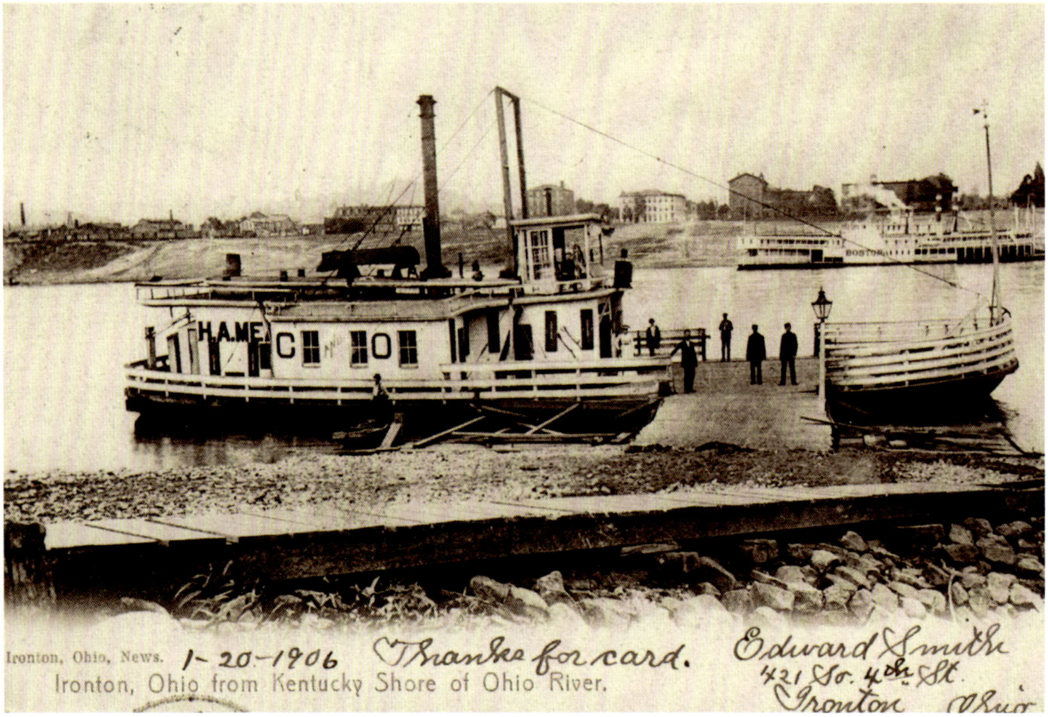

**IRONTON VIEWED FROM THE KENTUCKY SHORE:** A small steamboat is docked on the bank of the Ohio River from the Russell, Kentucky side. Downtown Ironton is across the river in the background with the side steamer *Boston* docked. This postcard photograph dates from around 1905.

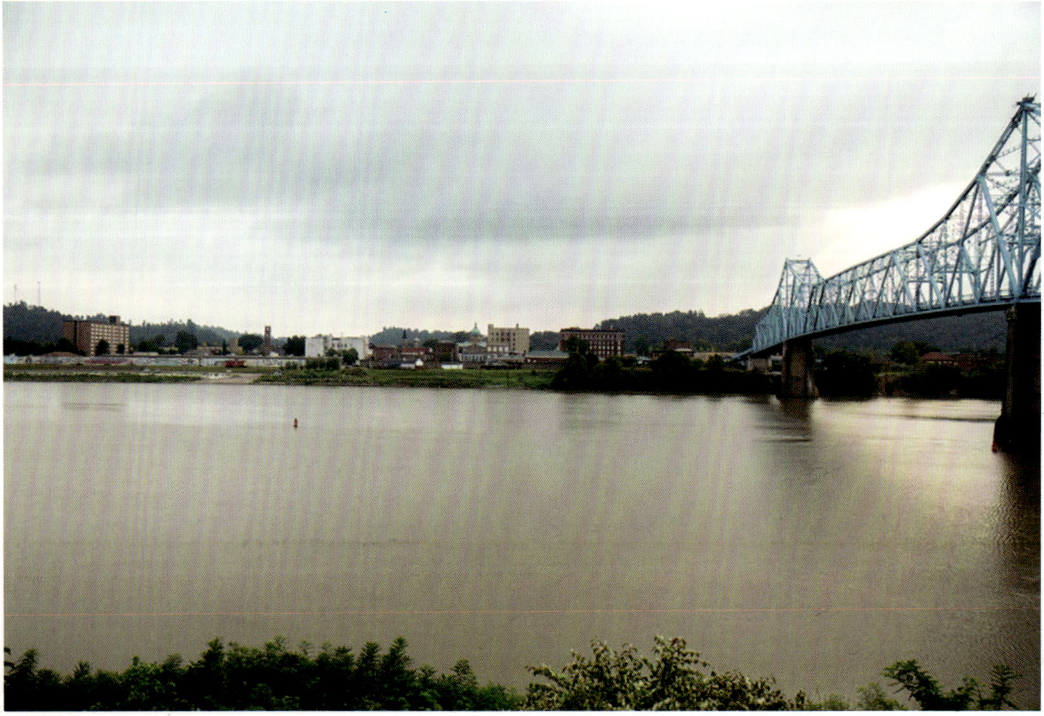

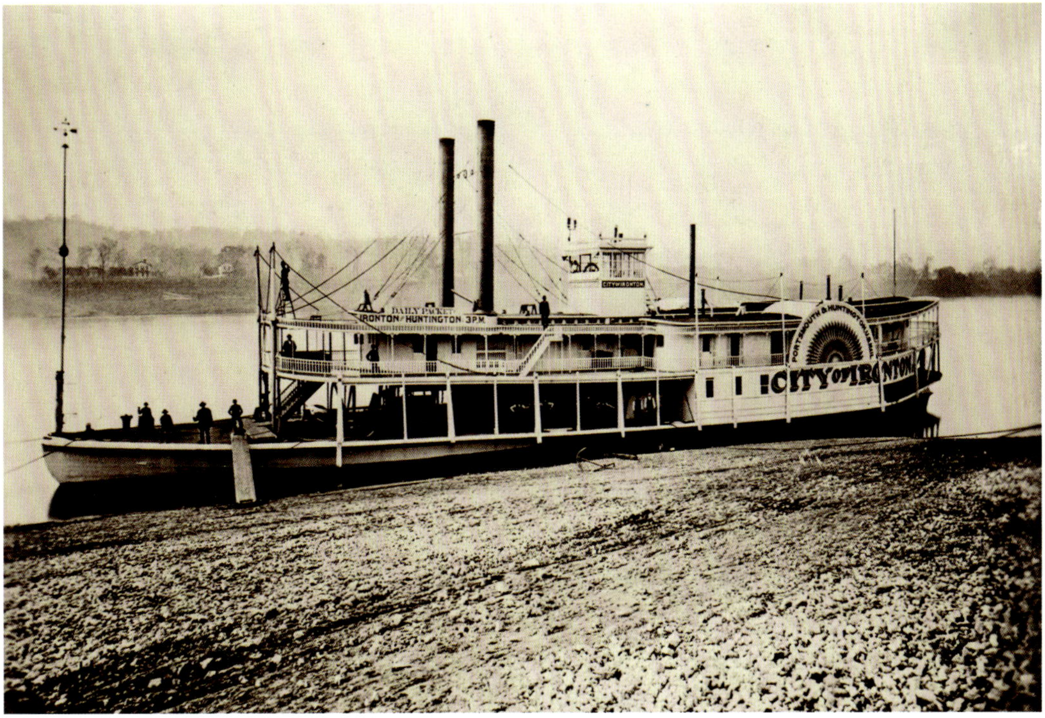

CITY OF IRONTON: For many years the old steamer *City of Ironton* transported passengers between Portsmouth and Huntington twice daily. As the railway became more reliable, cheaper, and much quicker, travelers opted for that mode between cities thus ending the era of passenger travel along the Ohio.

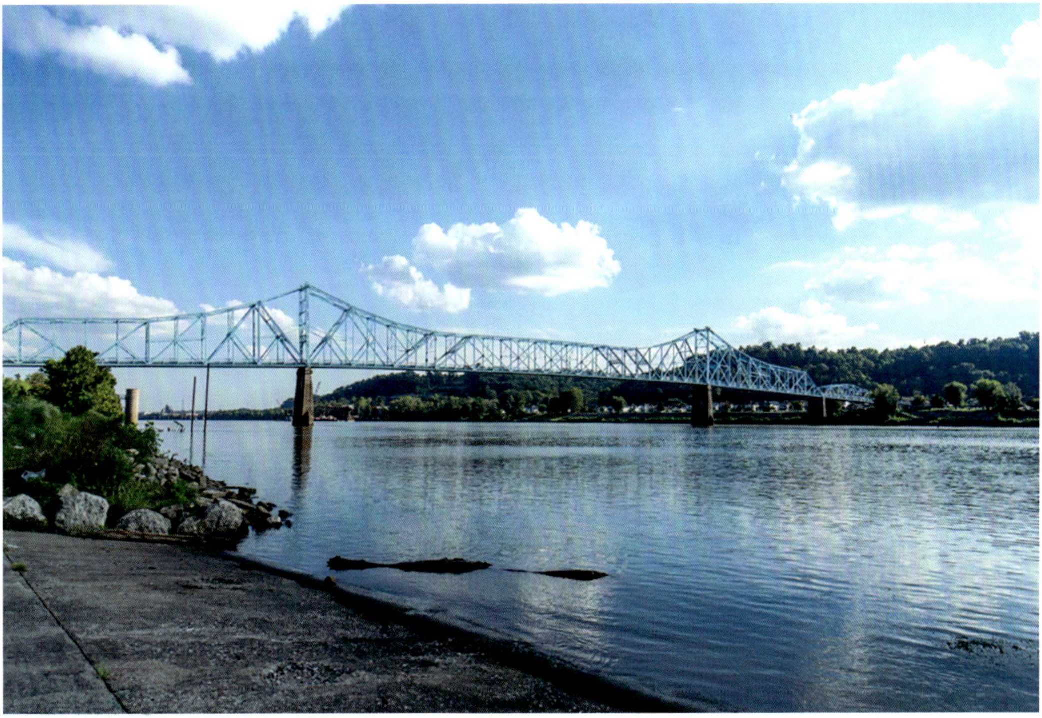

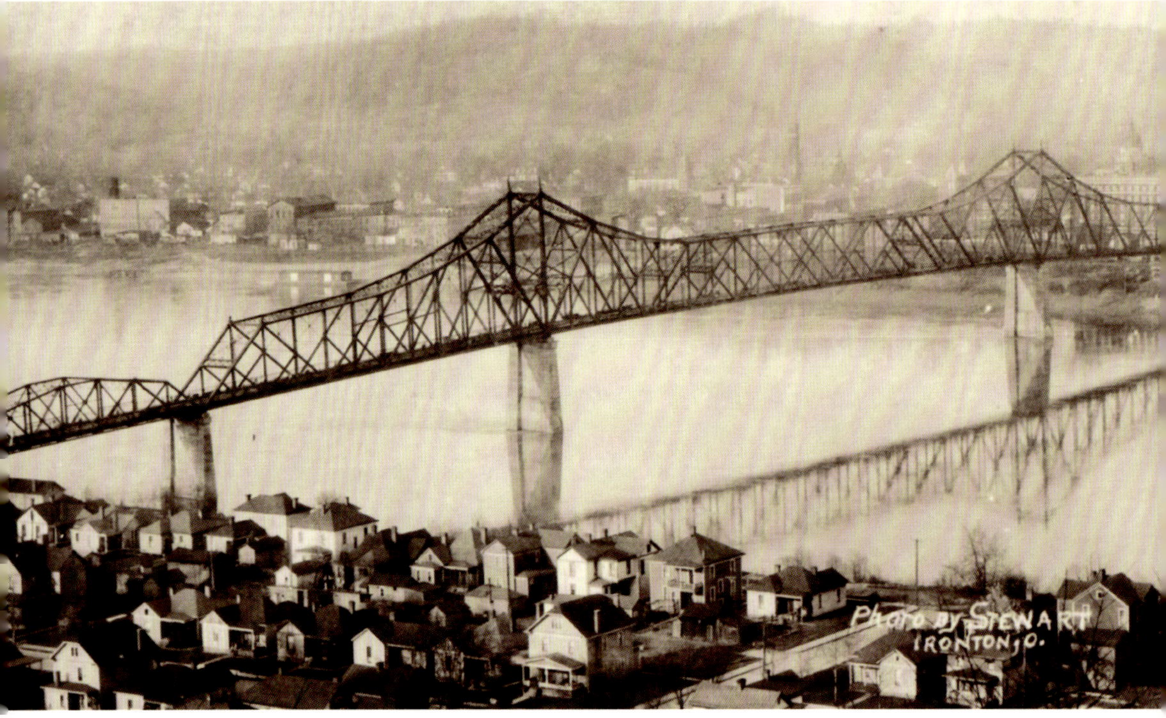

THE IRONTON RUSSELL BRIDGE: Opened to traffic in 1922, this was the first bridge between the north and south banks of the Ohio River in the tri-state area. It began its life painted in a dark color, however for many years the span has been light blue. The structure is due to be replaced not long after the publication of this book.

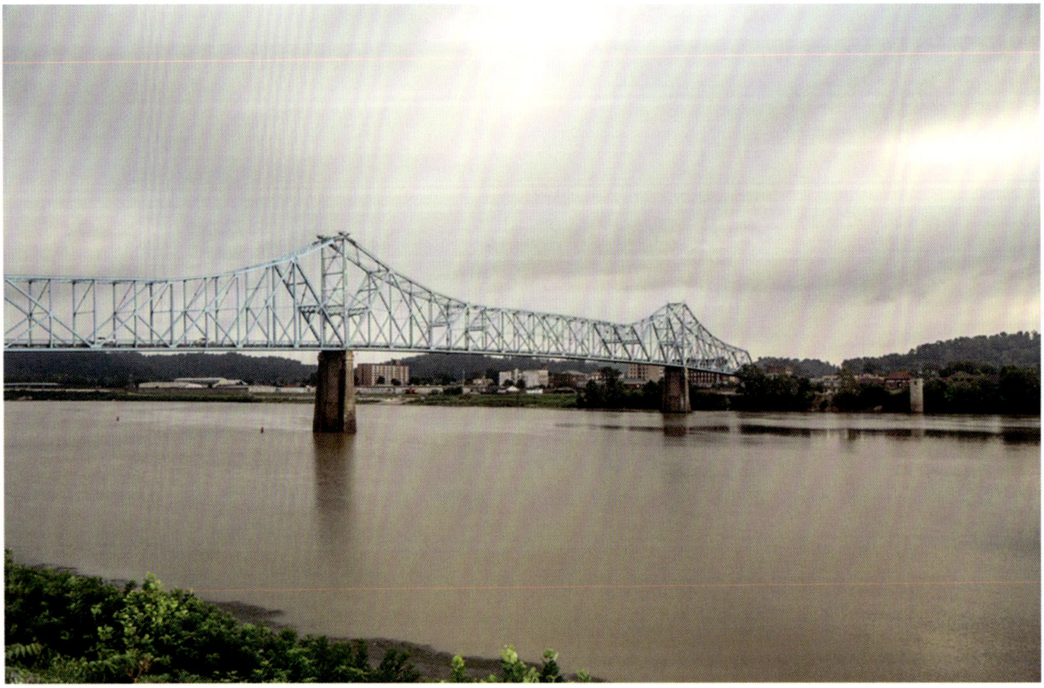

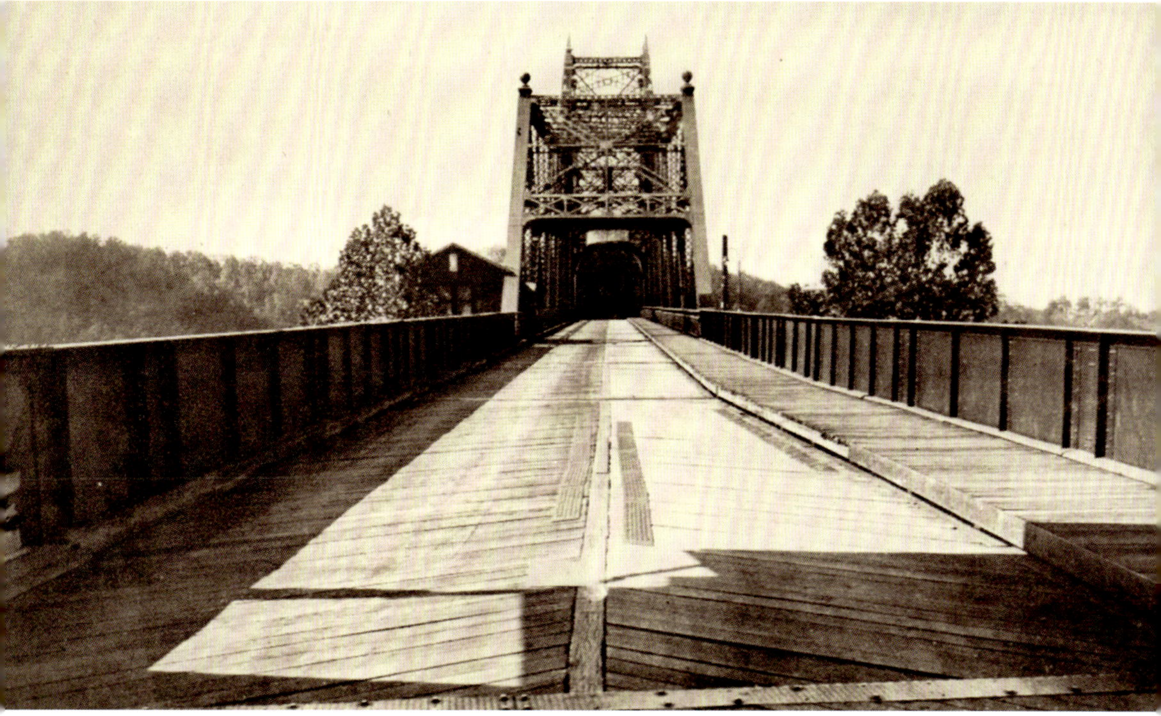

THE FIRST TOLL BOOTH: In the older undated photograph the toll both was located to the left of the bridge as a vehicle traveled south from Ironton to Russell. In the 1940s the booth was moved to the center of the road near this point. Tolls stopped being taken around 1978 and the booth was removed.

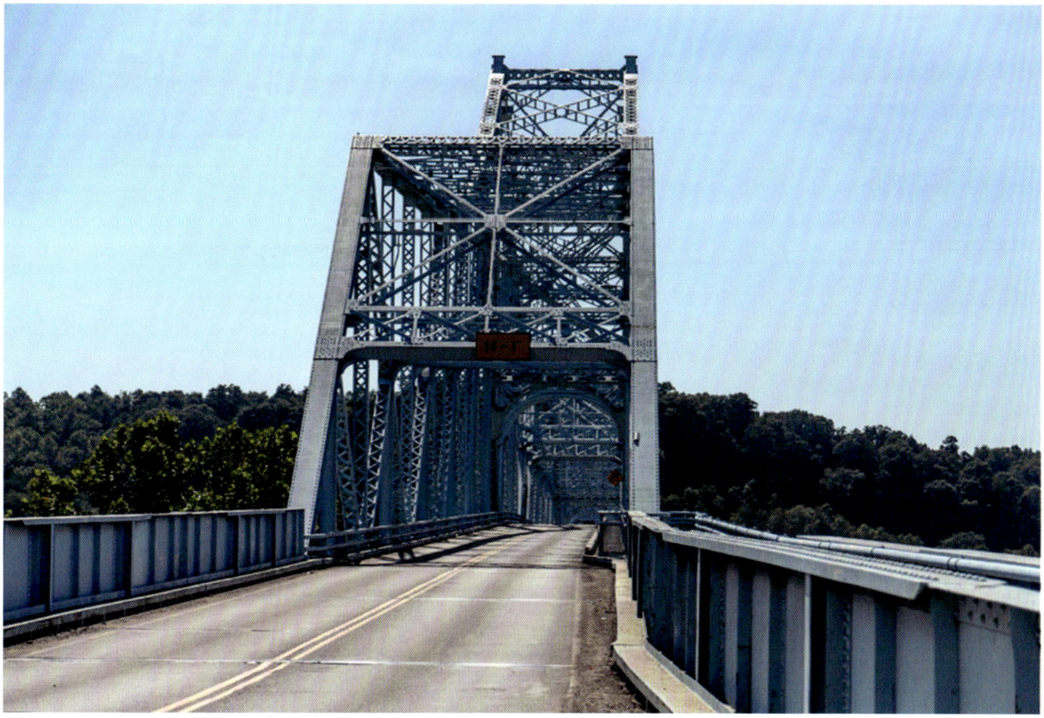

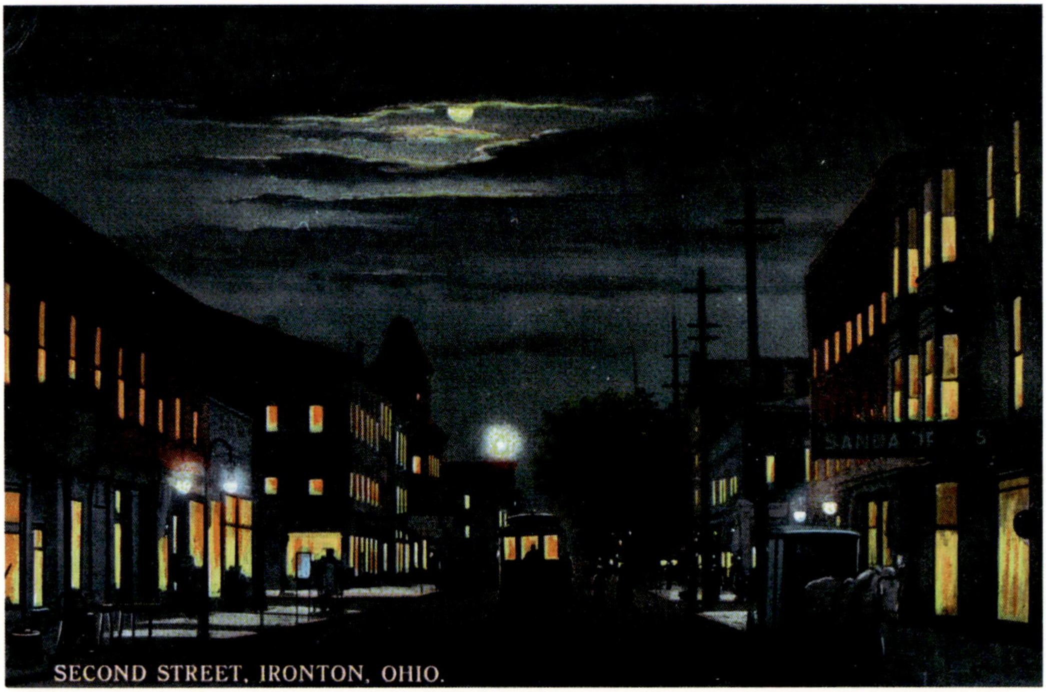

A STREETCAR IN IRONTON: Ironton's second street is lit up by electricity and gas in the old postcard from around 1900. Currently, many people visit the 2nd street area in order to dine at one of the area's finest Italian Restaurants, *Melini Cucina*.

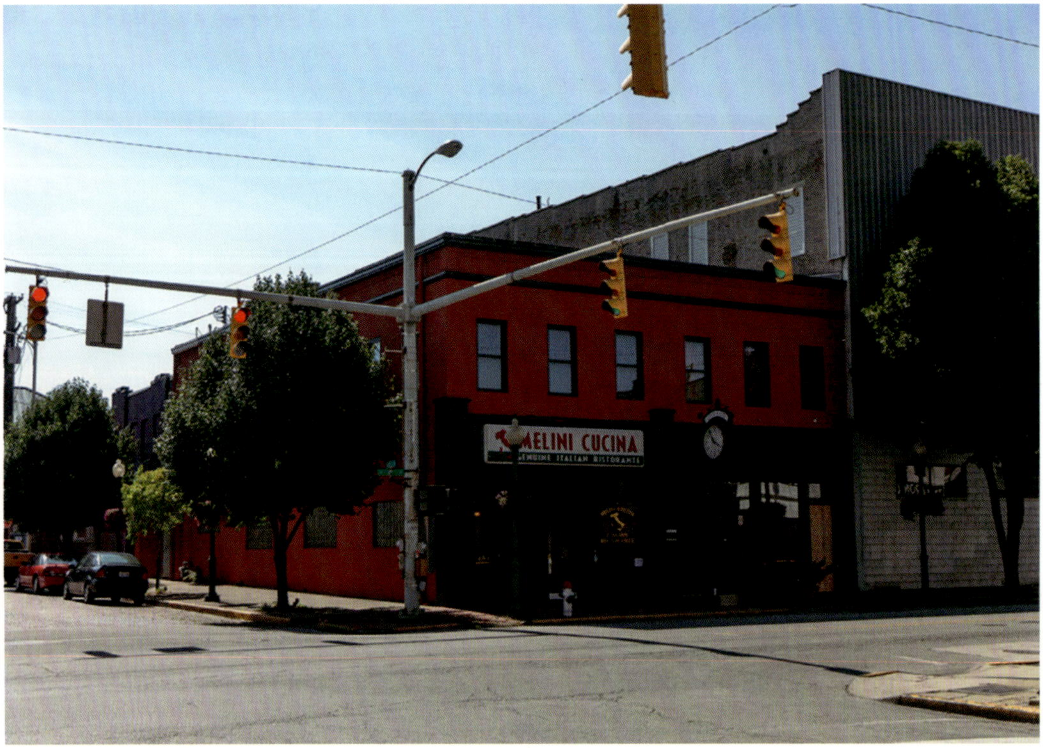

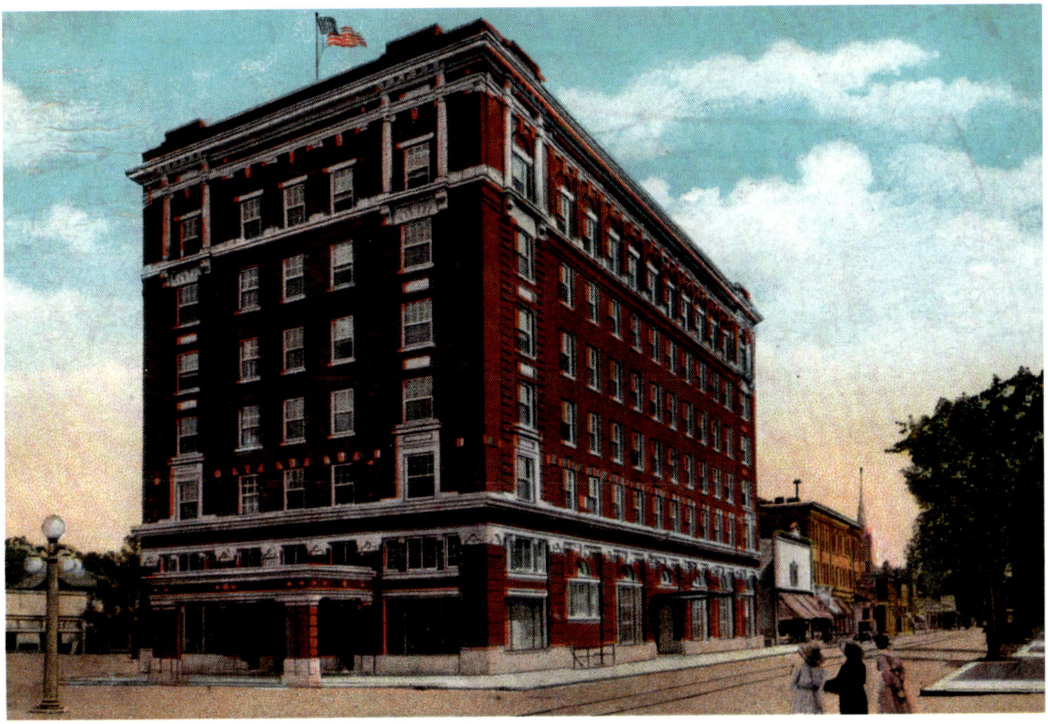

THE MARTING HOTEL: The red brick Marting Hotel has been a familiar fixture in the Ironton cityscape since it opened its door in 1921. After a major transformation in the late 1990s the building houses elderly citizens with a new name, Park Avenue Apartments.

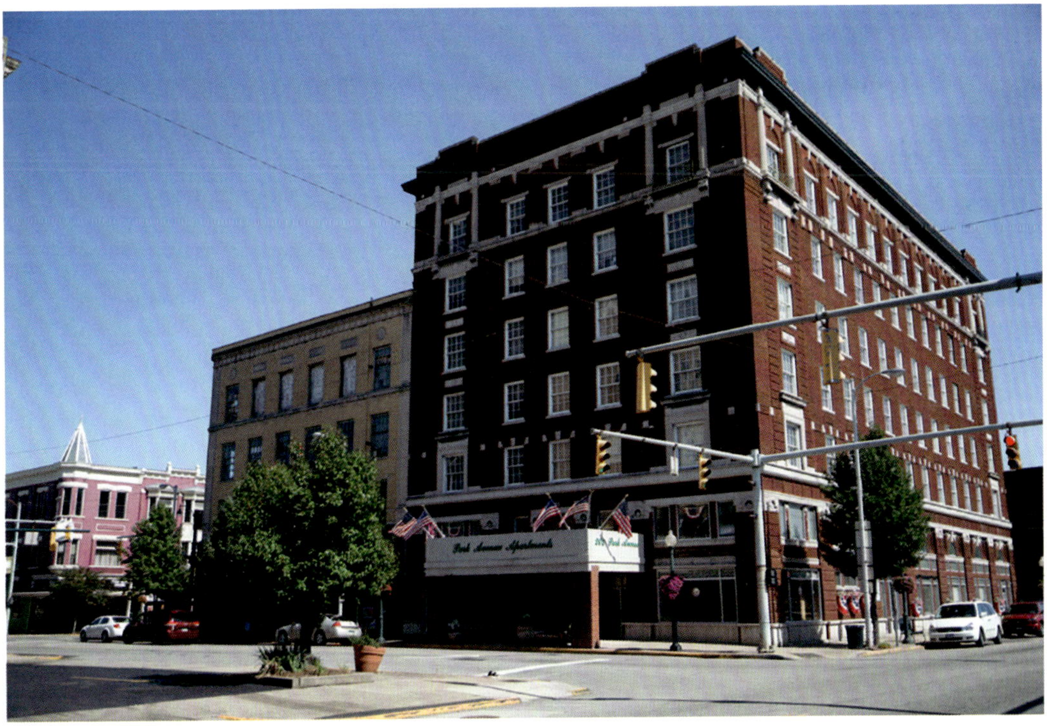

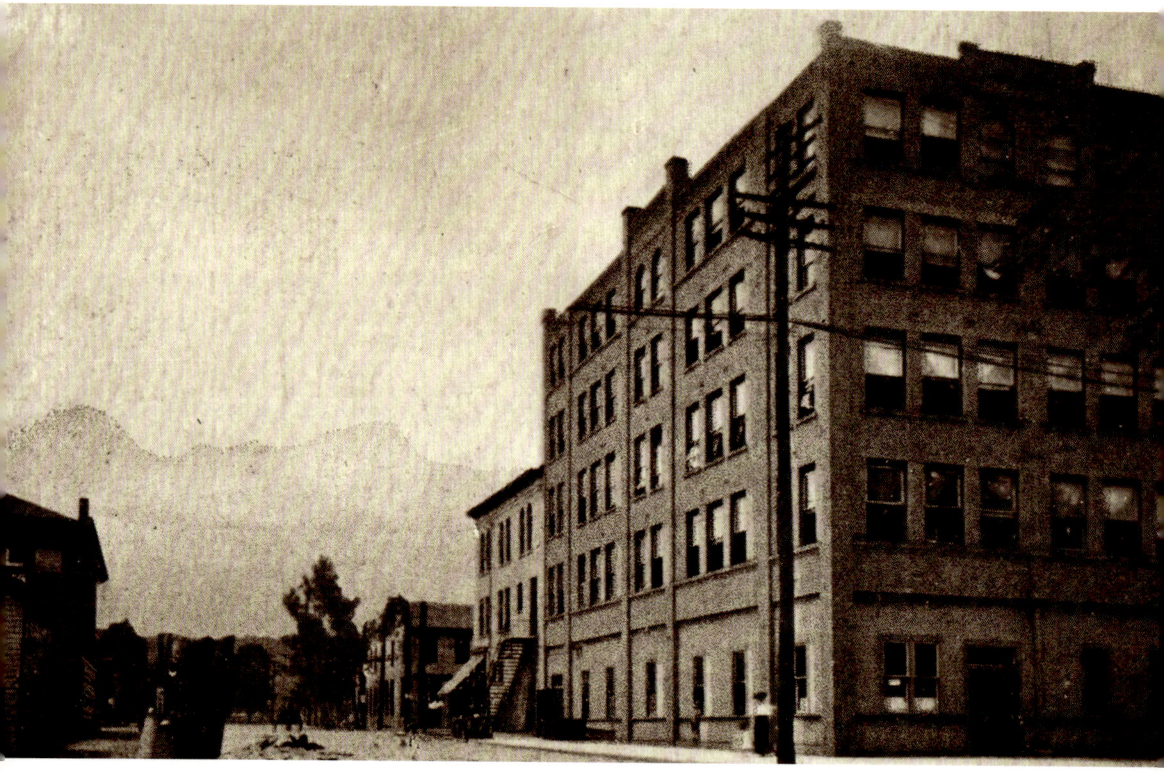

THE OLD CIGAR FACTORY: The factory building still stands at the corner of Vernon Street and 3rd. The city of Ironton was well known for the iron produced there, however over the years many other businesses have developed and thrived in the city.

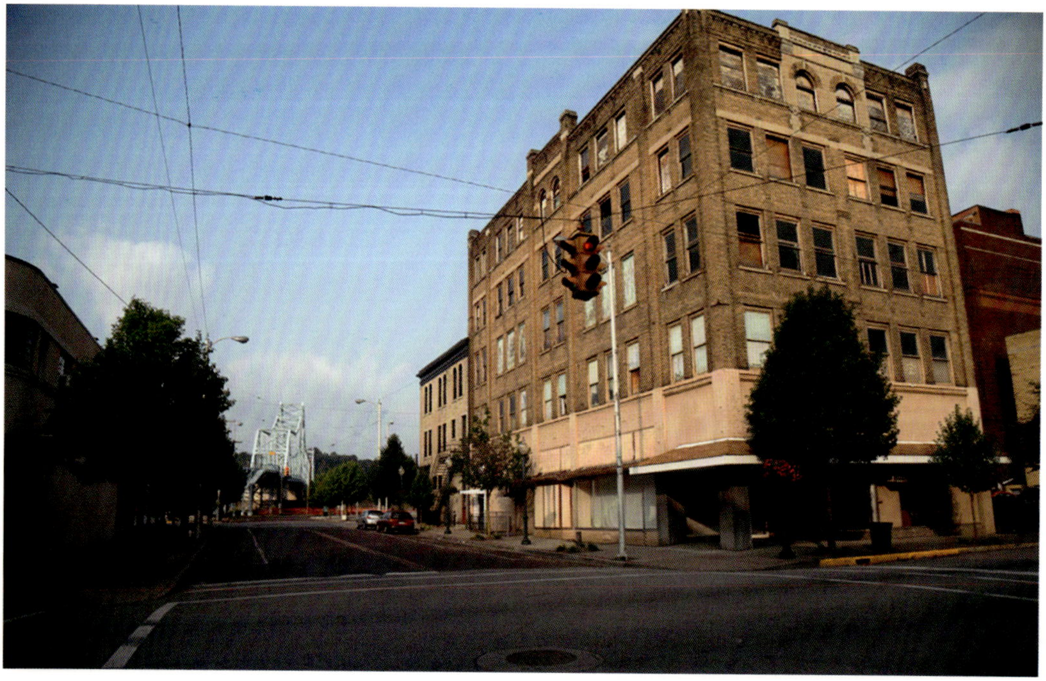

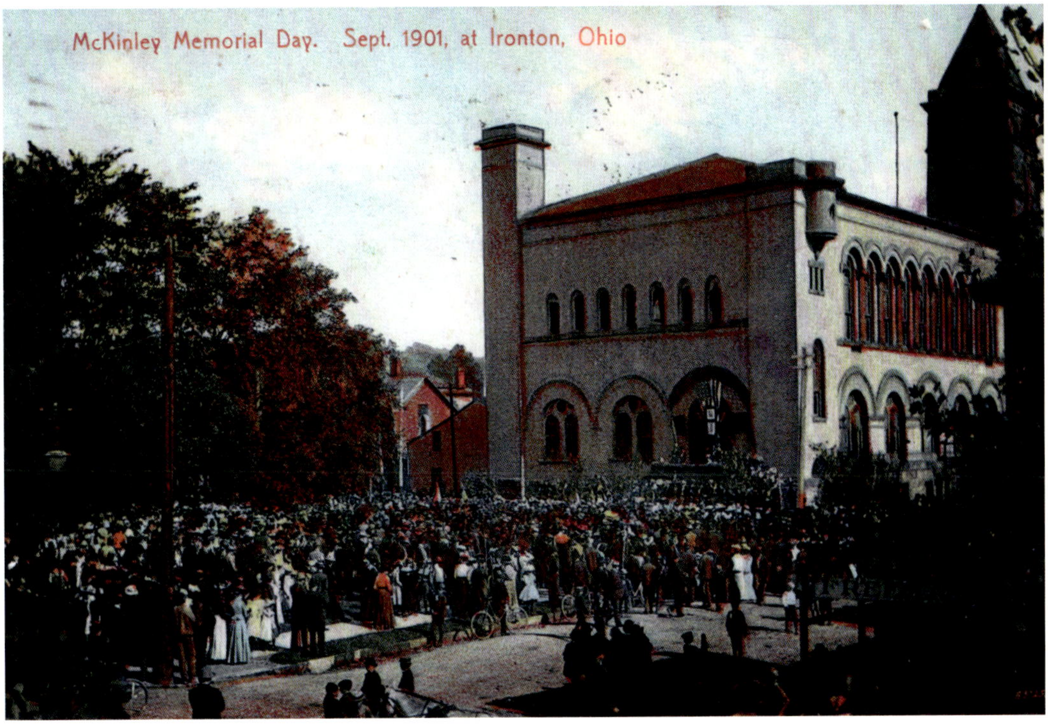

McKinley Memorial Day. Sept. 1901, at Ironton, Ohio

OHIO'S SON: When Ohio's own William McKinley—the 25th President of the United States—was assassinated in 1901, Ironton built a memorial for their fallen son in the front of Memorial Hall. It was rebuilt in 1905 after a fire, but has been recently demolished due to safety concerns.

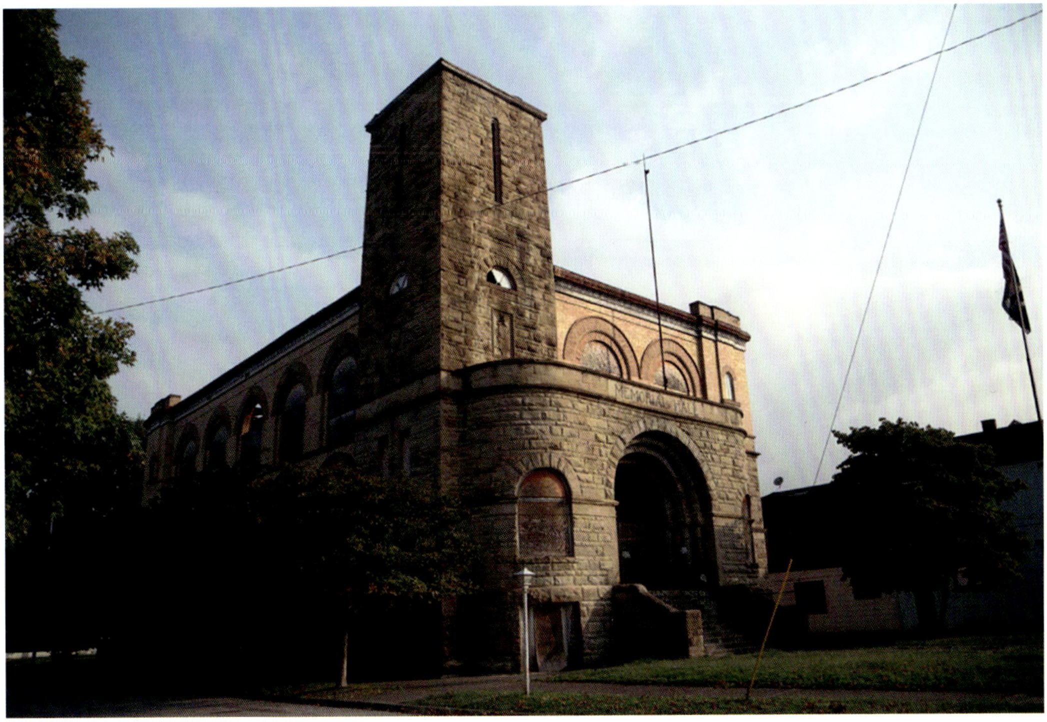

MEMORIAL HALL

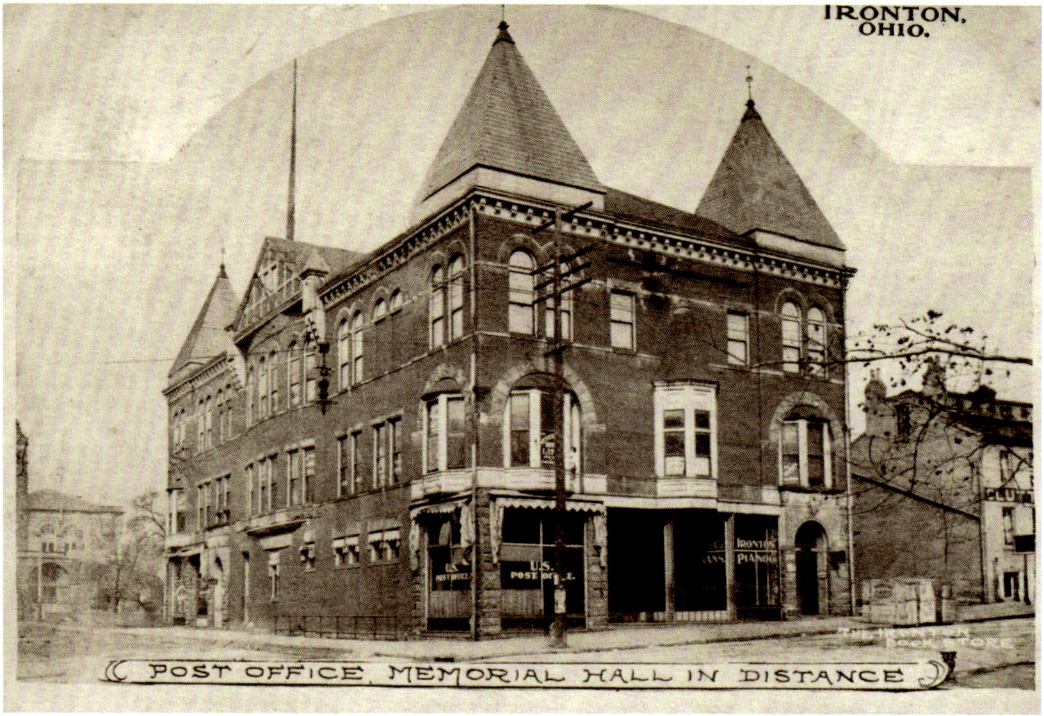

THE OLD POST OFFICE: The Victorian-styled U.S. Post Office served Ironton for many years. Other organizations also used the same building. At the time writing, this building—which stands across the road from the courthouse—continues to house several local businesses.

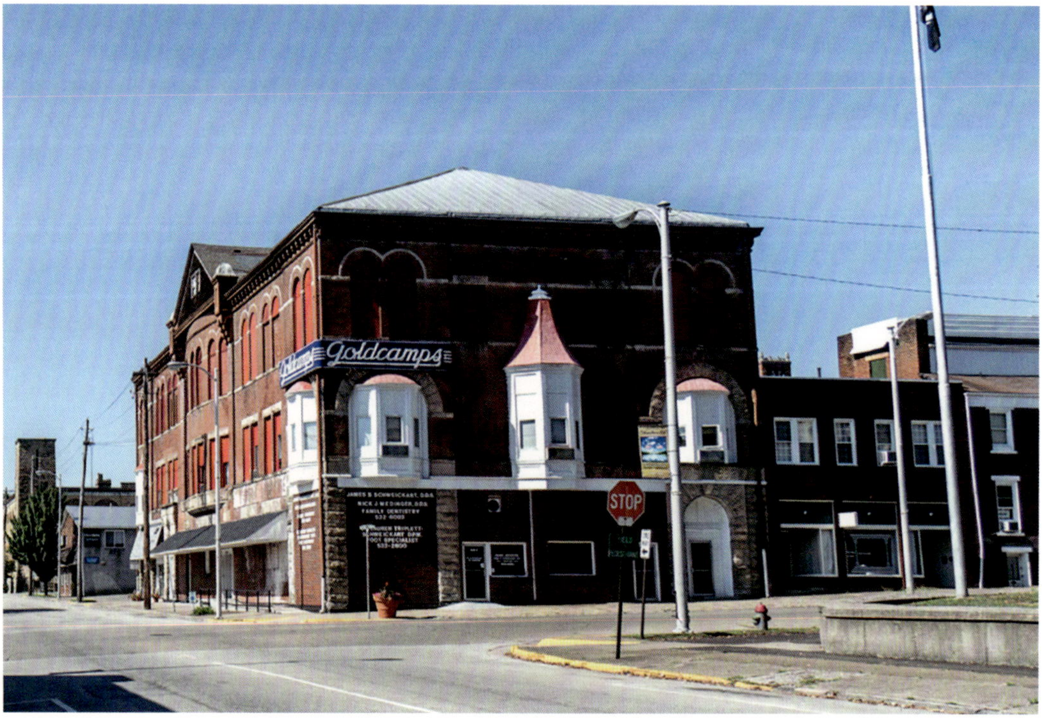

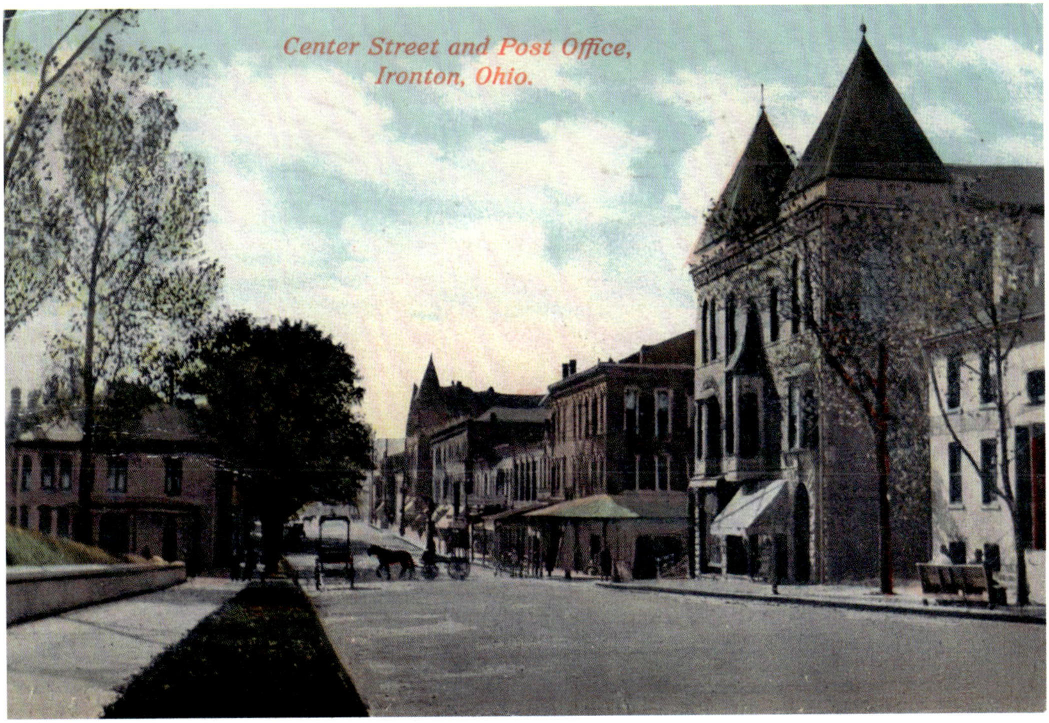

CENTER STREET: This postcard of Center Street dates from *c.* 1900. The Post Office can be seen to the left together with several horse-drawn wagons. Today many of the buildings remain the same as they were 116 years ago, but horse power is no longer needed.

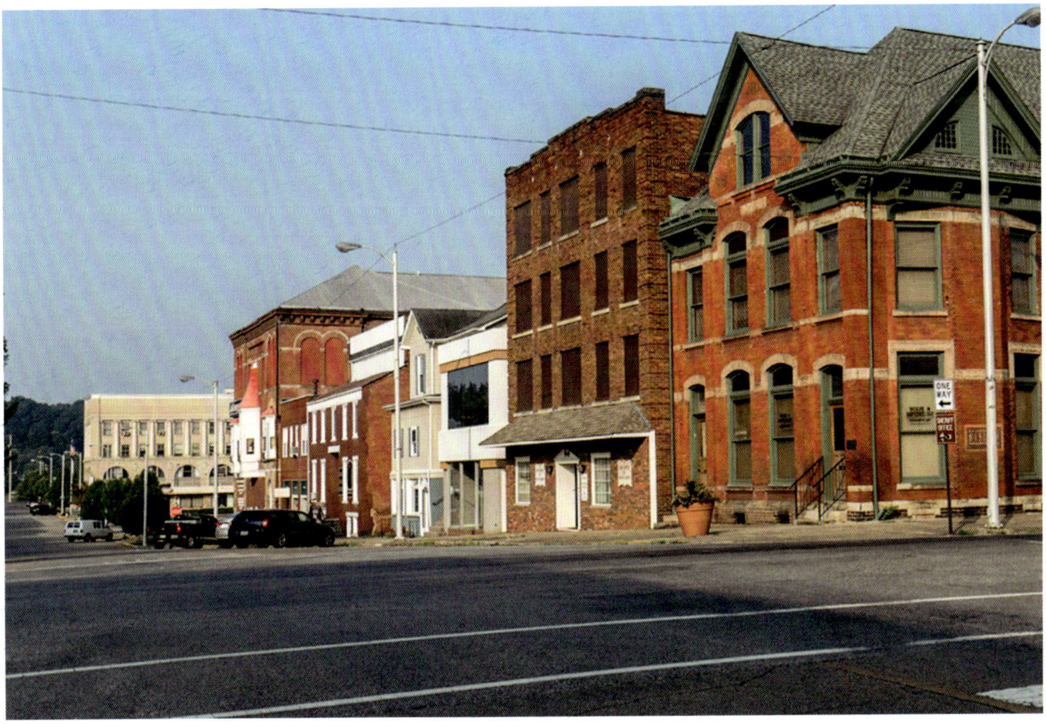

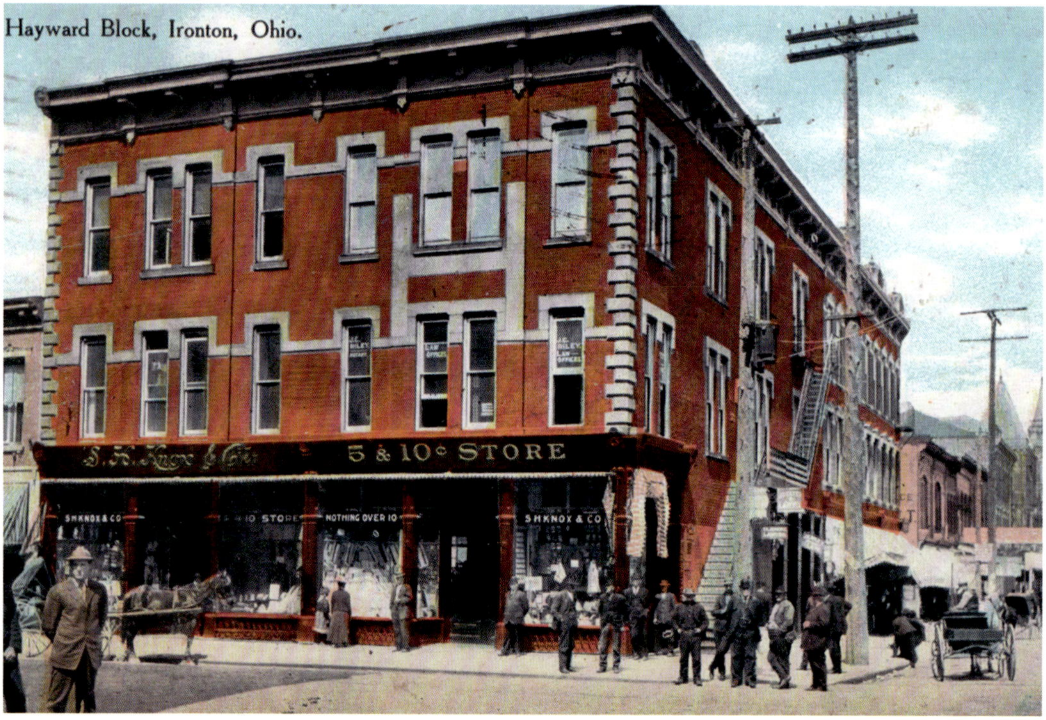

Hayward Block, Ironton, Ohio.

HAYWARD BLOCK, IRONTON: Similar to today's dollar store, advertisements on the windows of Ironton's old 5 & 10 cent Store declare that they sell nothing over 10 cents. At some point, the building was remodeled to what we have at the Hayward Block location today.

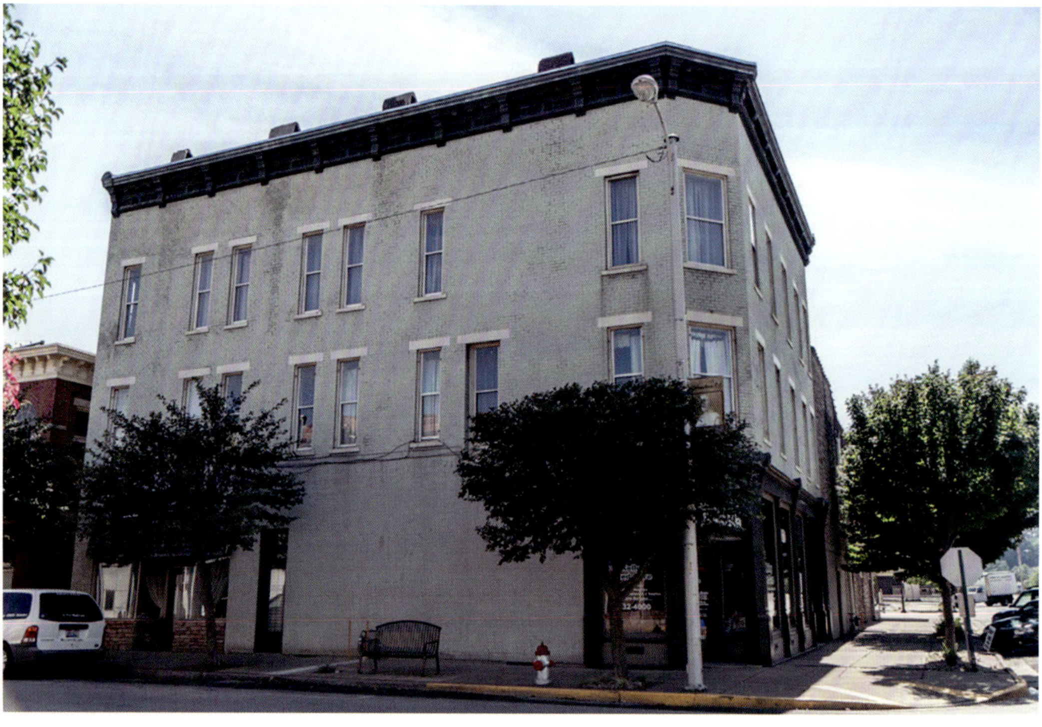

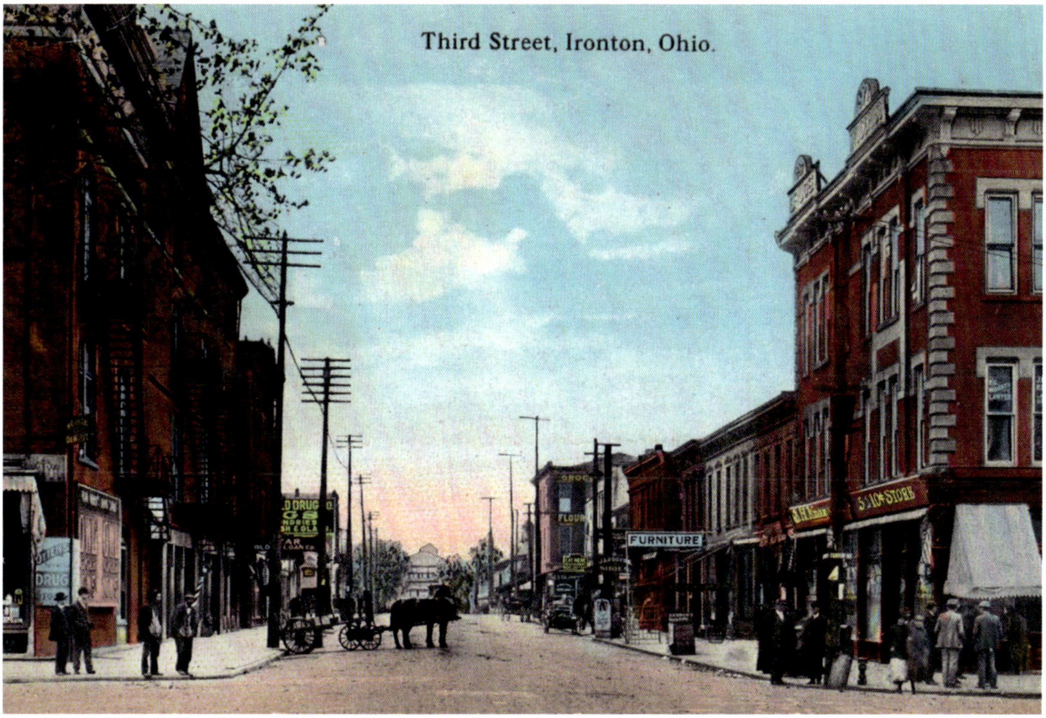

Third Street, Ironton, Ohio.

3rd Street: A drug and furniture store is visible in the postcard view of Ironton's 3rd Street from 1905. As of the writing of this book there are many available office and store spaces along this street. One of the more appealing structures on 3rd Street houses a Mexican restaurant on the street level.

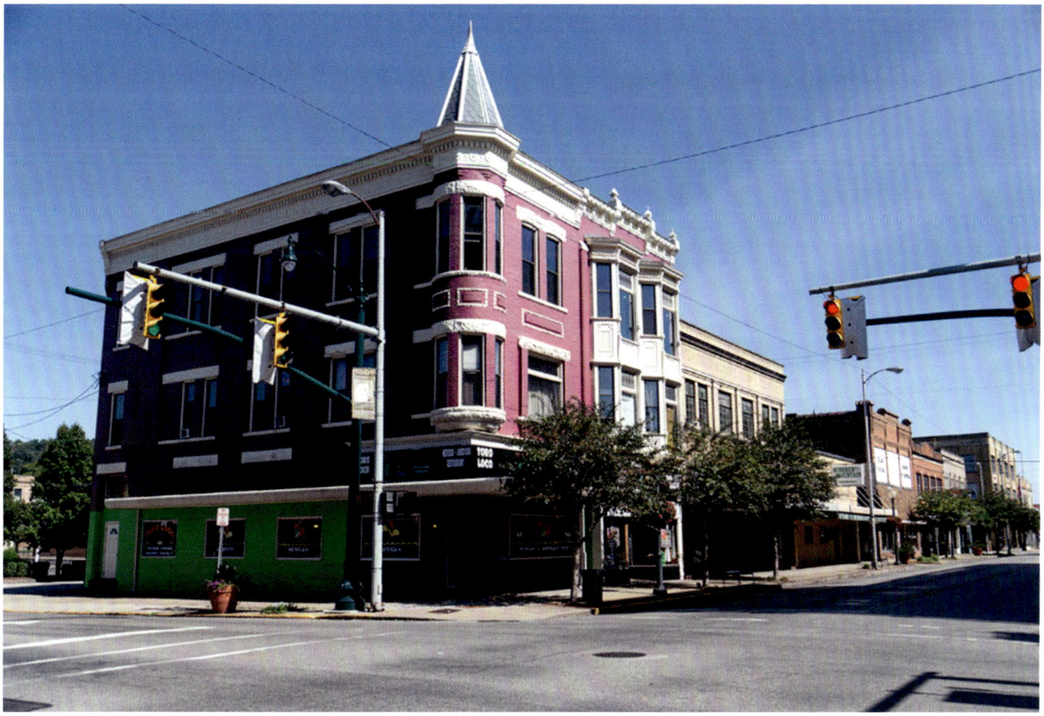

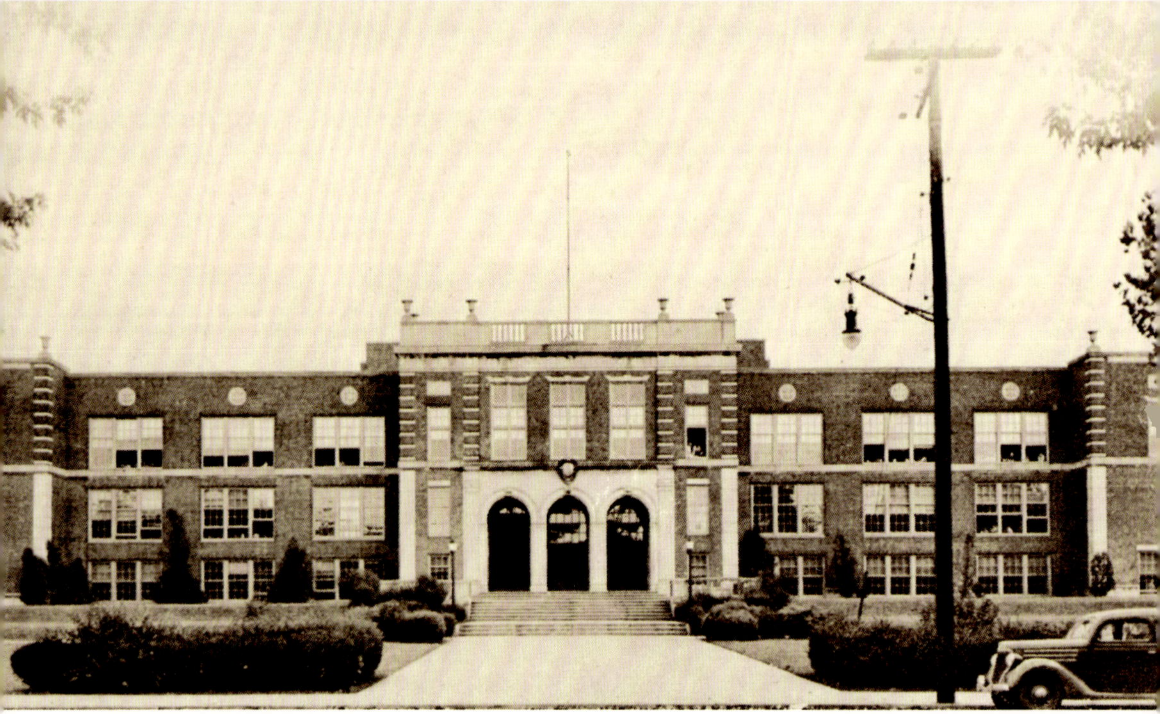

**IRONTON HIGH SCHOOL:** Originally built in 1922, Ironton High School had around 80 percent of the school demolished and rebuilt. The original front entrance was saved and with the new addition maintains its 1922 characteristic look. The city is very proud of this new home of the Fighting Tigers.

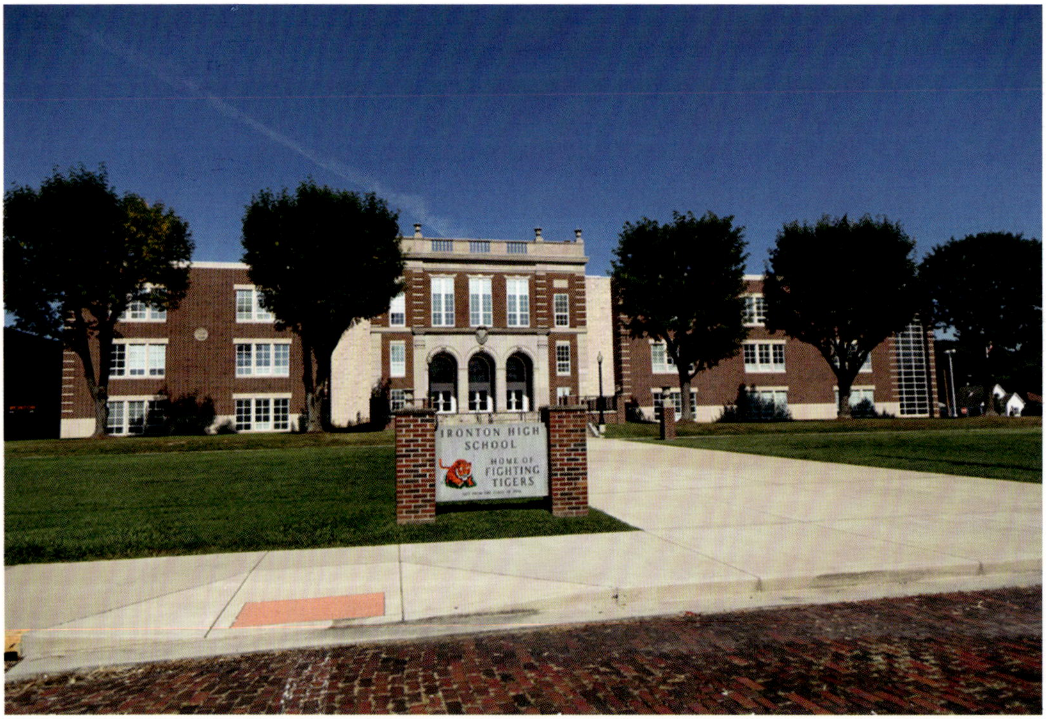

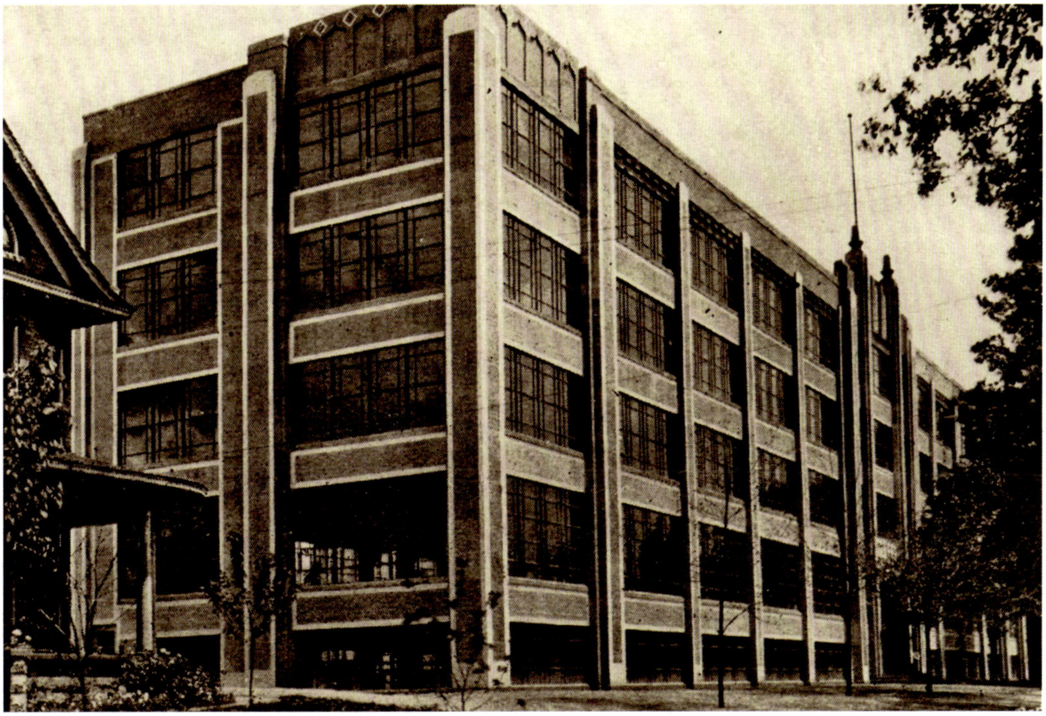

**IRONTON ART DECO:** On the east side of the city stands the five story tall old Shelby Shoe Factory. Built by Roger Shelby in the mid-1920s it has employed many hundreds of people of its time. The date of the construction is easy to see due to the Art Deco style of the façade.

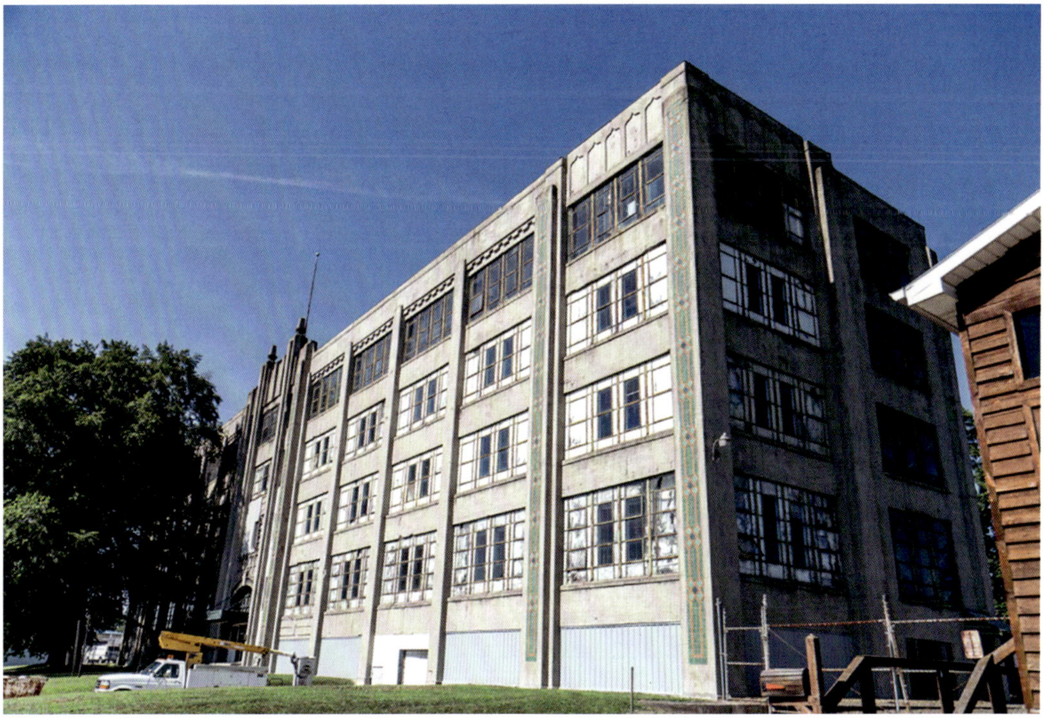

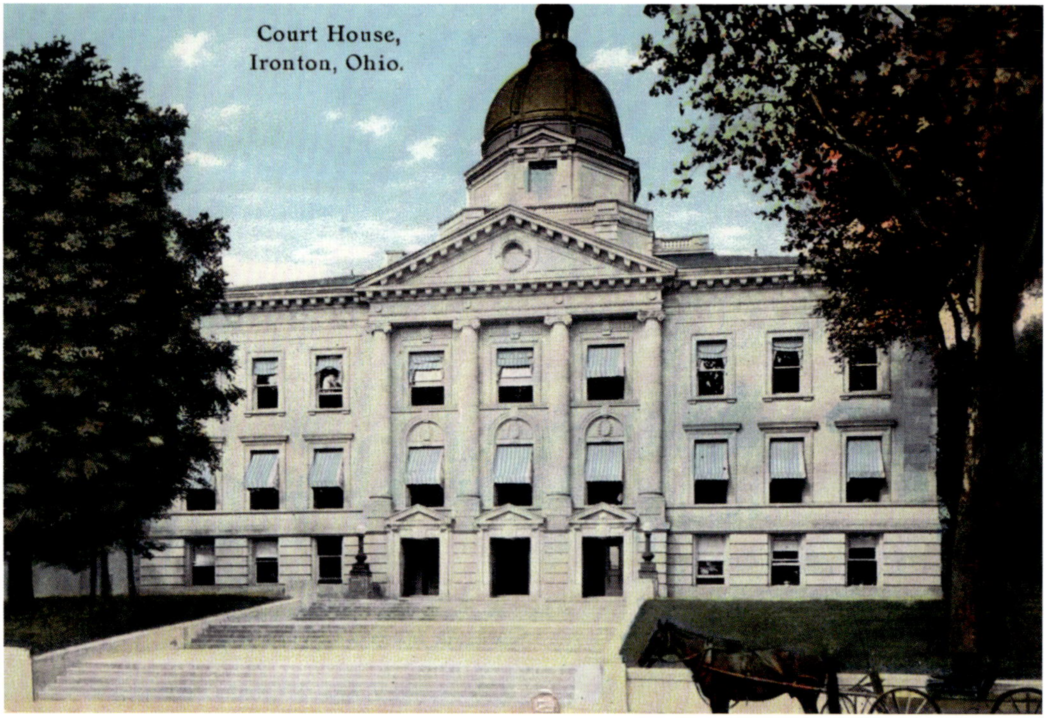

Court House,
Ironton, Ohio.

THE LAWRENCE COUNTY COURTHOUSE: The Courthouse in the center of Ironton was built in 1907 after the previous courthouse had burned. Like many neoclassical-style structures of the time, this building had Ionic columns and included a large dome at the center.

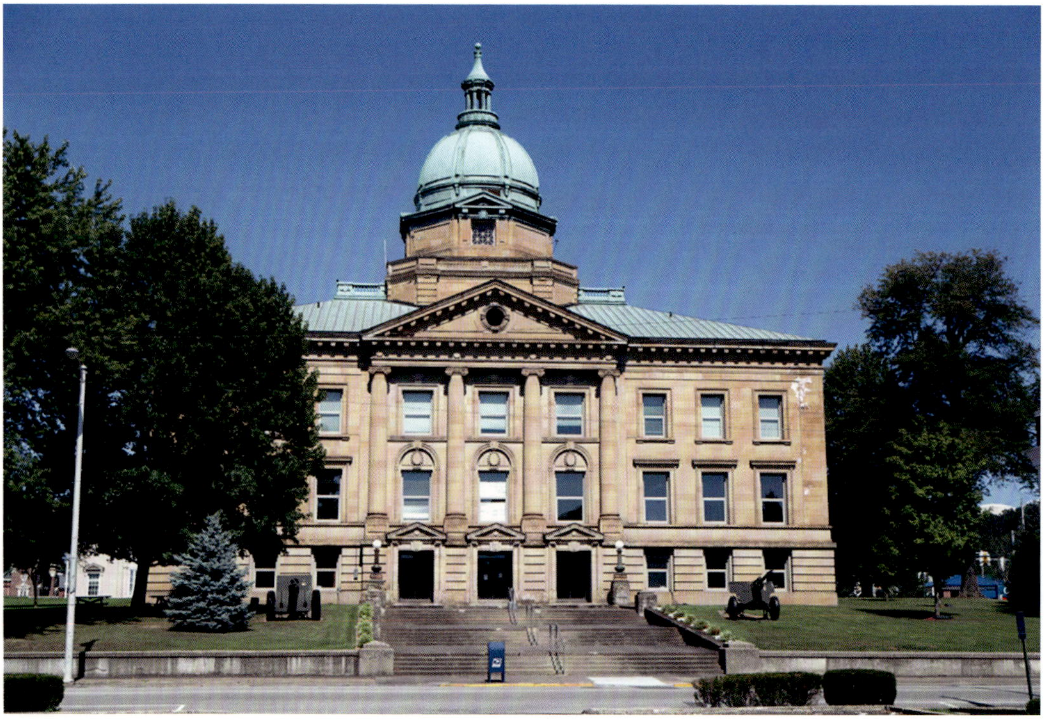

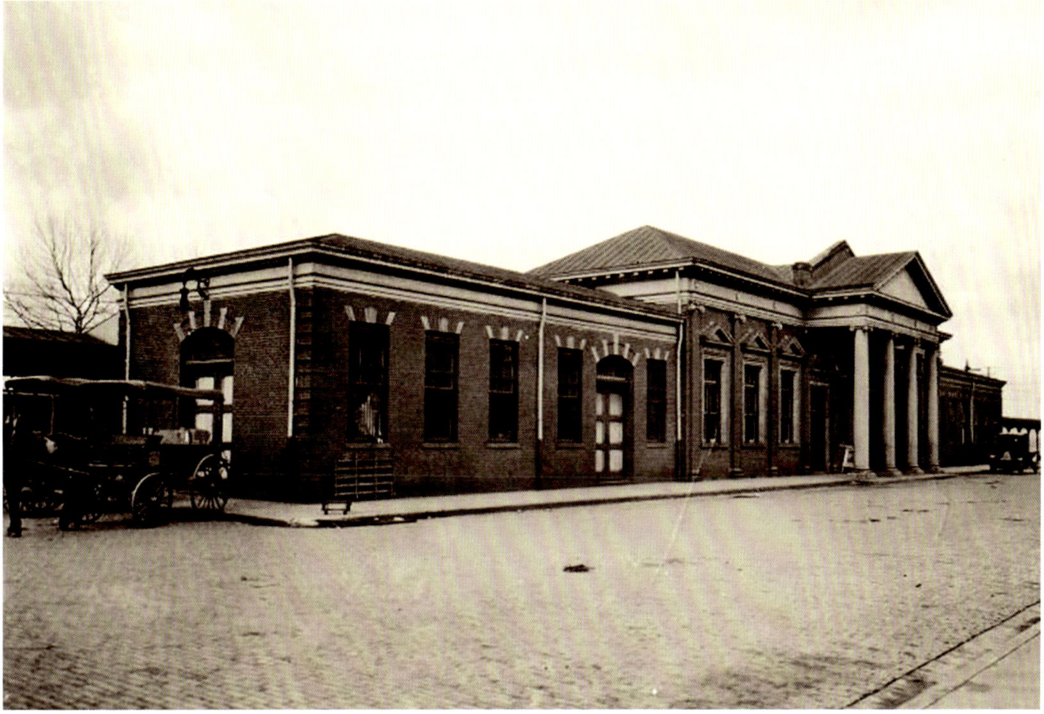

THE IRONTON NORFOLK AND WESTERN DEPOT: The depot is a single story neoclassical style structure that was built around 1905. During the structure's 50-year period as a train station, there are a few individuals around that remember catching trains here to attend a Cincinnati Reds baseball games.

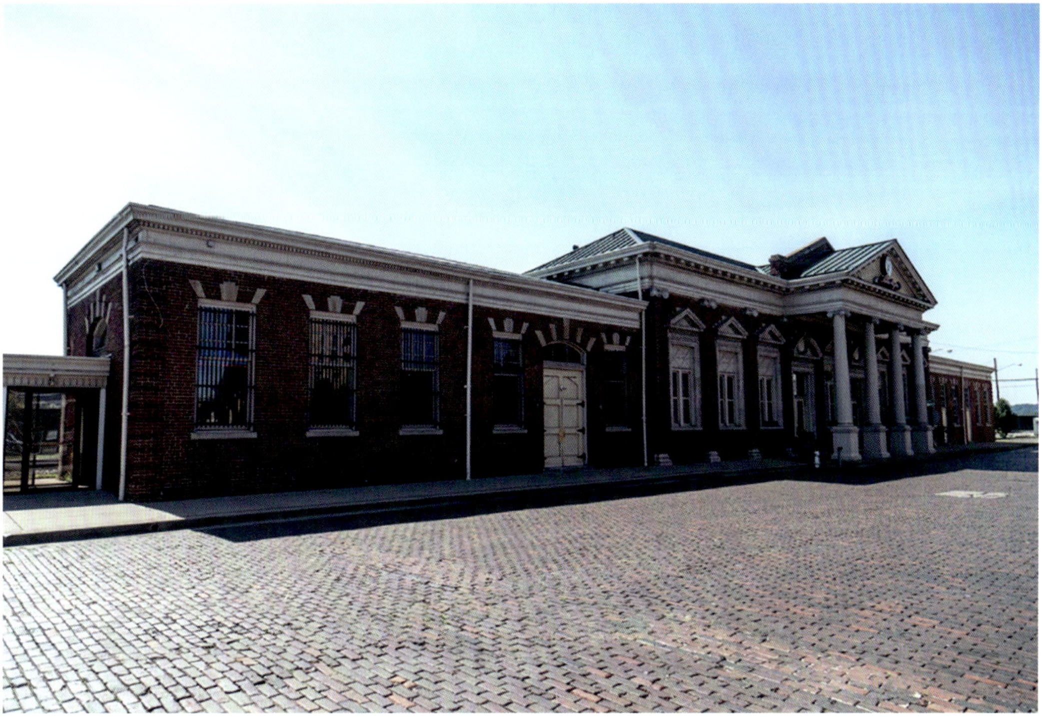

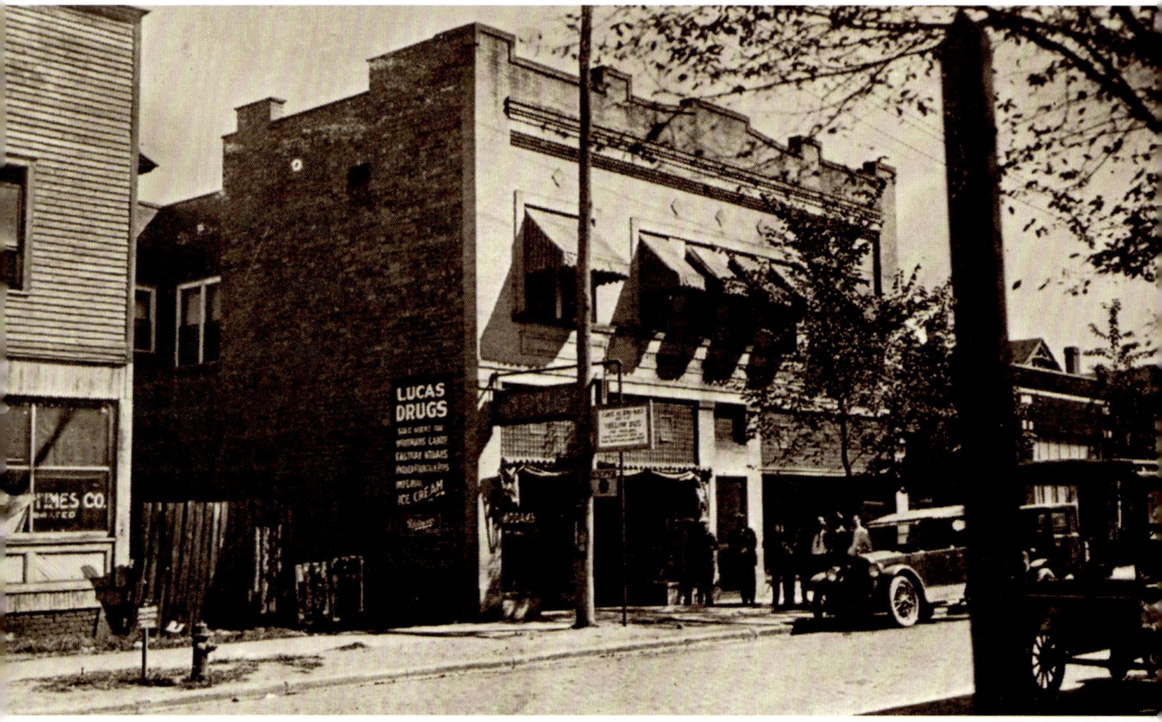

RUSSELL, KENTUCKY: Unlike Ironton, until recently Russell, Kentucky, was located in a dry county. Many individuals would walk or drive across the Ironton Russell Bridge to obtain alcohol. Russell has several antique shops as well as several vacant storefronts available for rent or purchase.

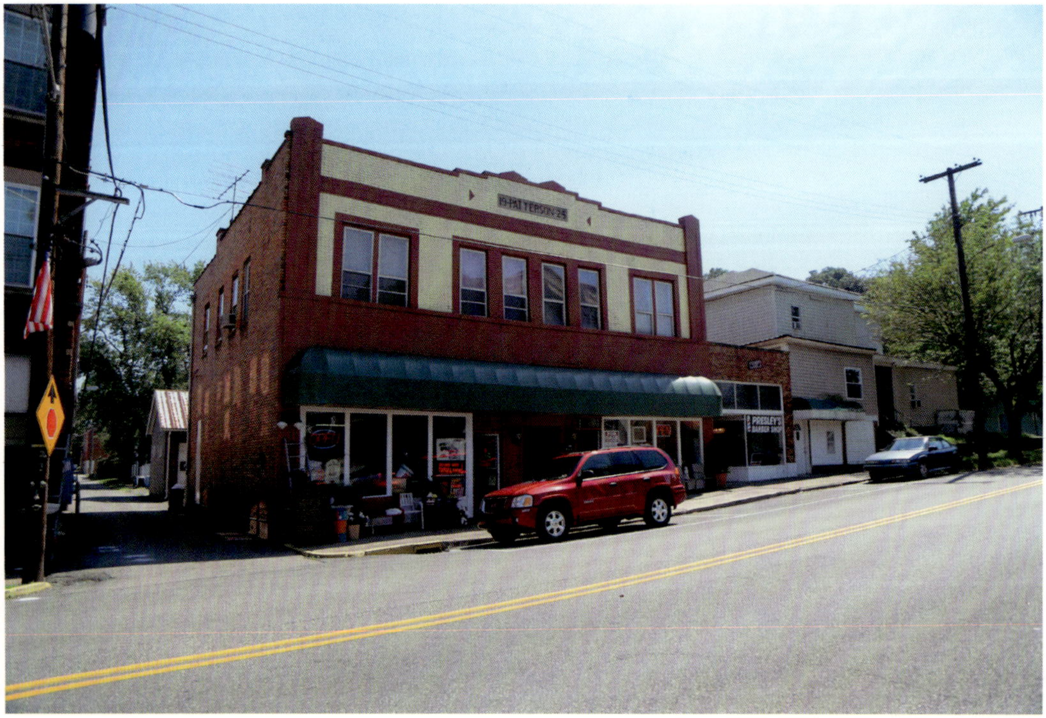

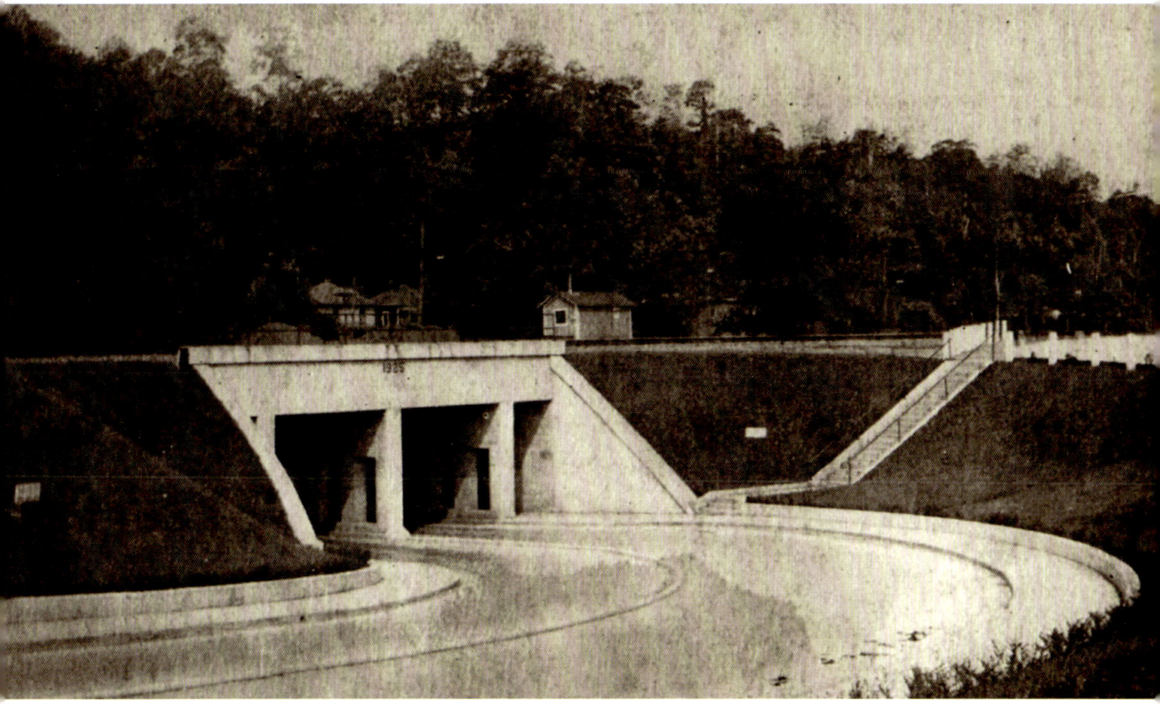

**The Russell Underpass:** Built in 1925 under the railway tracks, the Russell underpass is as familiar as the Ironton Russell Bridge to people of Greenup County. The city of Russell can trace its beginning back to Jeff More, an early pioneer of the area. Eventually the city was named after John Russell who purchased the area in the late 1860s.

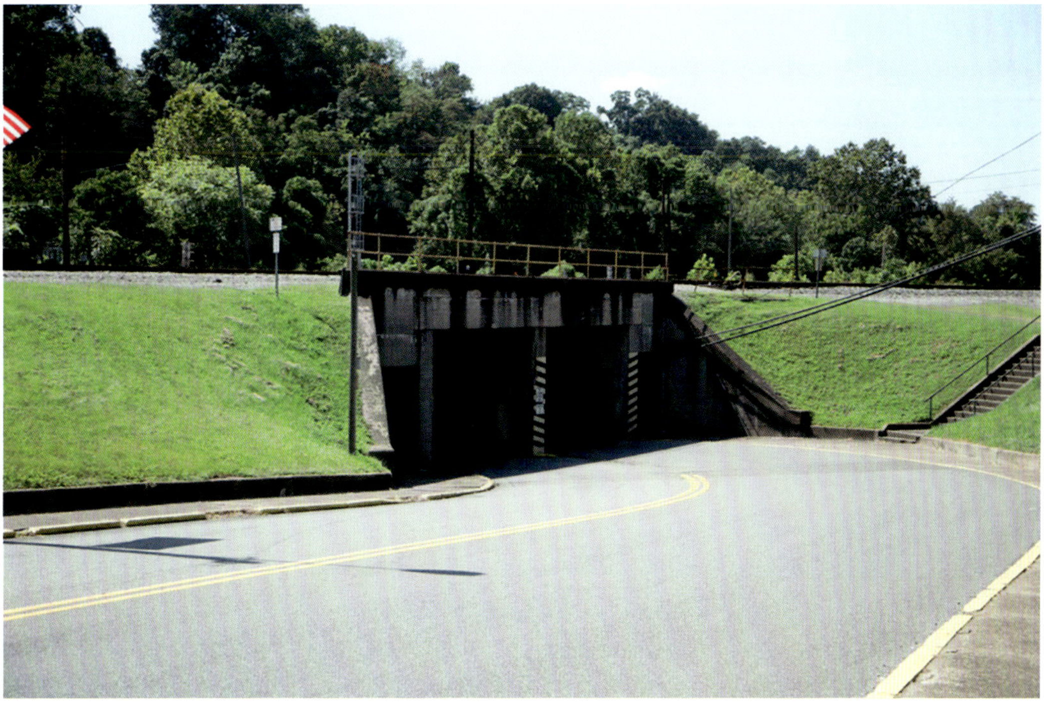

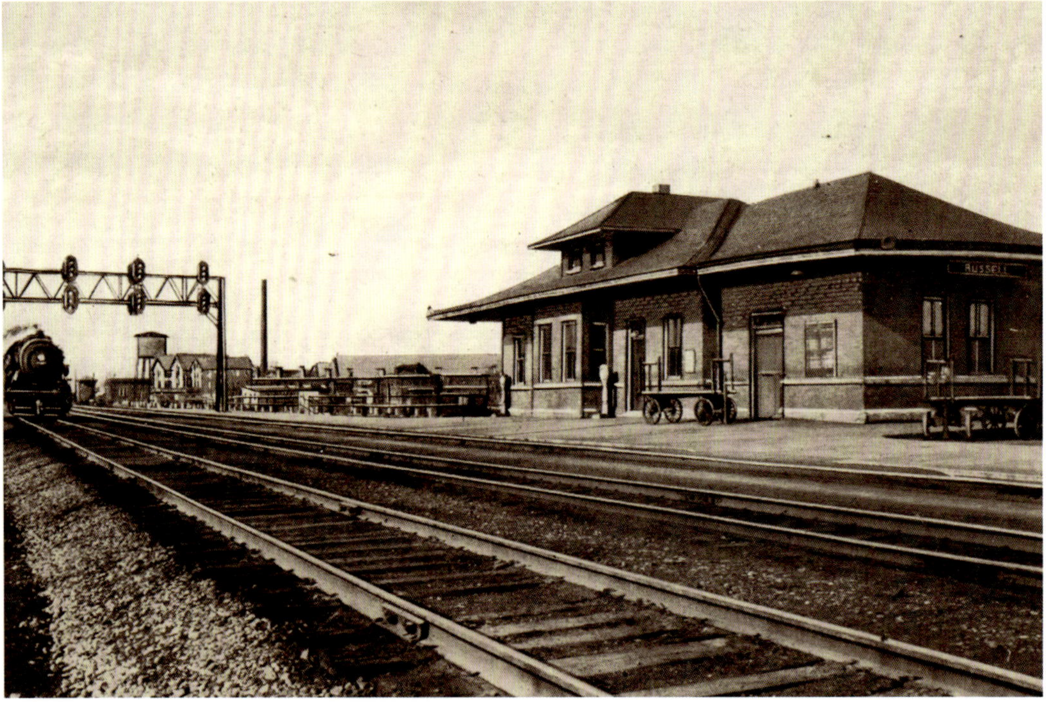

**THE CHESAPEAKE AND OHIO RAILROAD:** Russell has been a railroad town since the Chesapeake and Ohio Railroad came in 1889. Eventually the C&O would construct shops, roundhouse, and the very large rail yards. The depot has been a fixture in the community for many years and has changed little over the years.

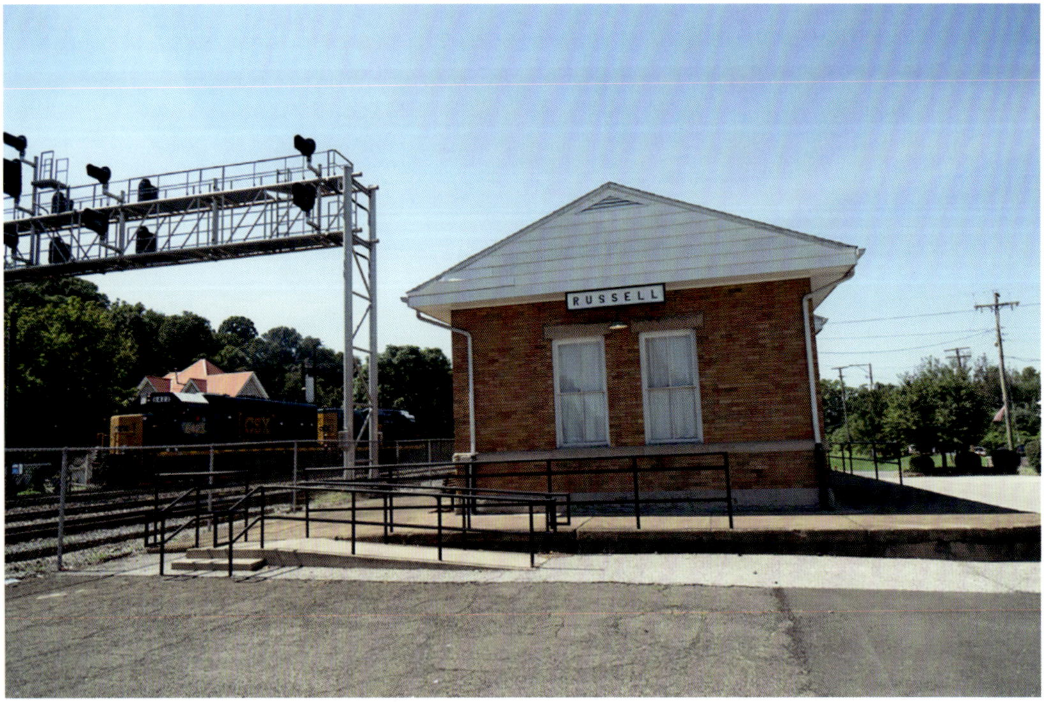

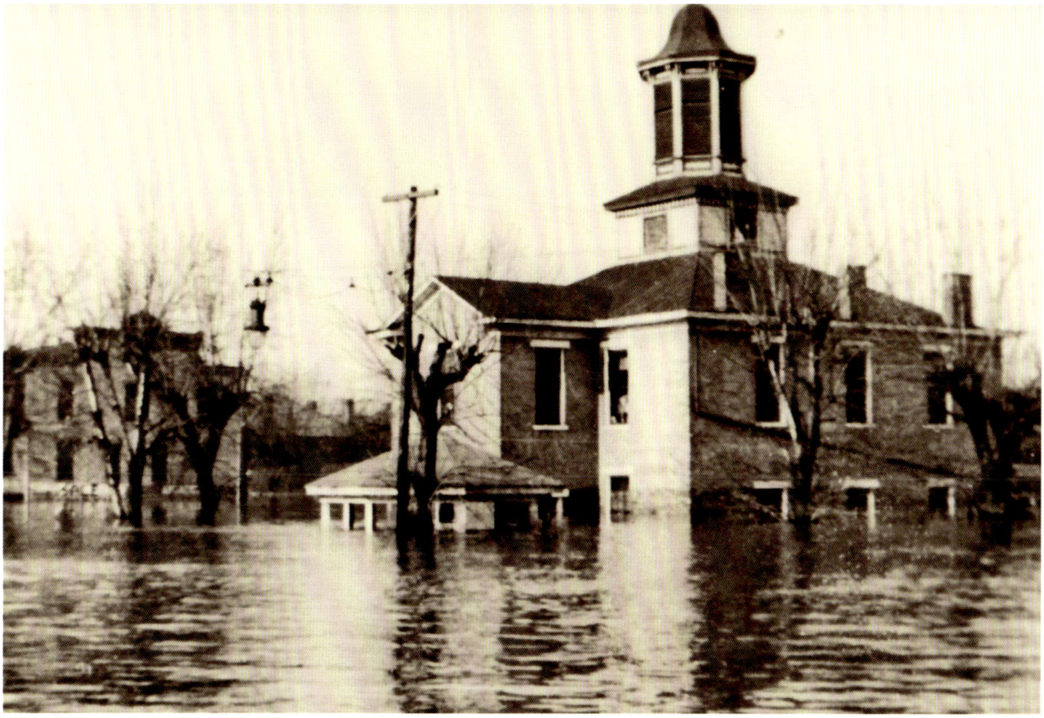

THE OLD COURTHOUSE: Greenup was once referred as "Hang town" because of the number of hangings handed down to offenders in Greenup's original courthouse. That courthouse, built in 1812, suffered through many damaging floods as pictured in this postcard during the flood of 1913.

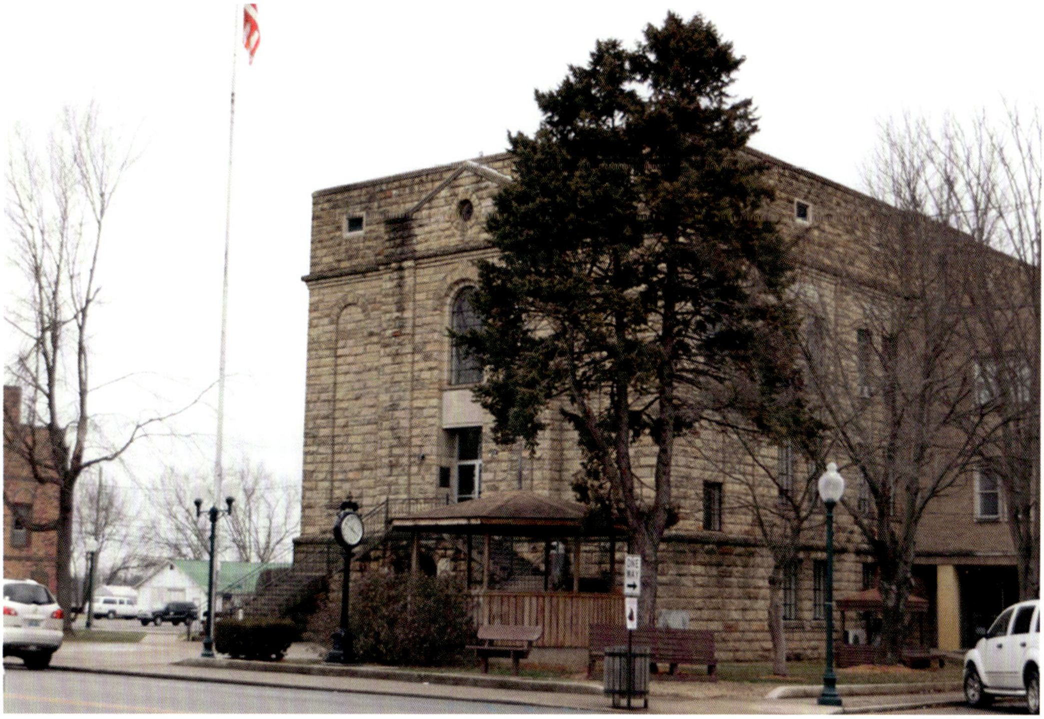

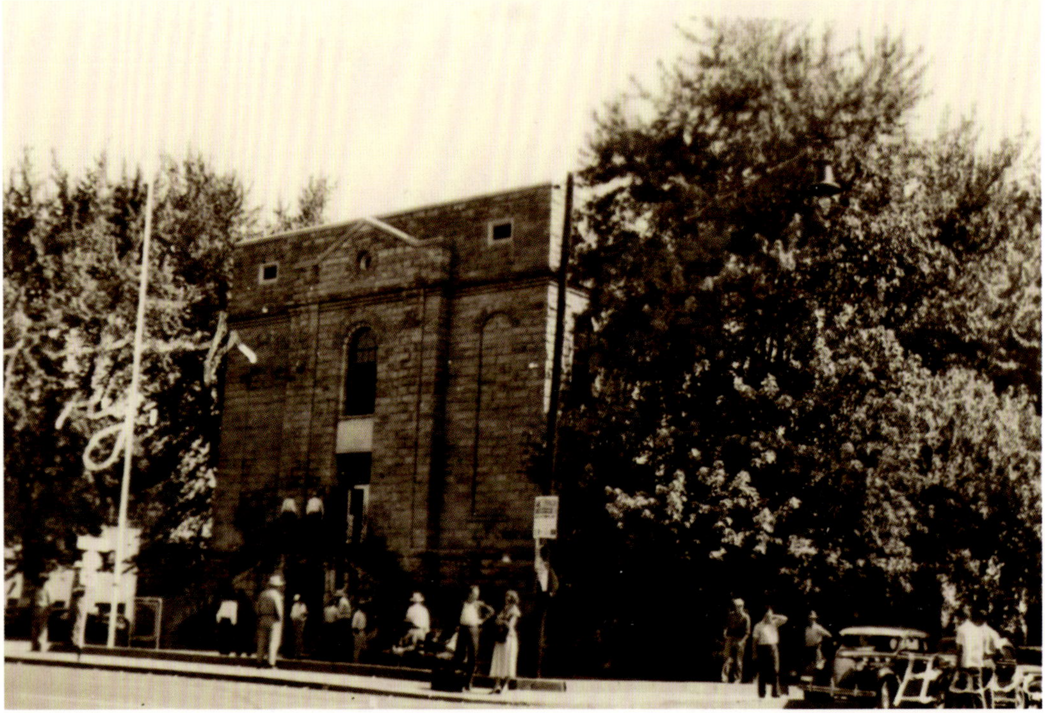

**THE NEW COURTHOUSE:** Today's courthouse came about because of President Franklin D. Roosevelt's new deal program. The stones were cut nearby and hauled to Greenup where the newly employed masons worked tirelessly to complete the building the county has today.

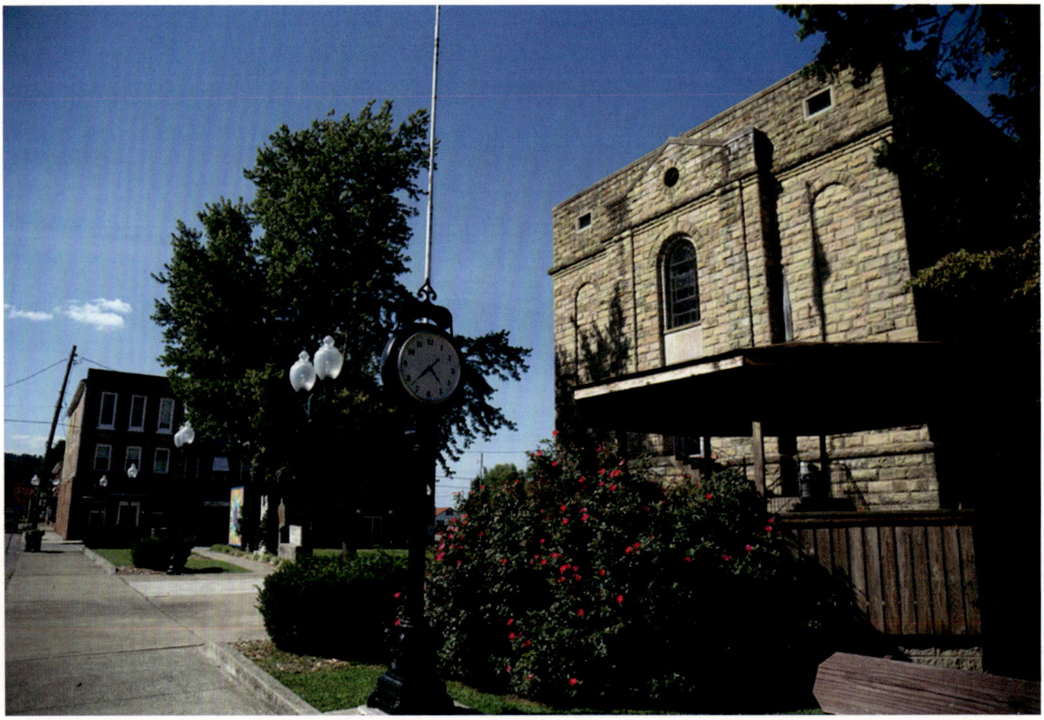

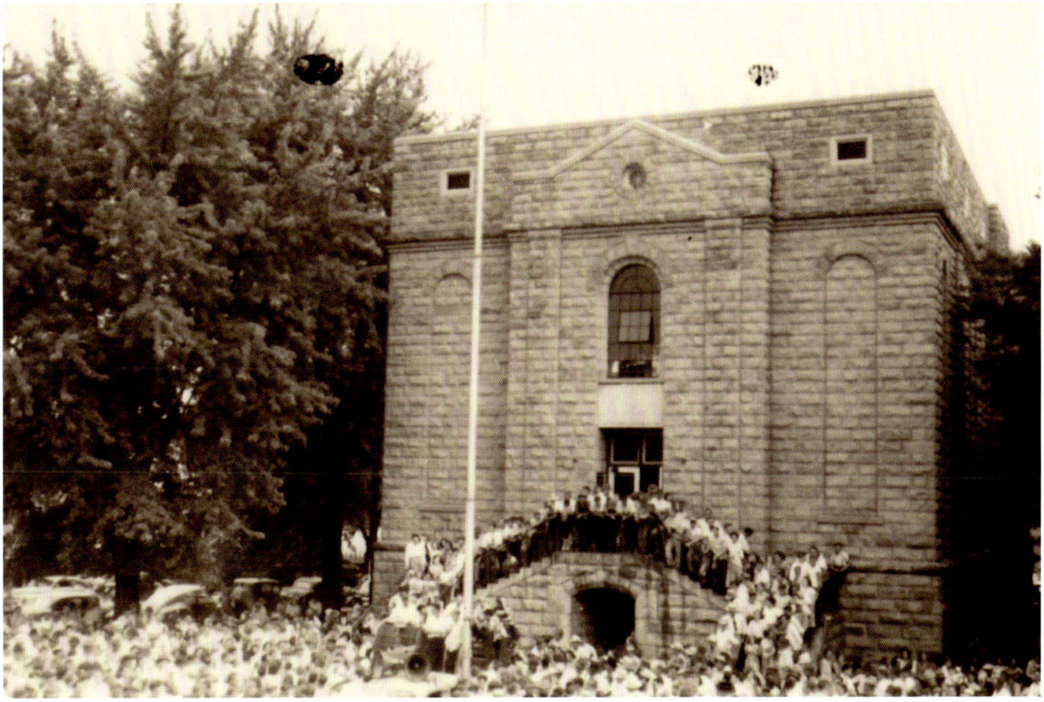

OLD FASHION DAYS: Thousands of residents throughout Greenup County were in attendance as the newly constructed courthouse was dedicated in the early 1940s. Greenup hosts their annual "Old Fashion Days" early every October and the Greenup County Courthouse is the center of activity during the celebration.

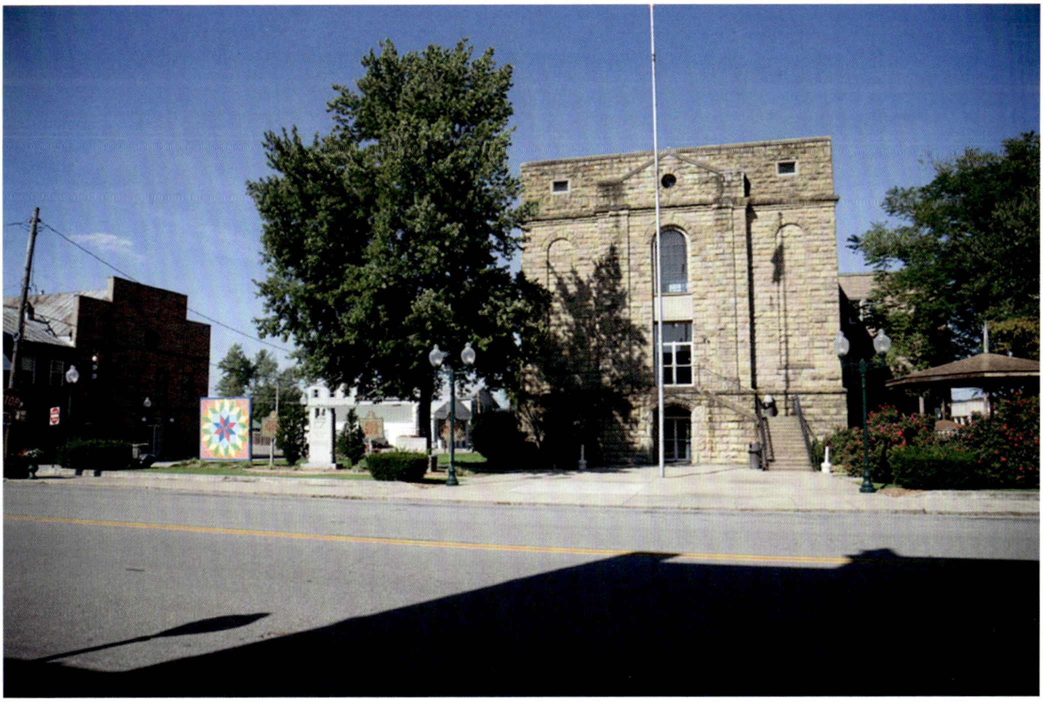

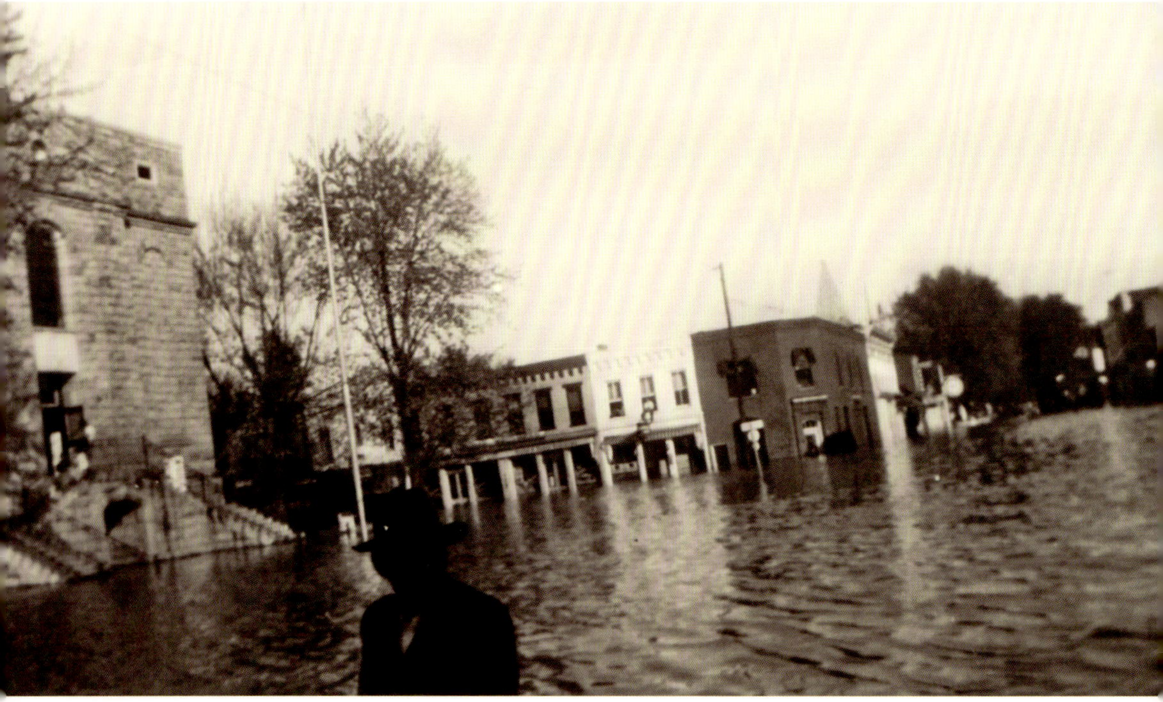

**The Flood of 1941:** The first flood to impact the activities as well as the structure of the new courthouse happened in 1941. The older photograph shows the bottom entrance of the courthouse as well as businesses along Harrison Street inundated with several feet of water.

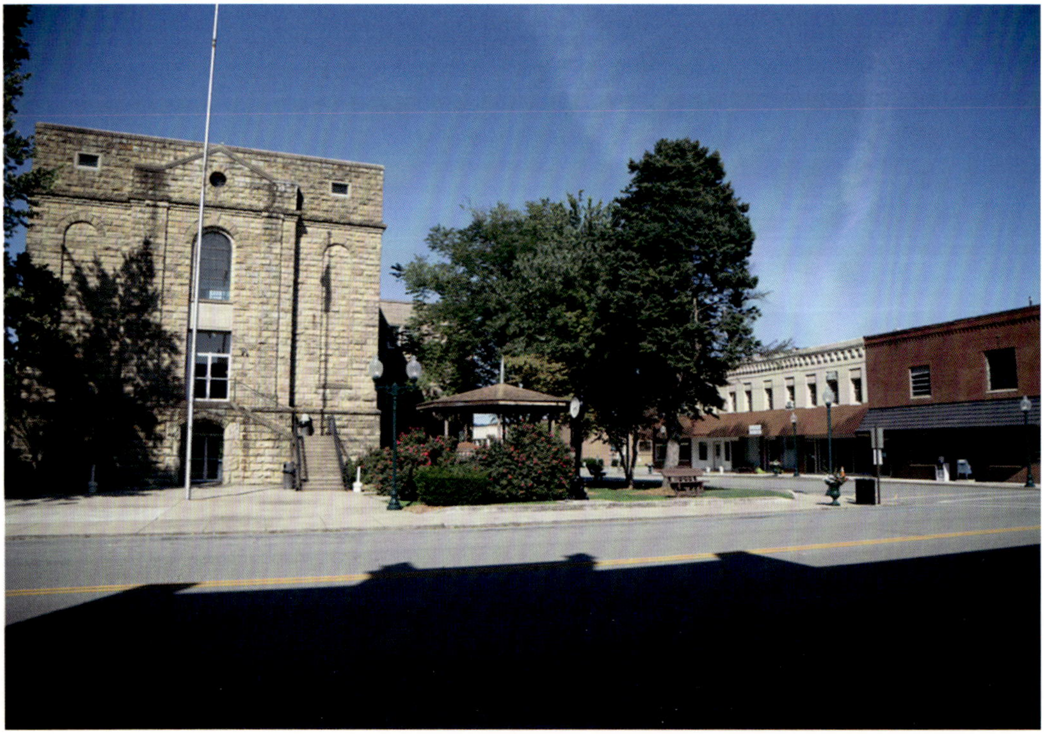

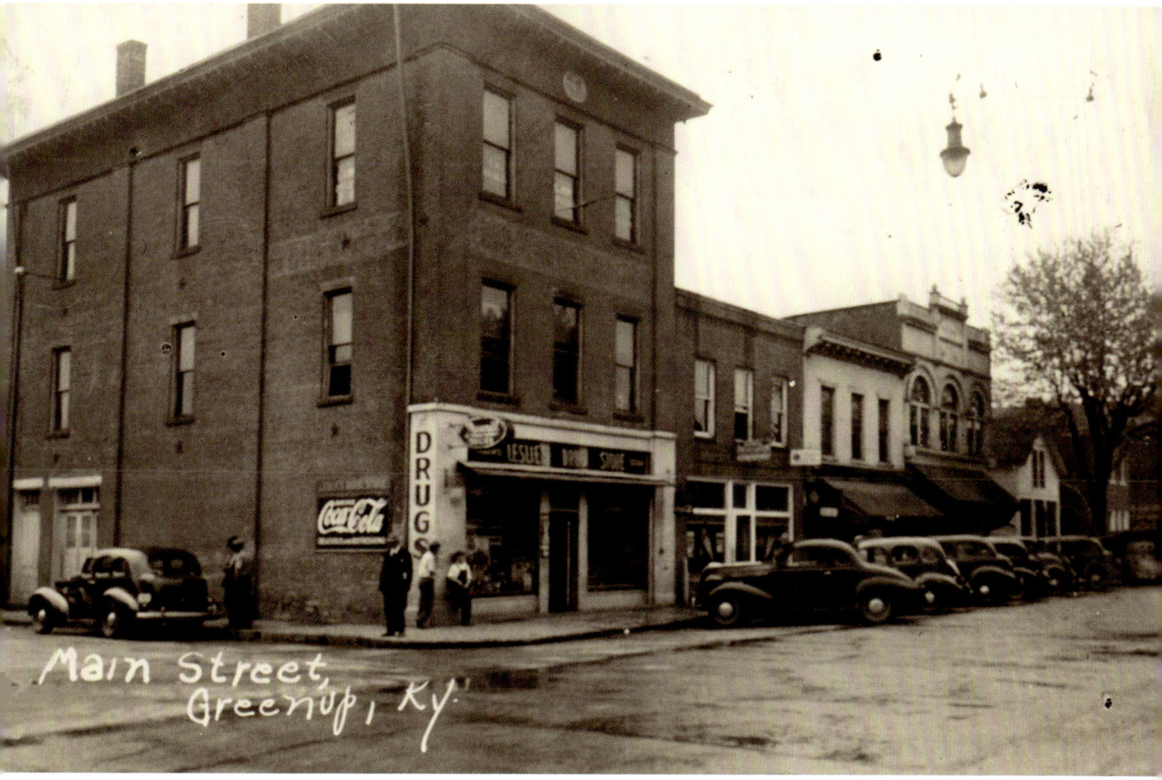

LESLIE'S DRUG STORE: Famed author Jesse Stuart loved his visits to Leslie's Drug Store on the corner of Main Street and Harrison Street. Even today many can recall walking into the store and ordering their chocolate sodas. Before becoming a drug store, it was Leslie Curry Motor Company and a gas station.

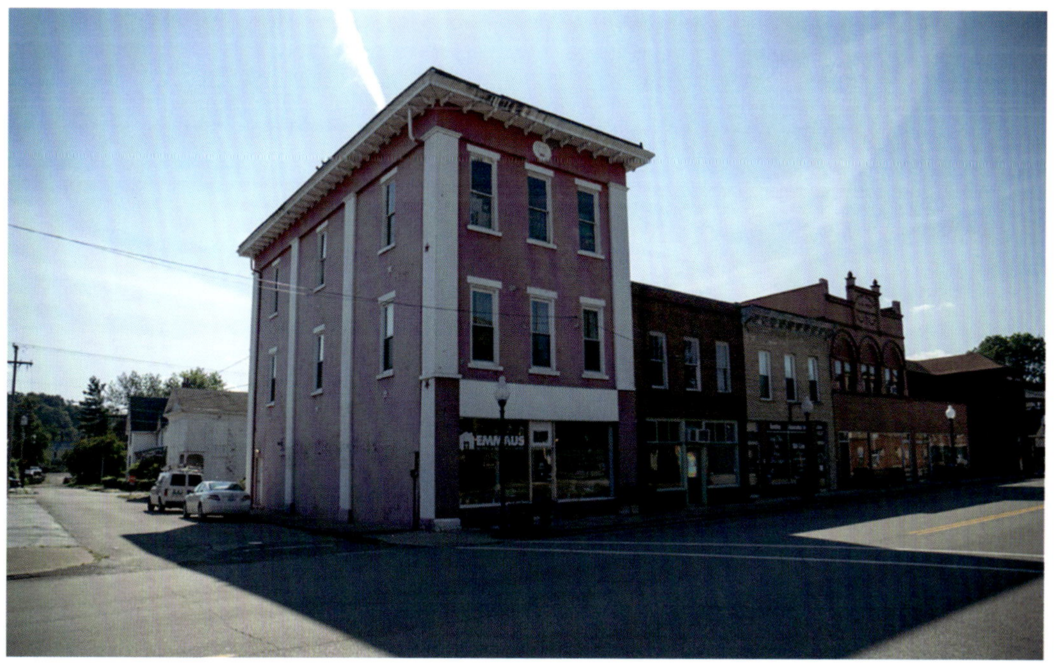

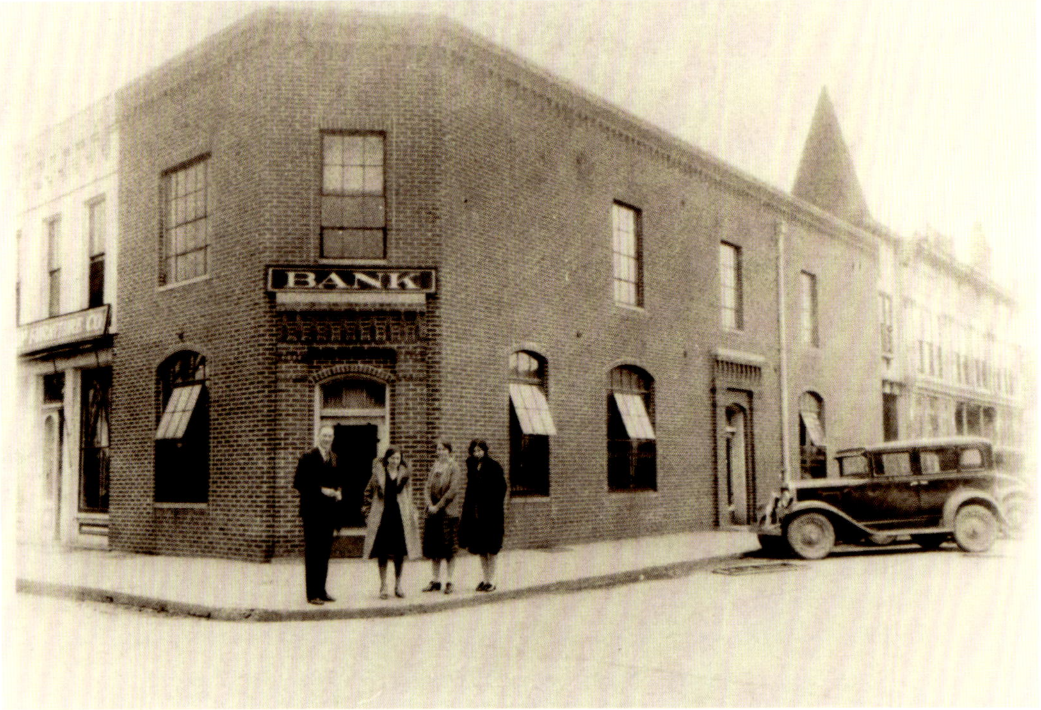

THE CORNER OF MAIN AND HARRISON: The bank on the corners of Main Street and Harrison Street has retained its familiar façade since the 1890s. The corner doorway has welcomed many Greenup County generations through great floods and deep snows.

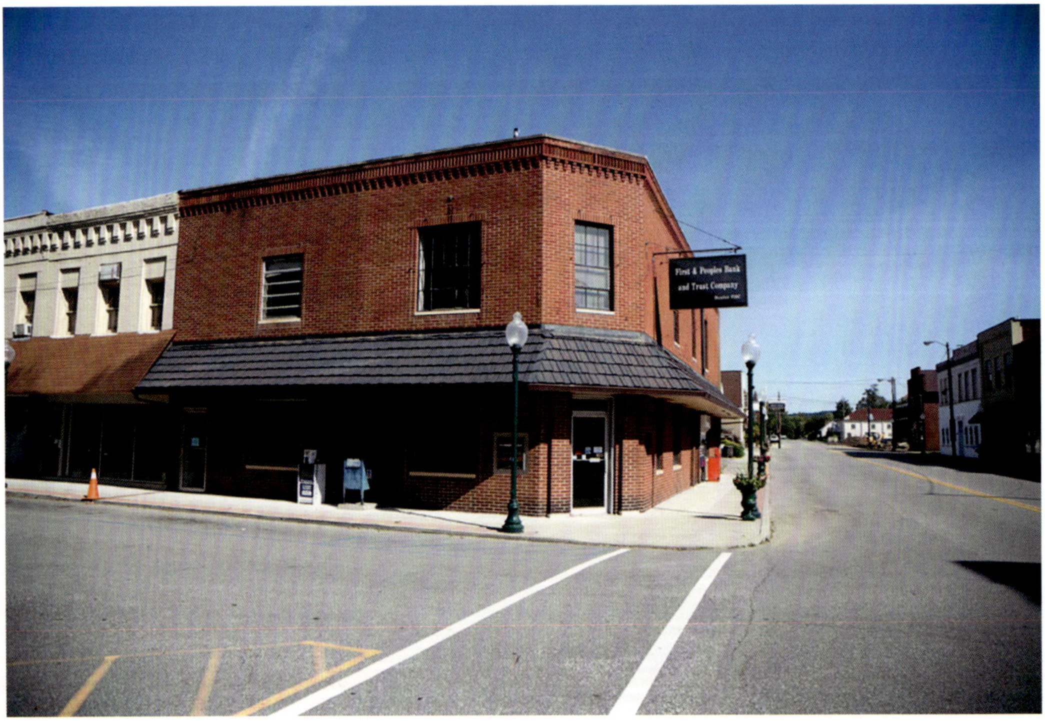

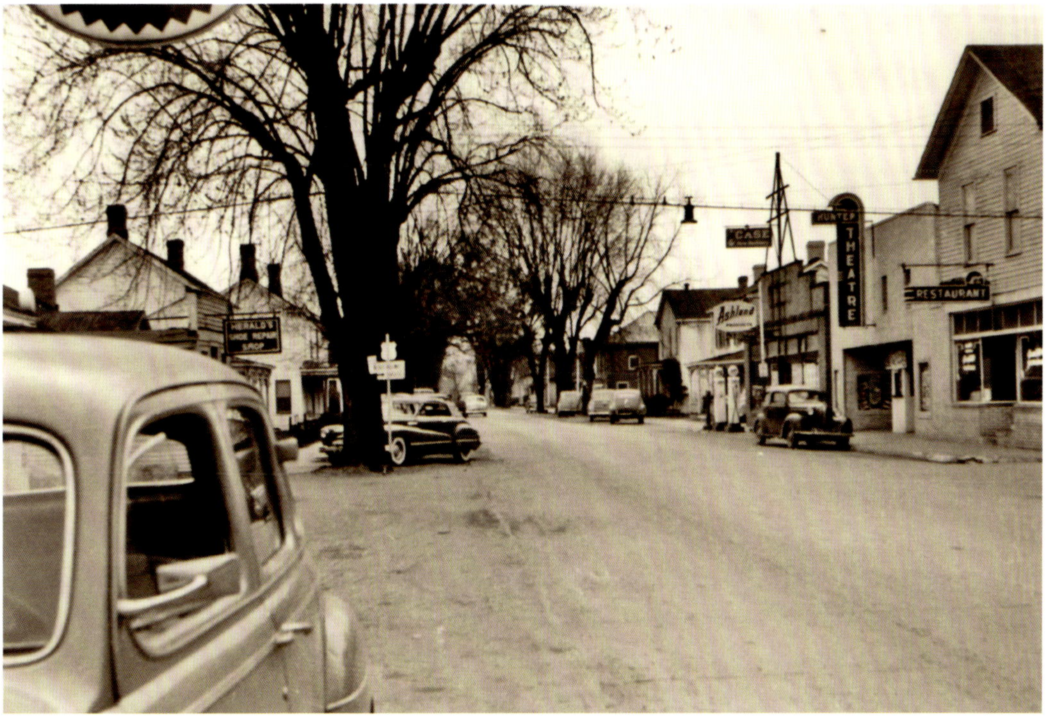

THE GAS STATION AND THEATRE: The older photograph shows an Ashland gas station, the Hunter Theatre, and Gambill's Restaurant. The new main Greenup County Public Library was built where these structures once stood. Once again young and old alike frequent the area but now in search of knowledge.

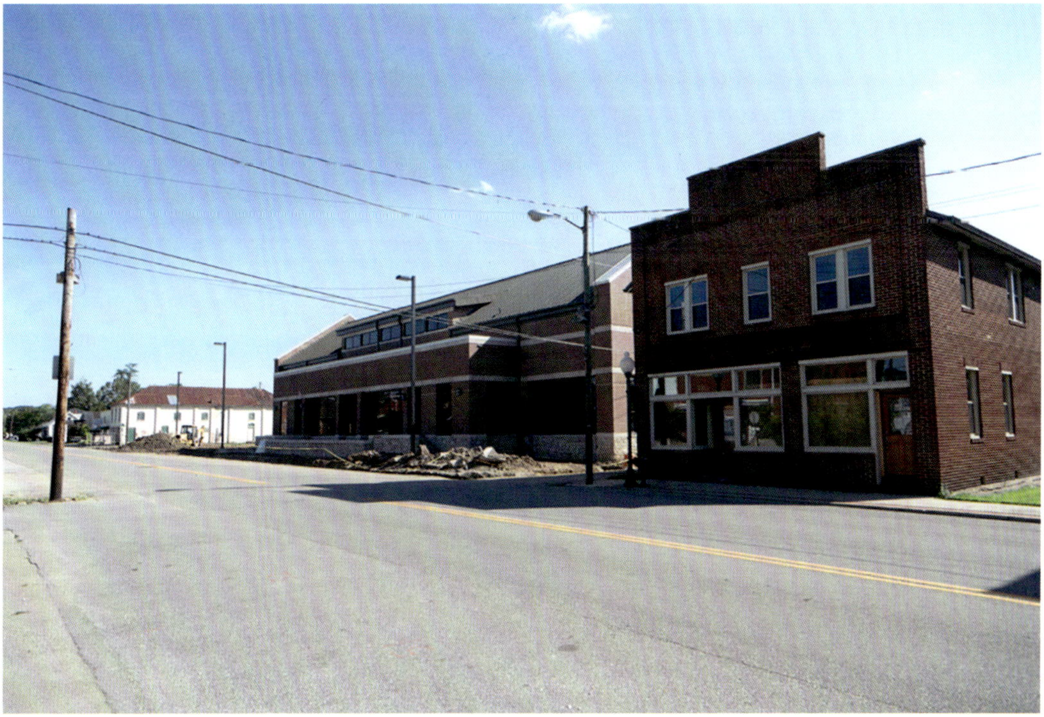

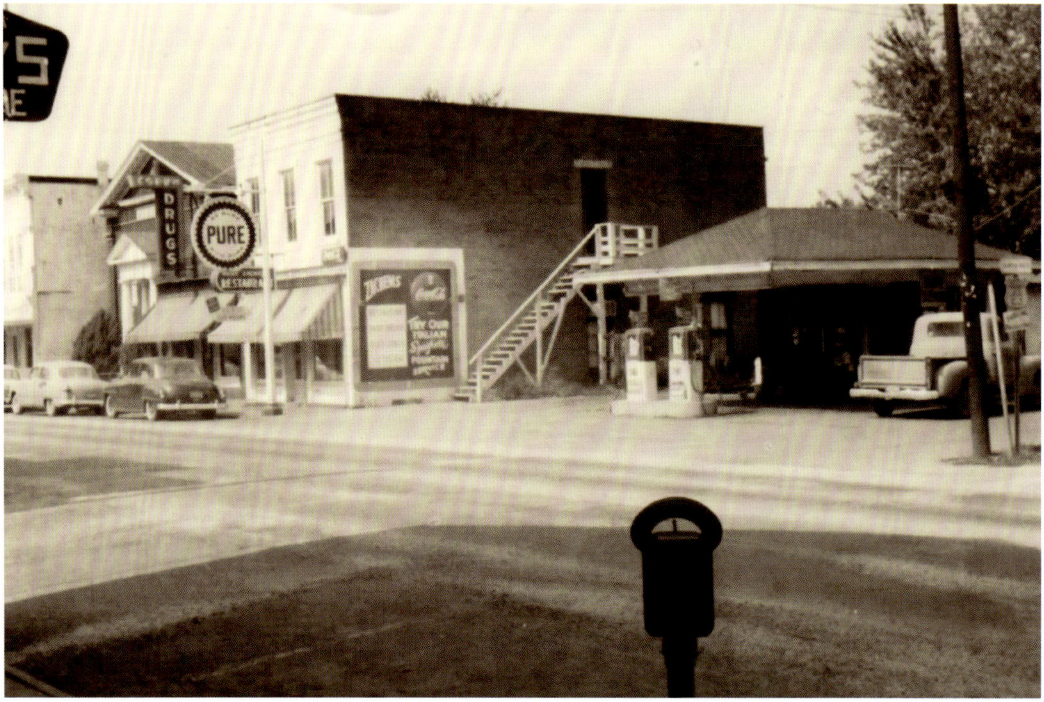

THE TWO-PUMP GAS STATION: Main Street looking north at Corum's Drug Store, Zachems' Restaurant, and the little two-pump gas station that continues to operate as Quillen's Garage as of the printing of this book. Greenup had several filling stations in the downtown area, now most everything is located on the highway outside of downtown.

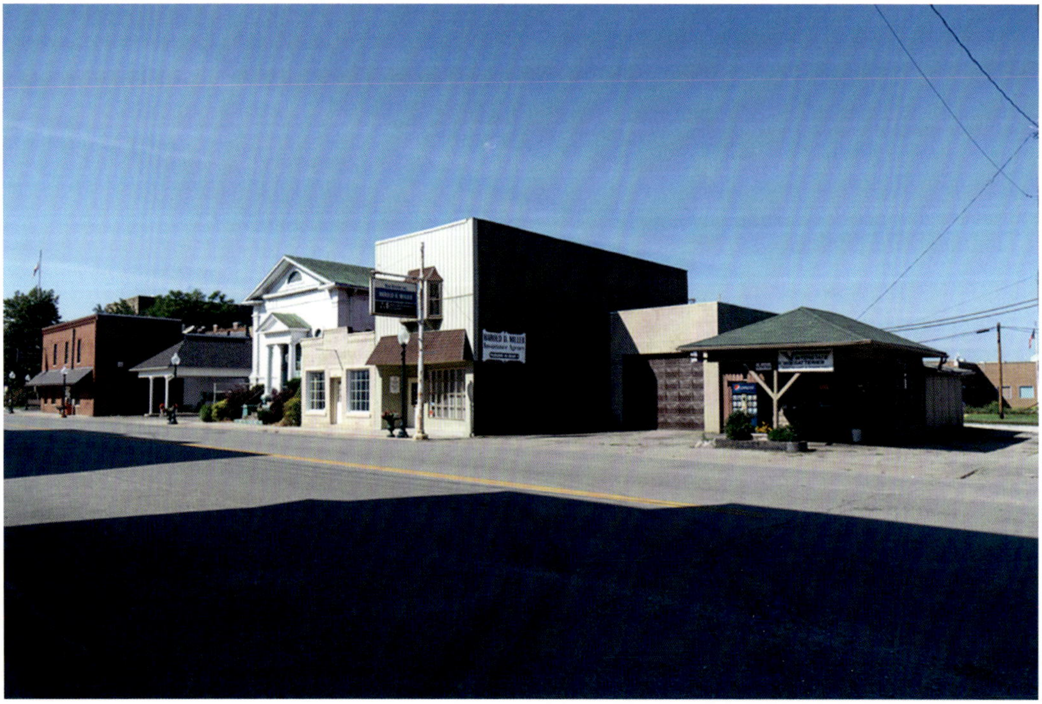

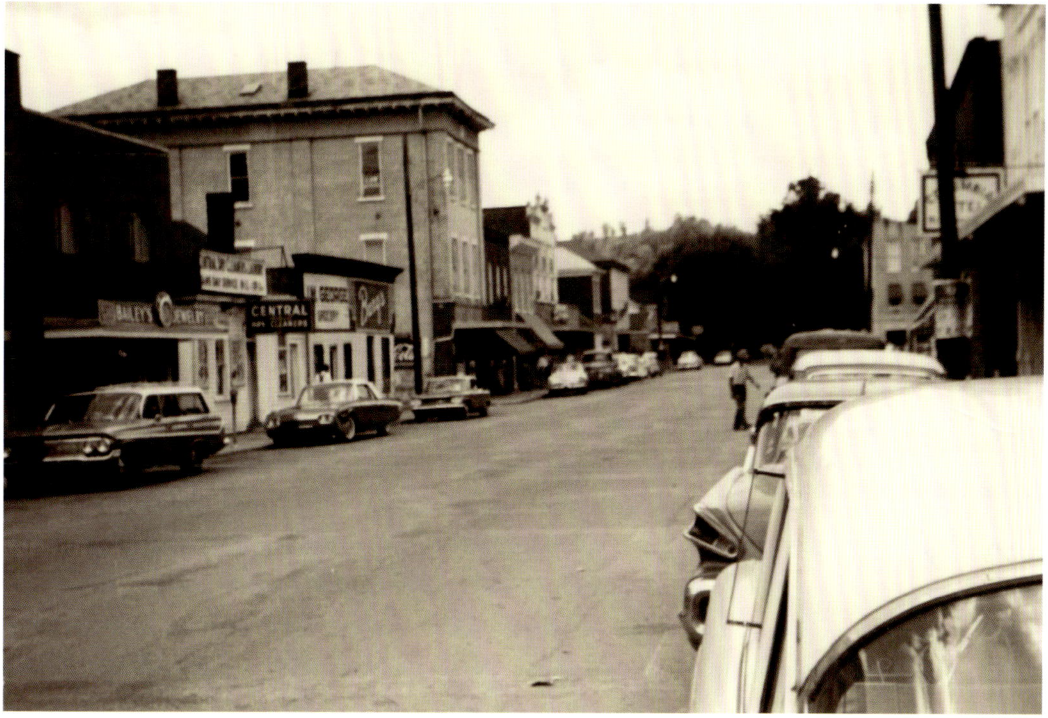

LOOKING EASTWARD ON MAIN STREET IN THE EARLY 1960S: The town had many businesses that surrounded the county courthouse. From the Greenup's early development to just around 40 years ago, the courthouse square served as the center of legal as well as civil affairs.

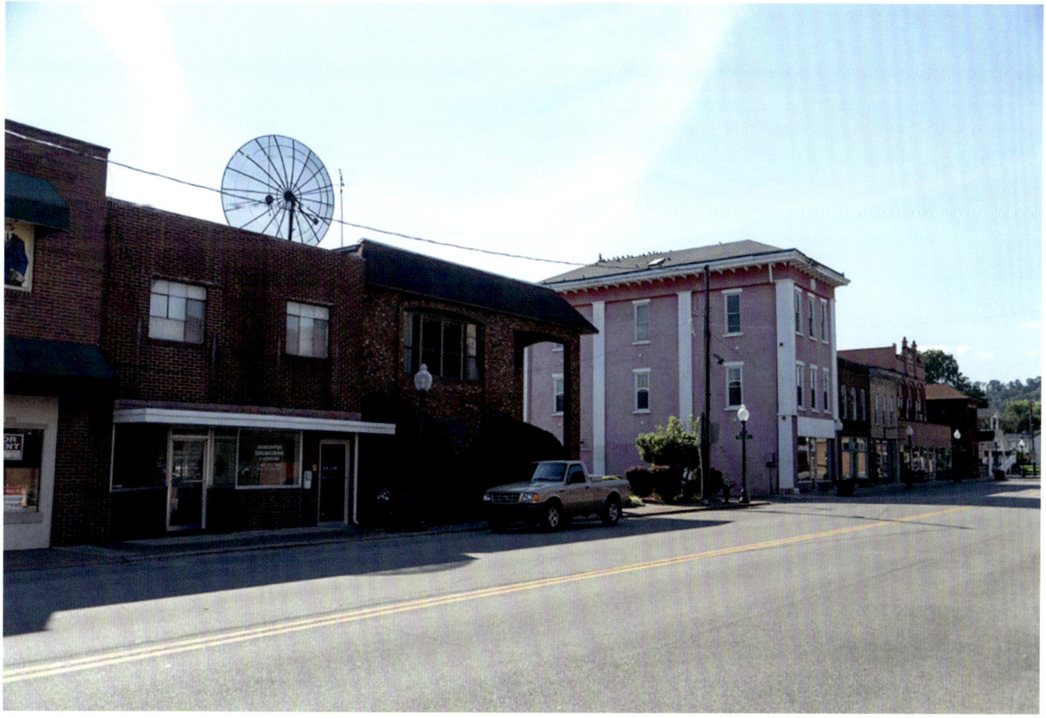

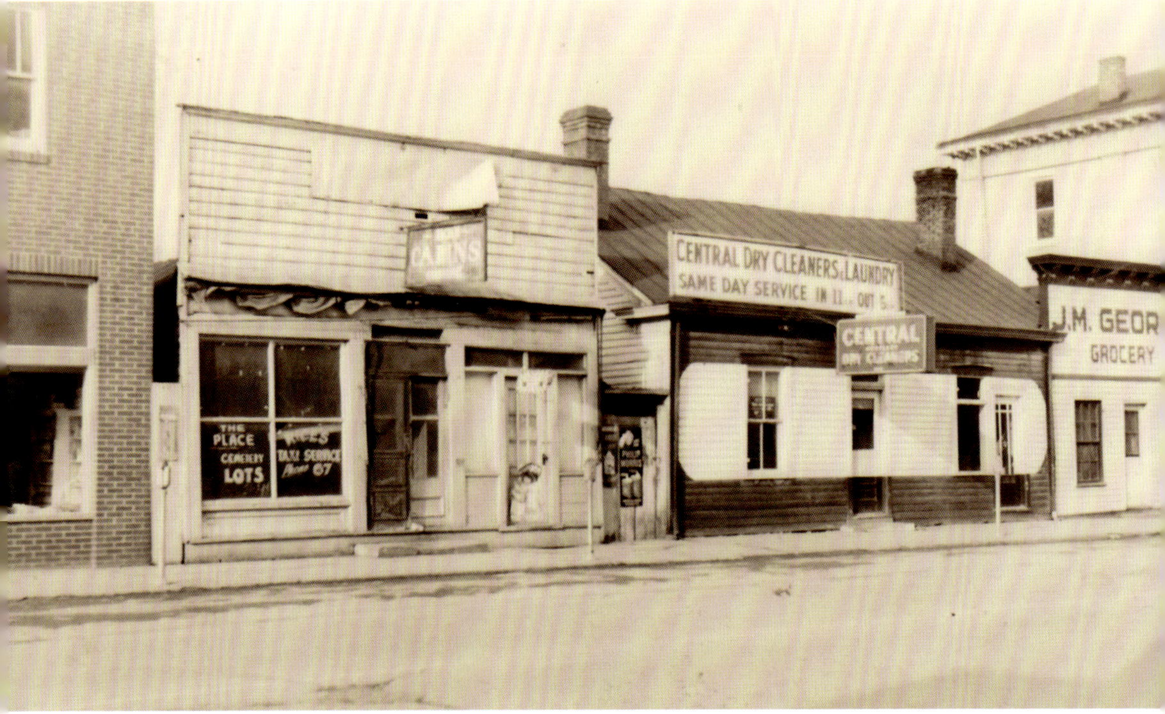

**The Last Wooden Buildings:** Pictured in the late 1950s are what turned out to be the last three business structures constructed from wood. Pictured here are a grocery, dry cleaners and a taxi service. The three buildings stood until the late 1970s to make way for law offices.

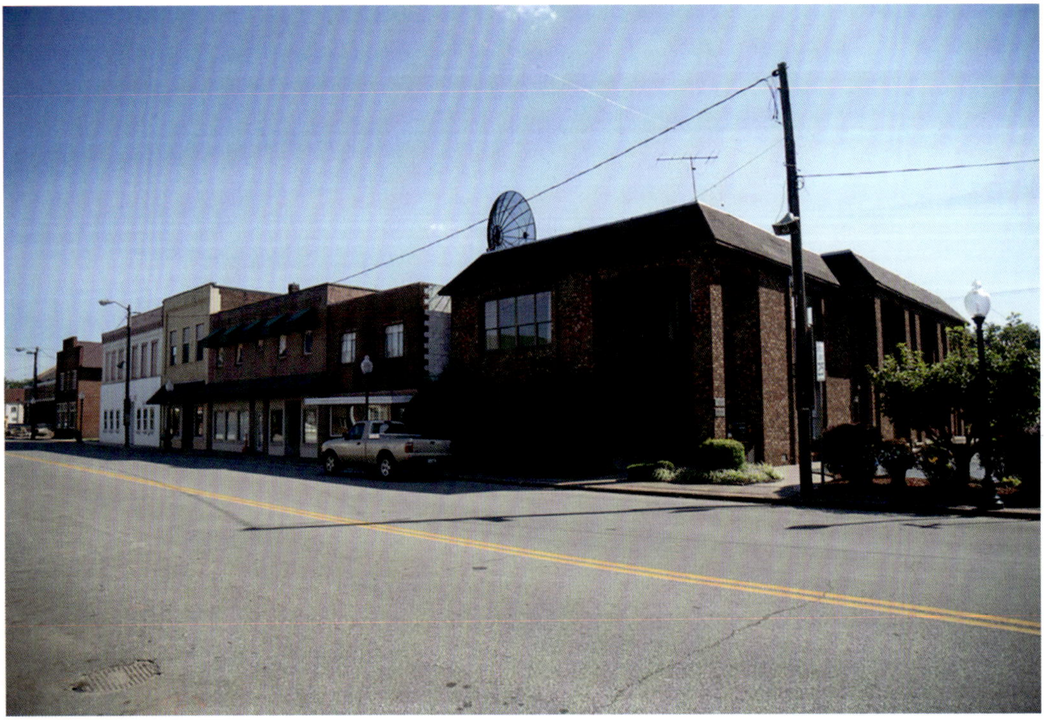

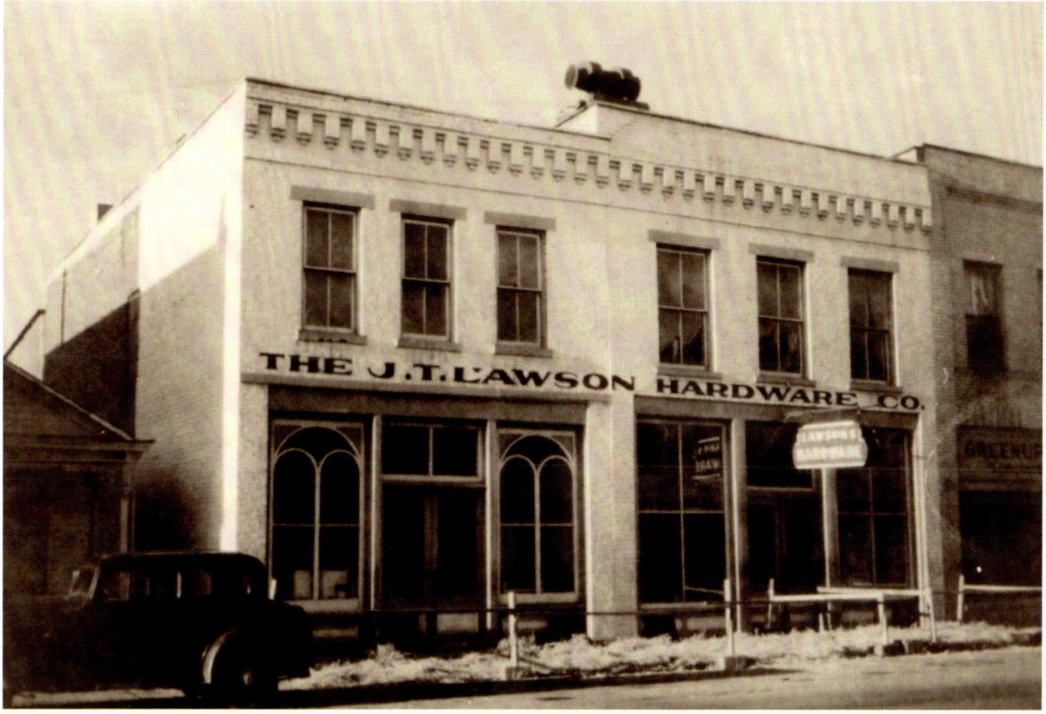

J. T. LAWSON HARDWARE: The photograph above is of the J. T. Lawson Hardware Company building. Several generations frequented the store to buy items for home remodeling and building projects. The volunteer fire alarm located on the roof alerted firefighters and scared children holding their ears to emergencies.

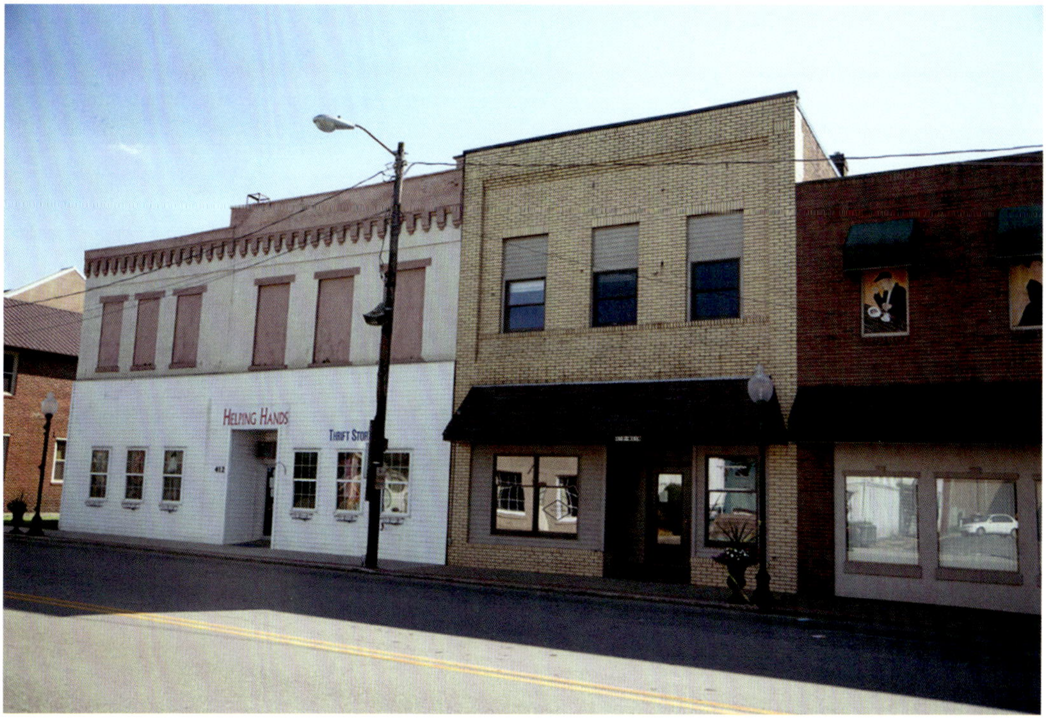

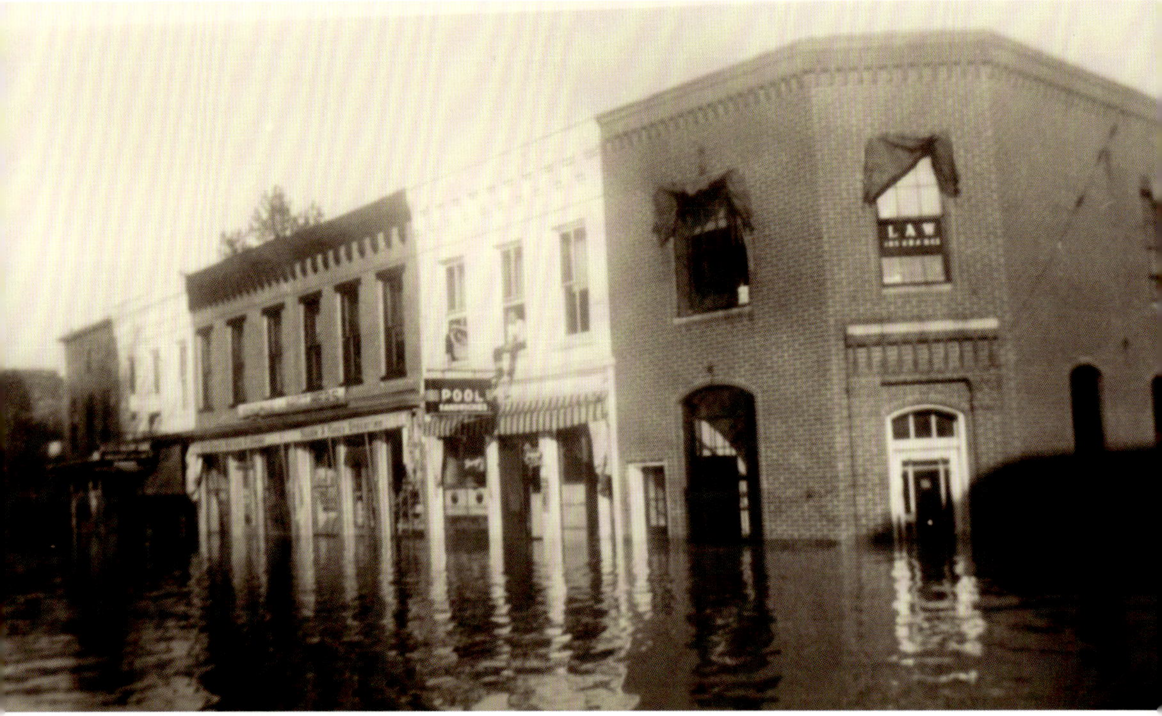

THE FLOOD OF 1941: The Ohio River has visited the streets of Greenup many times in the past. The photograph above shows the flood of 1941 along Harrison Street as renters of a second story apartment nonchalantly pose for the photograph. The last major flood to visit a Greenup street was in 1997.

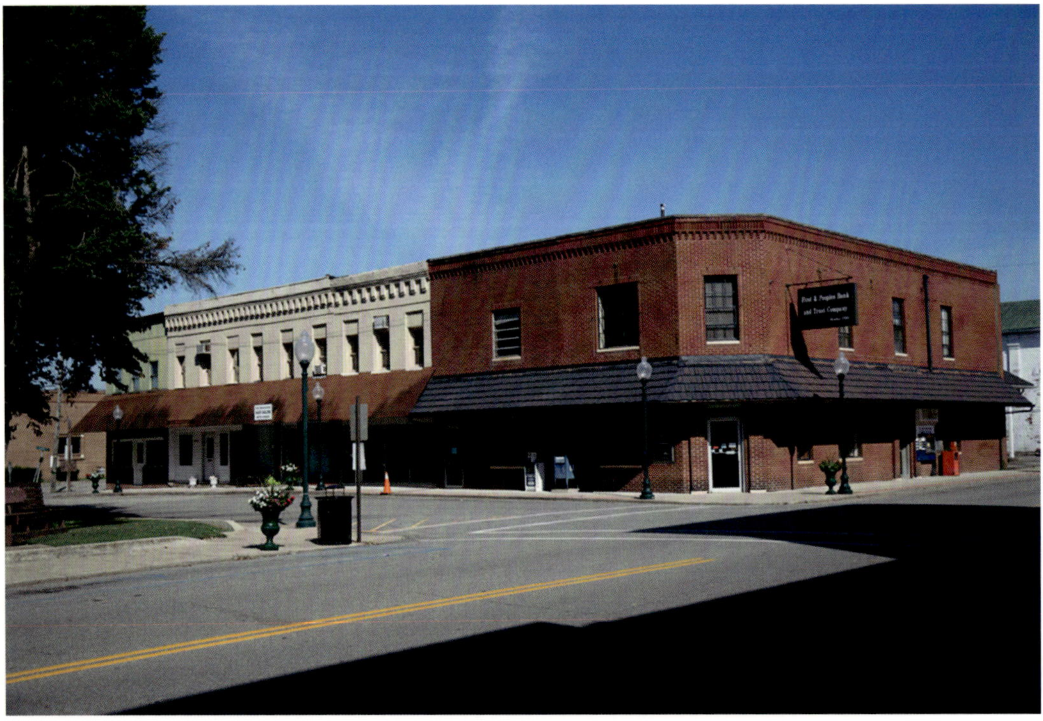

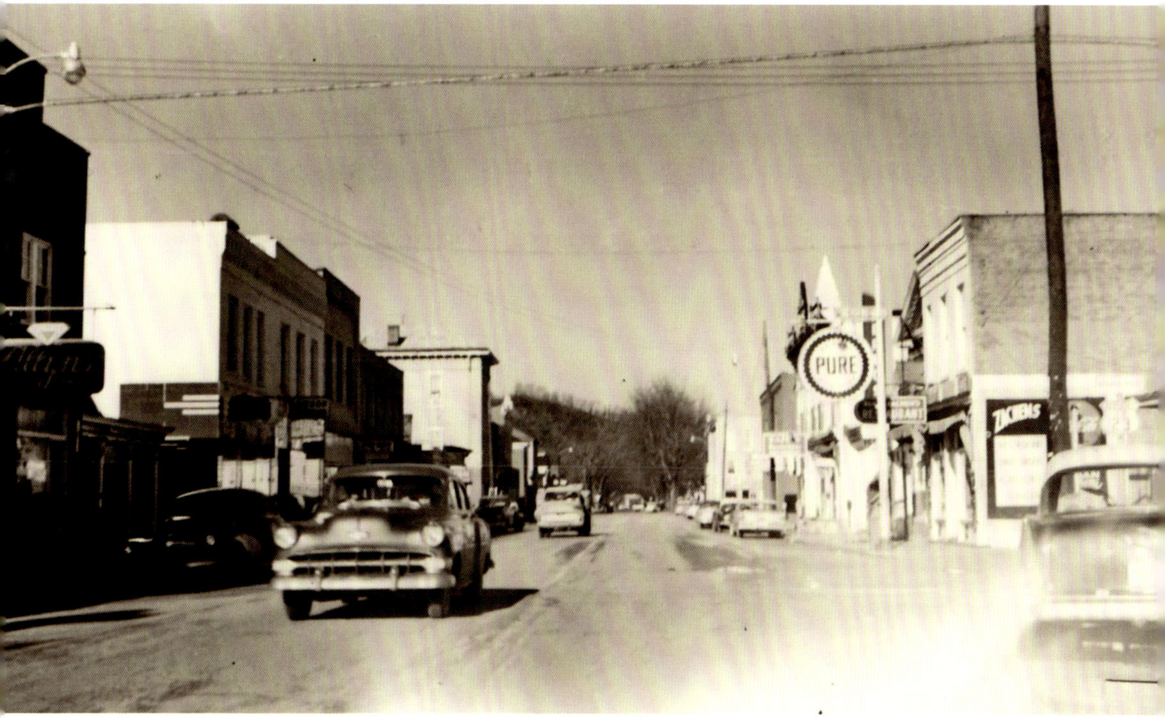

GREENUP IN THE 1950S: After the town of Greenup was laid out back in the early 1800s Main Street was the main focus for businesses for well over a century-and-a-half. With the development of out of town retail the business in the center has declined and traffic is much reduced.

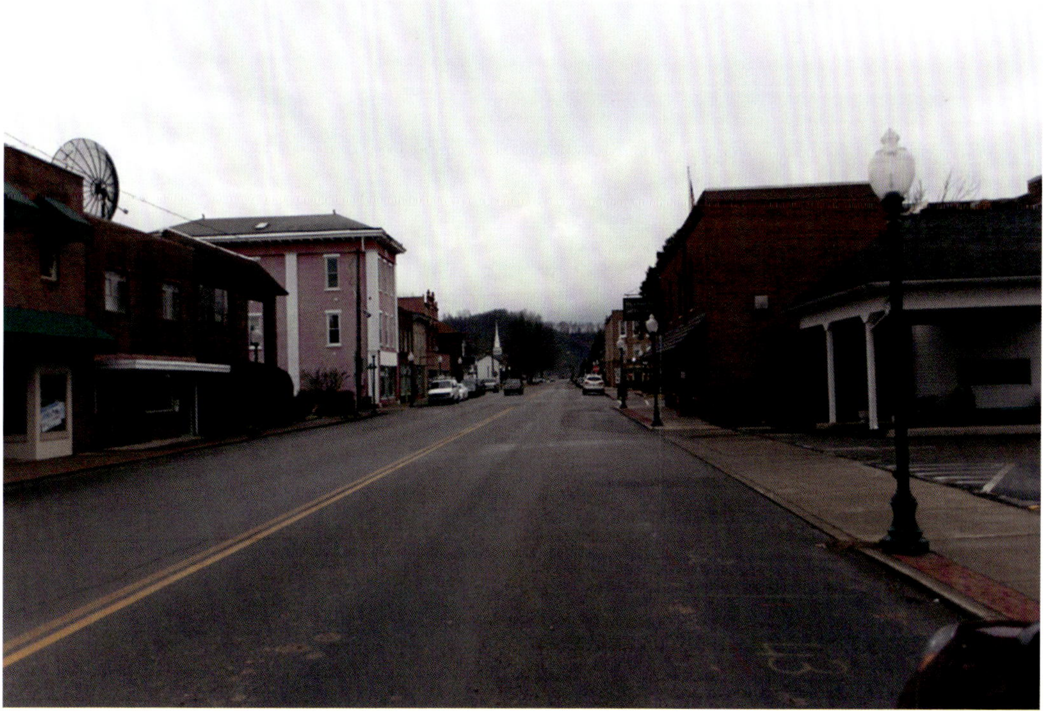

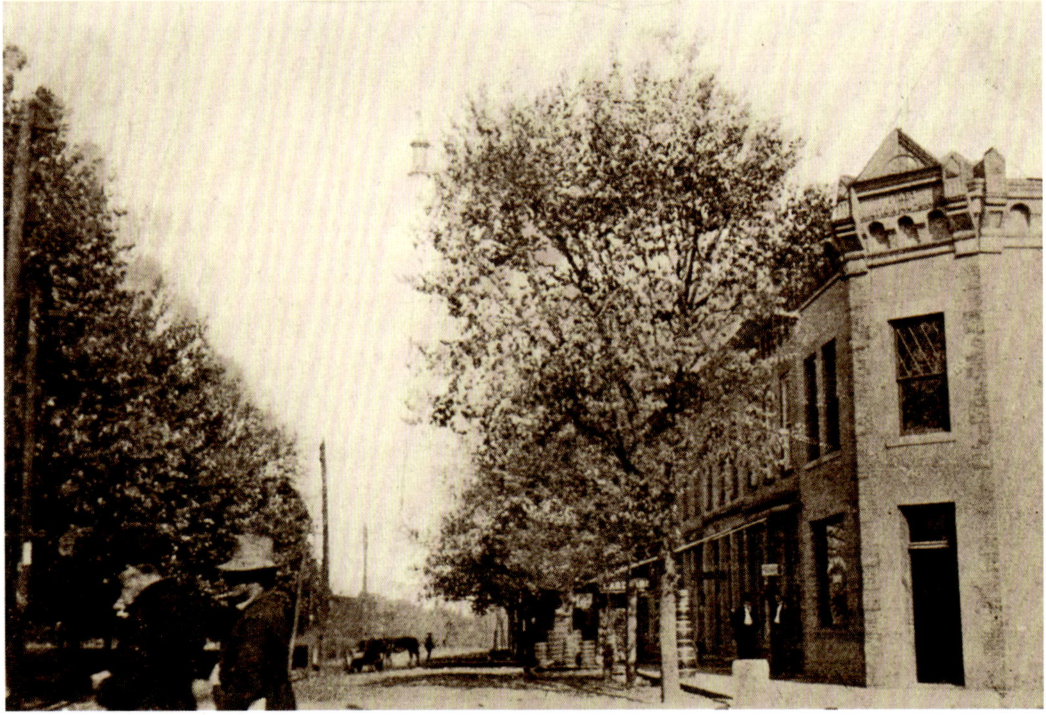

**THE OLD DIRT STREET:** The familiar corner bank entrance landmark is visible in the postcard photograph from around 1899. Men walk across the dirt Harrison and Main Street intersection toward the courthouse to chat about the goings on in the town and county.

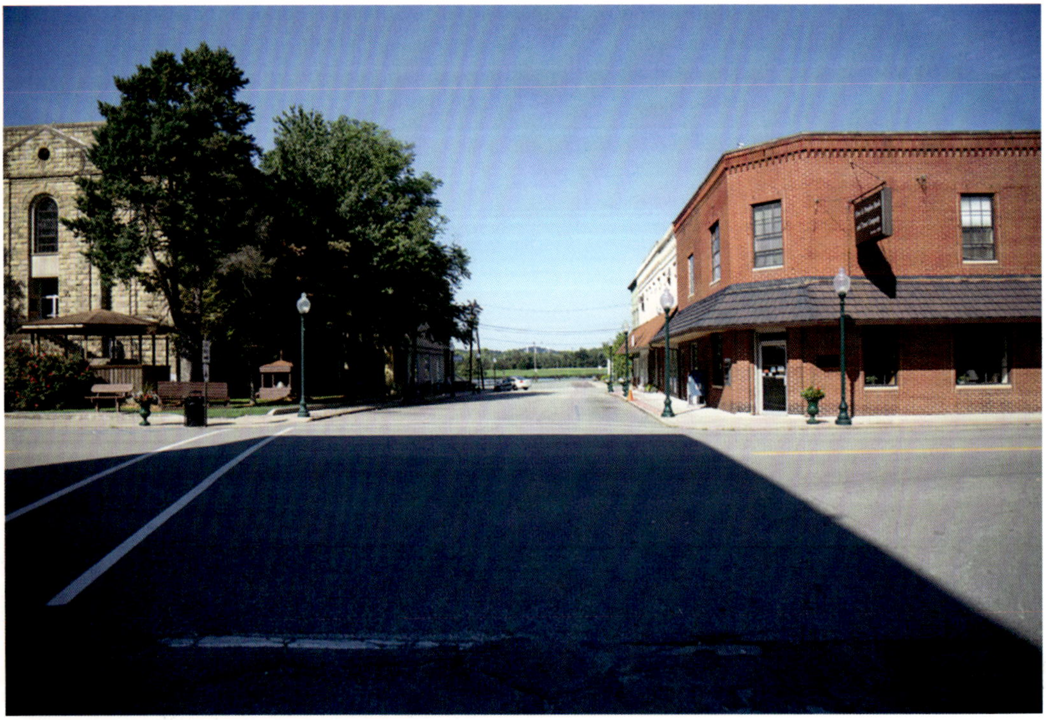

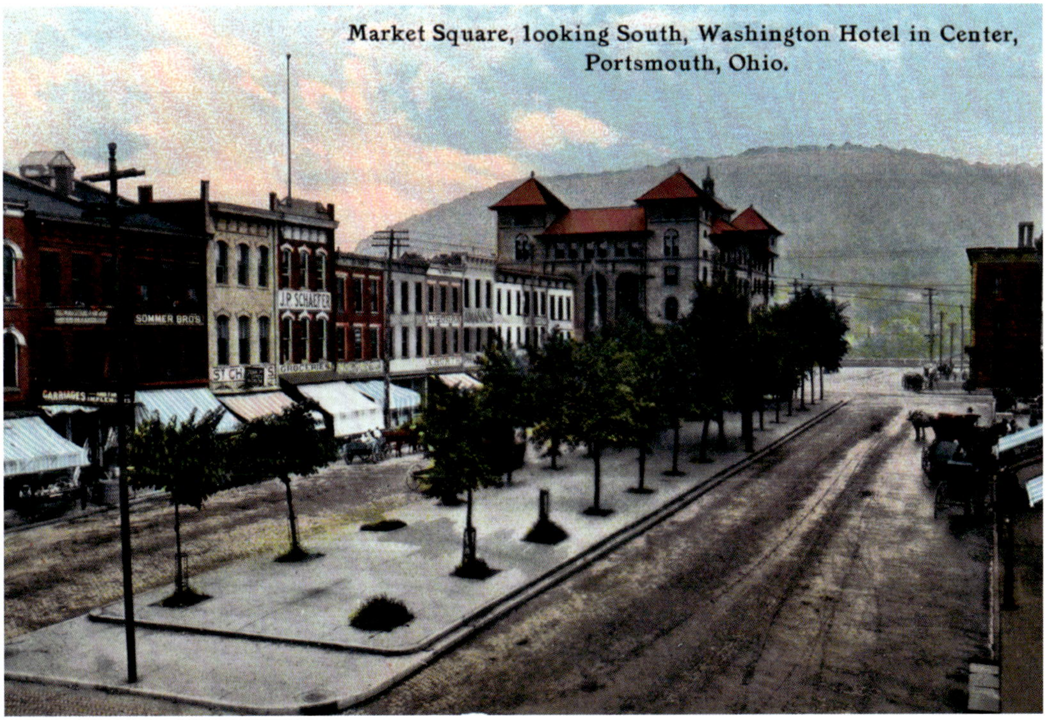

Market Square, looking South, Washington Hotel in Center, Portsmouth, Ohio.

MARKET SQUARE LOOKING SOUTH: Market Square as well as the Washington Hotel stands out in this postcard from 1905. In the photograph below we see that little has changed to the buildings in Market Street, but Washington House has lost its tiled pitched roofs.

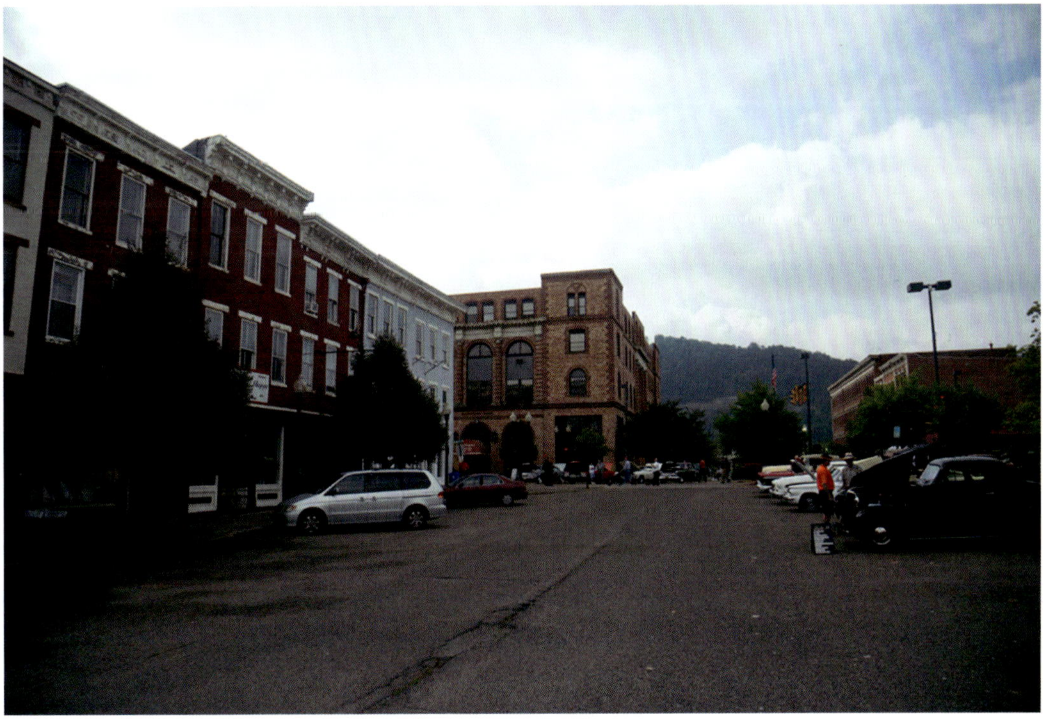

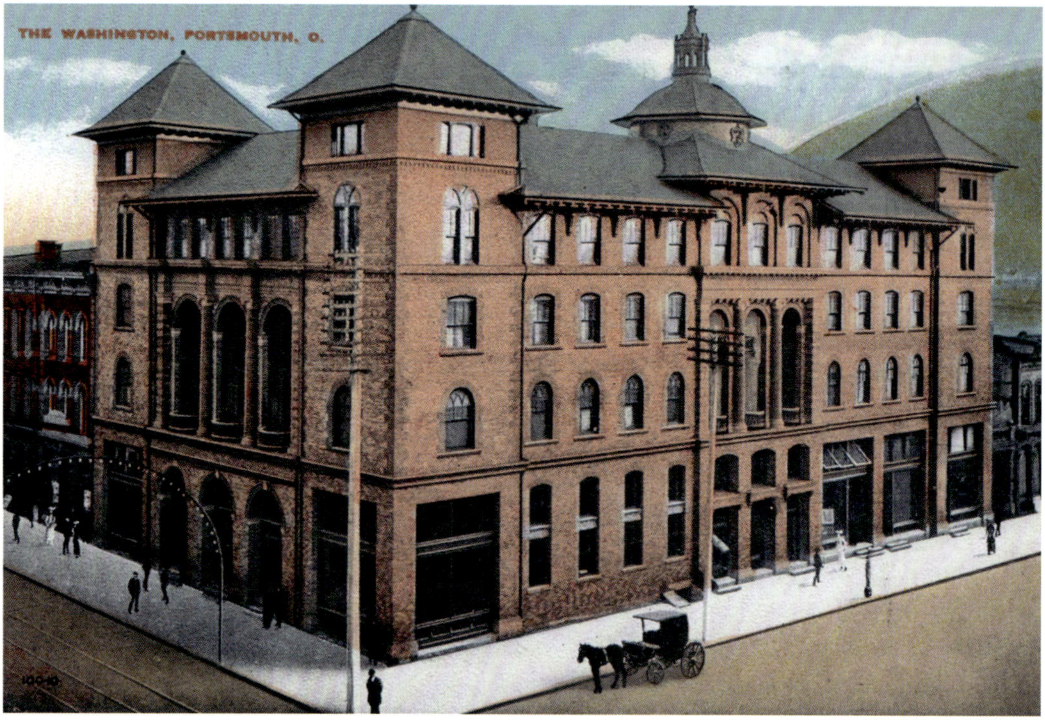

THE WASHINGTON: The Washington Hotel was built in 1900 on the south side of Market Square in order to accommodate travelers coming and going near both the B&O and C&O stations. The roof and dome are the main changes in the past 115 years.

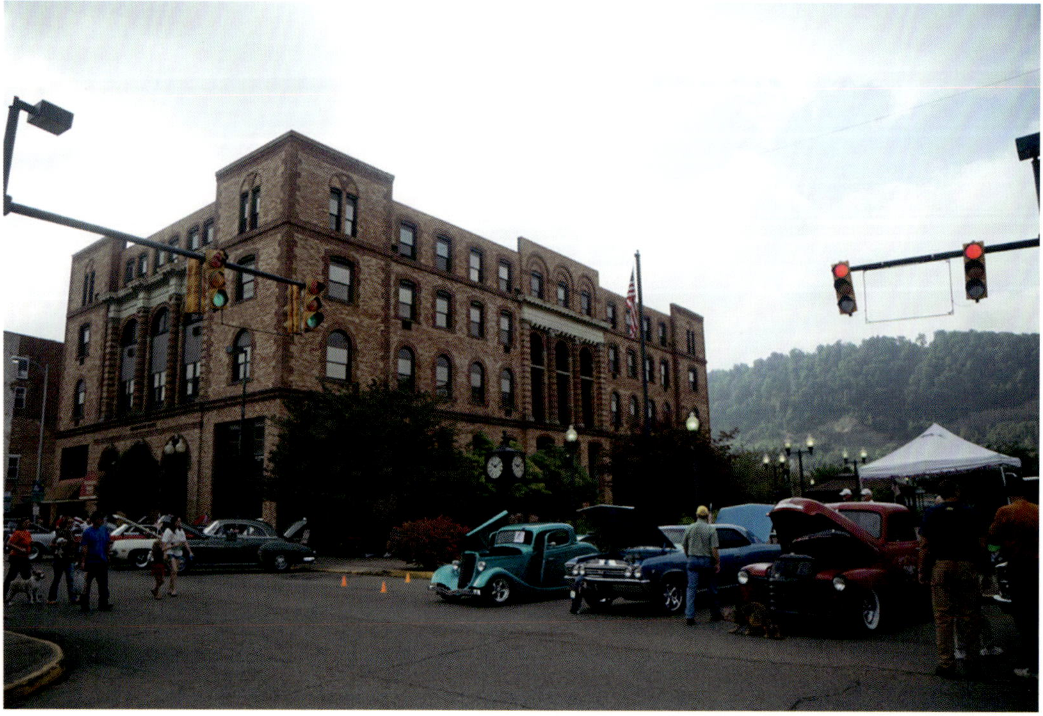

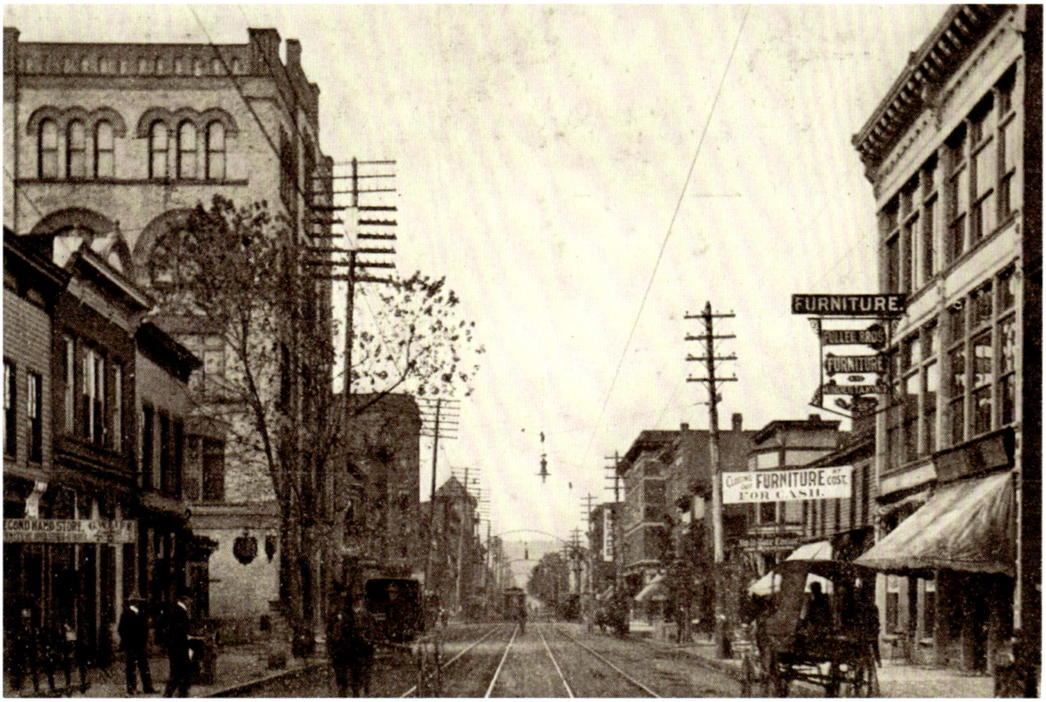

WEST SECOND STREET: Looking east along Second Street are furniture and second hand stores along the streetcar route. At the present time it is possible to pick out buildings along this street that are visible in the above photograph from well over a century ago. Sadly, many of the smaller wooden structures became victims to devastating floods.

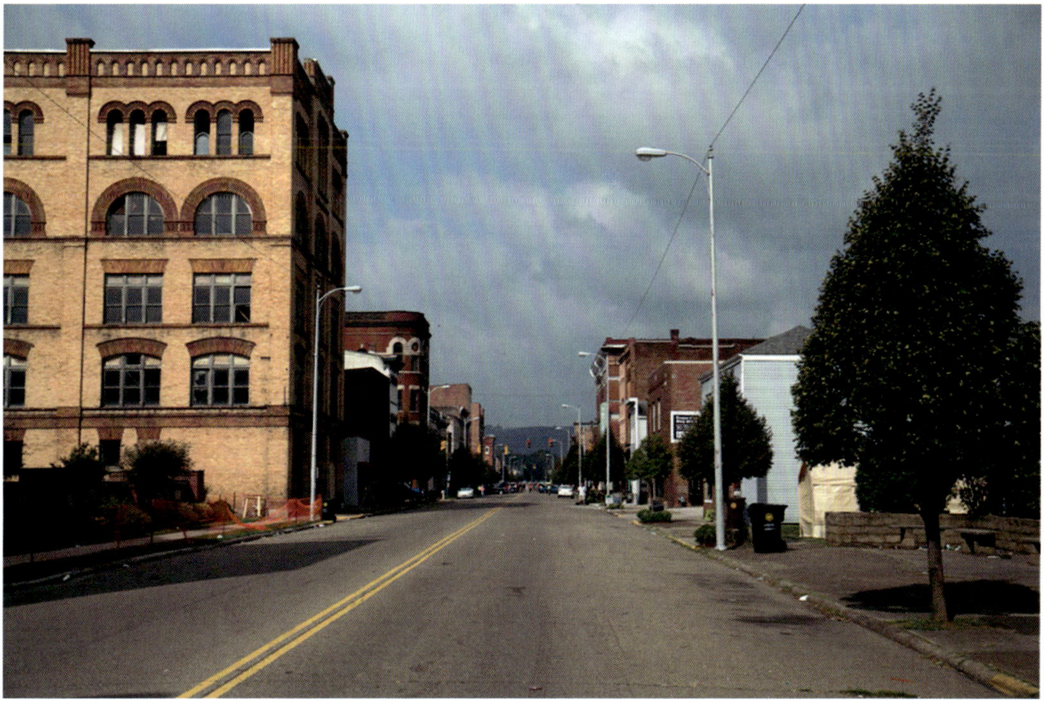

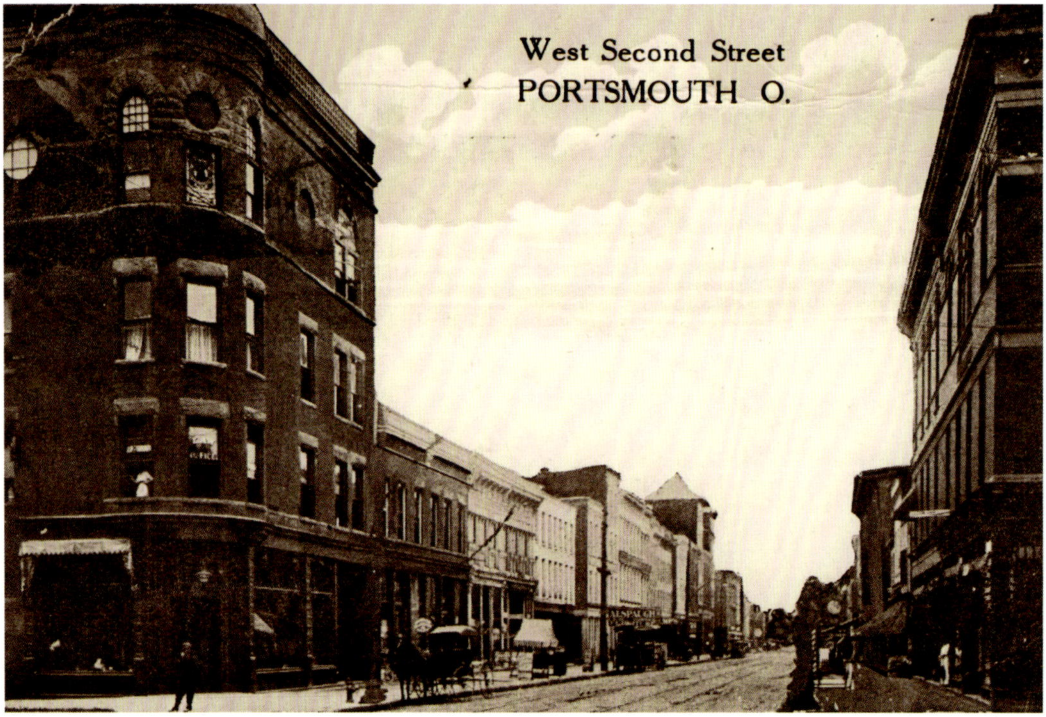

**West Second Street:** Horse and buggies line Second Street looking west in the above postcard photograph from *c.* 1905. The photographer has worked painstakingly on this postcard to erase all traces of telephone, electricity, and streetcar wires.

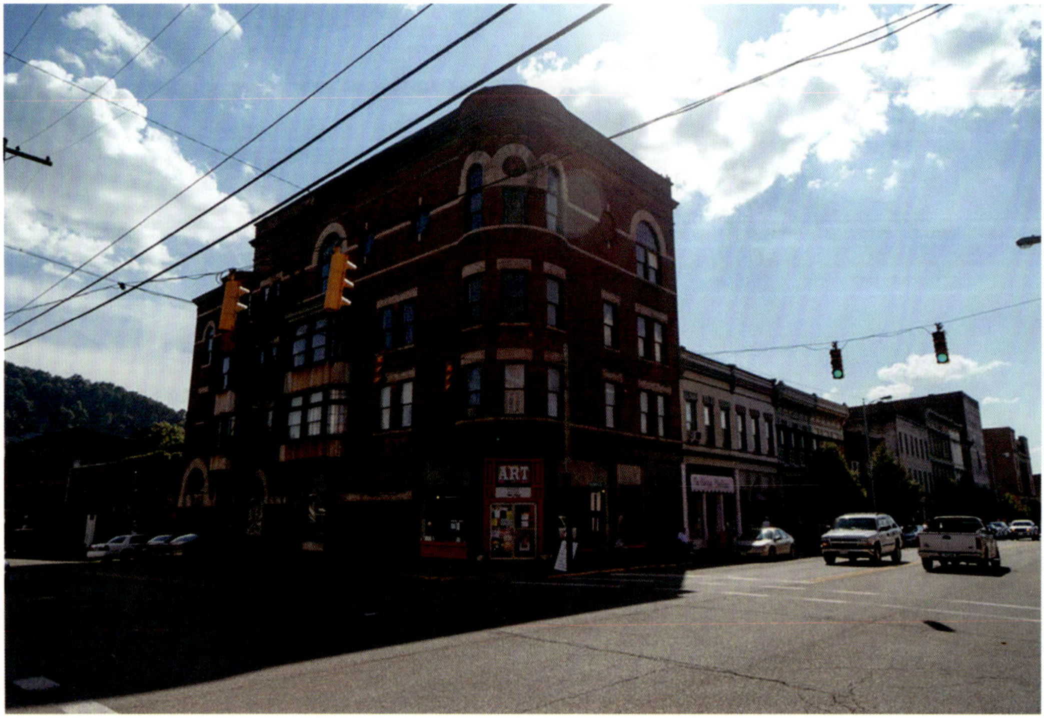

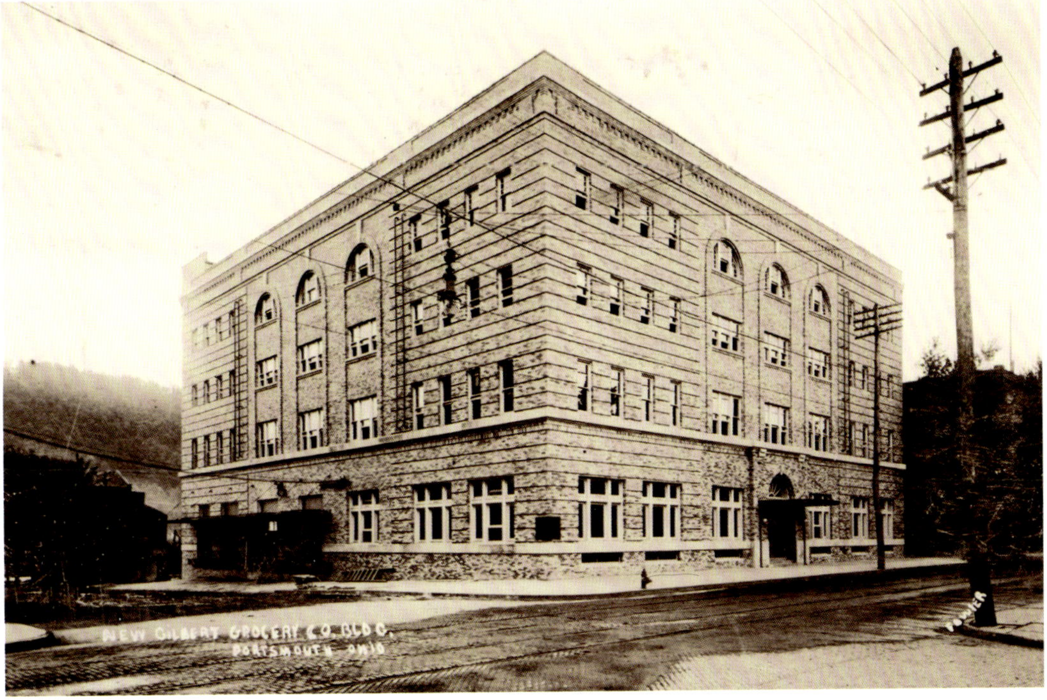

THE GILBERT GROCERY COMPANY WHOLESALE BUILDING: This was an extremely impressive structure when completed *c.* 1913. The original company headquarters was located not far away on Front Street but was completely destroyed by fire in October of 1910. The Gilbert Grocery Company had its beginnings in the early 1830s.

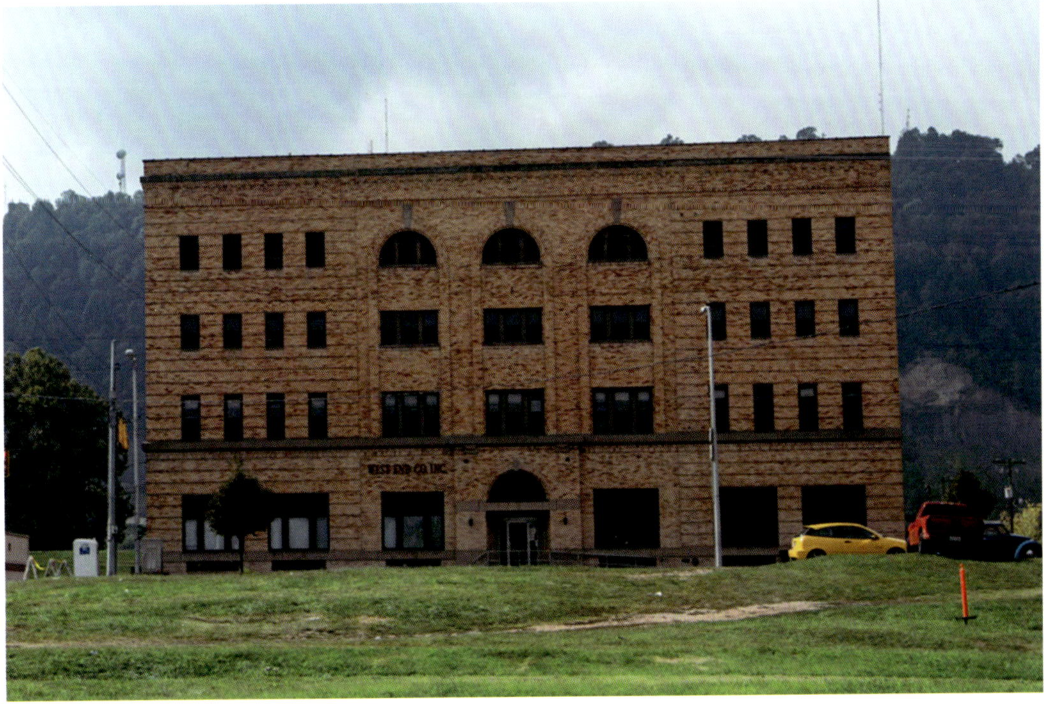

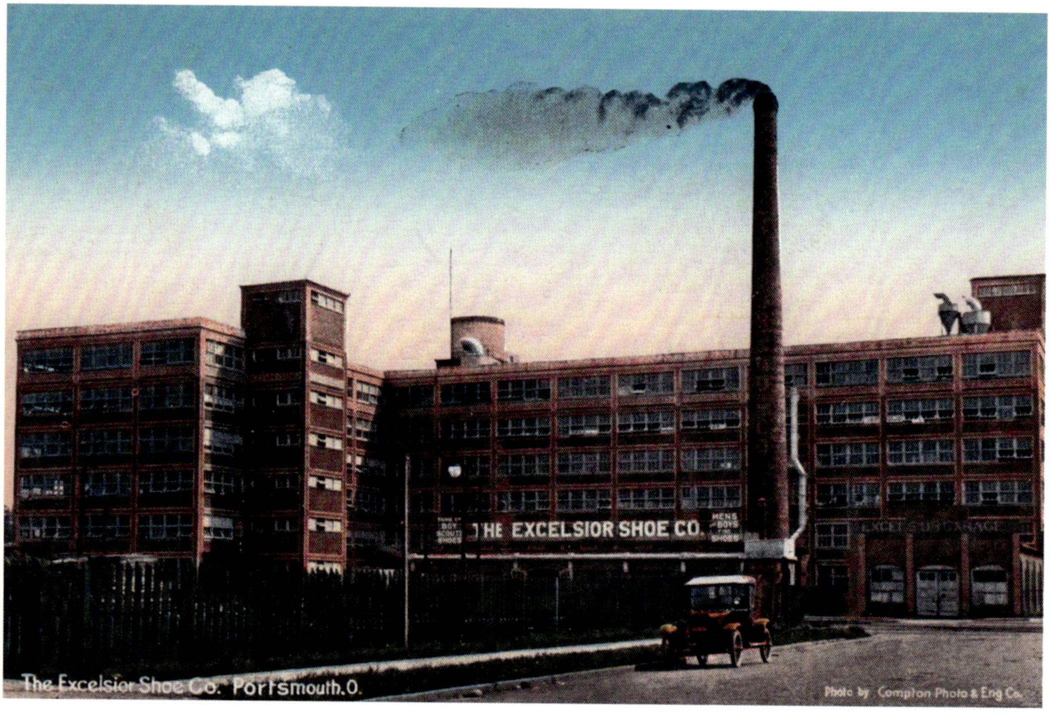

THE EXCELSIOR SHOE COMPANY: In this color postcard from the middle 1920s, the Excelsior Shoe Company is functioning at full capacity. The company was famous for manufacturing men and boy's shoes and boots. Especially popular for the Company was the official Boy Scout shoes with the scout seal on the lining.

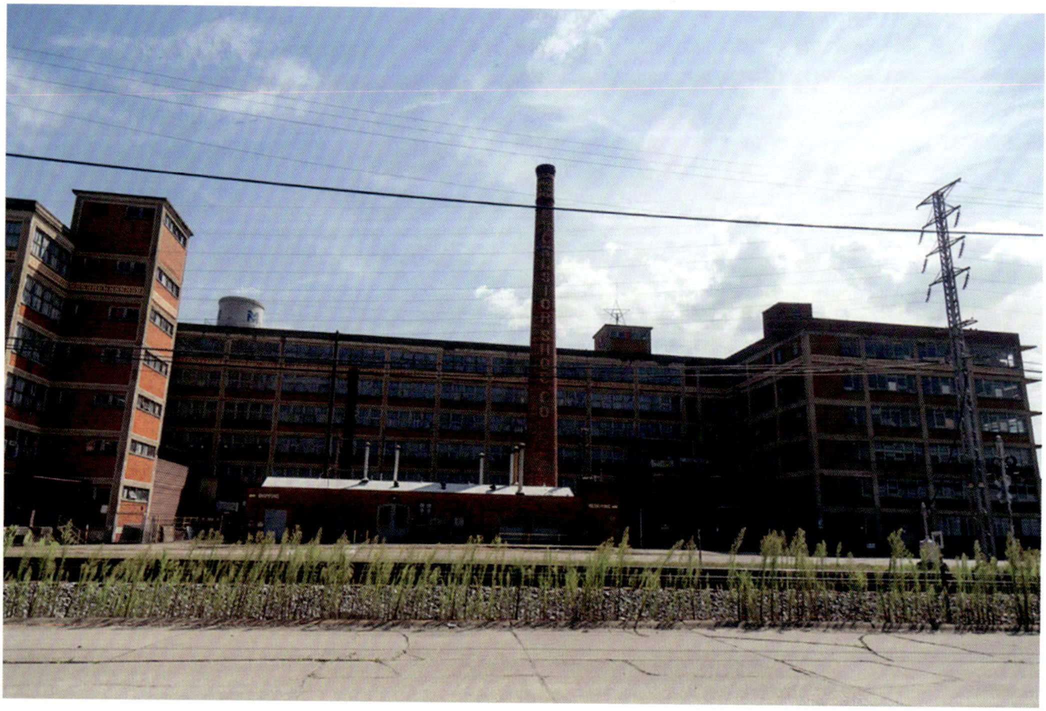

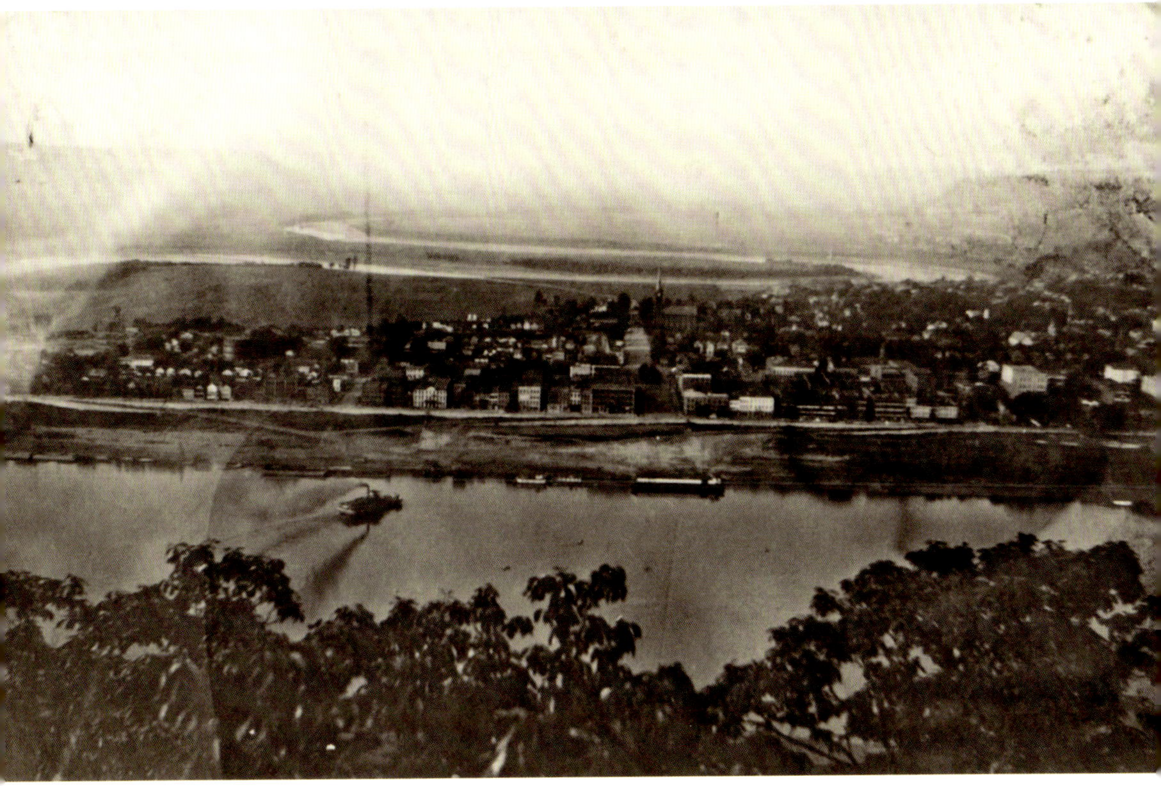

AN AERIAL VIEW: Most of West Portsmouth is visible in this photograph from *c.* 1915. The only way to cross the mighty Ohio River at this time was by steamboat that ran from Front Street near Market Square to South Portsmouth Kentucky.

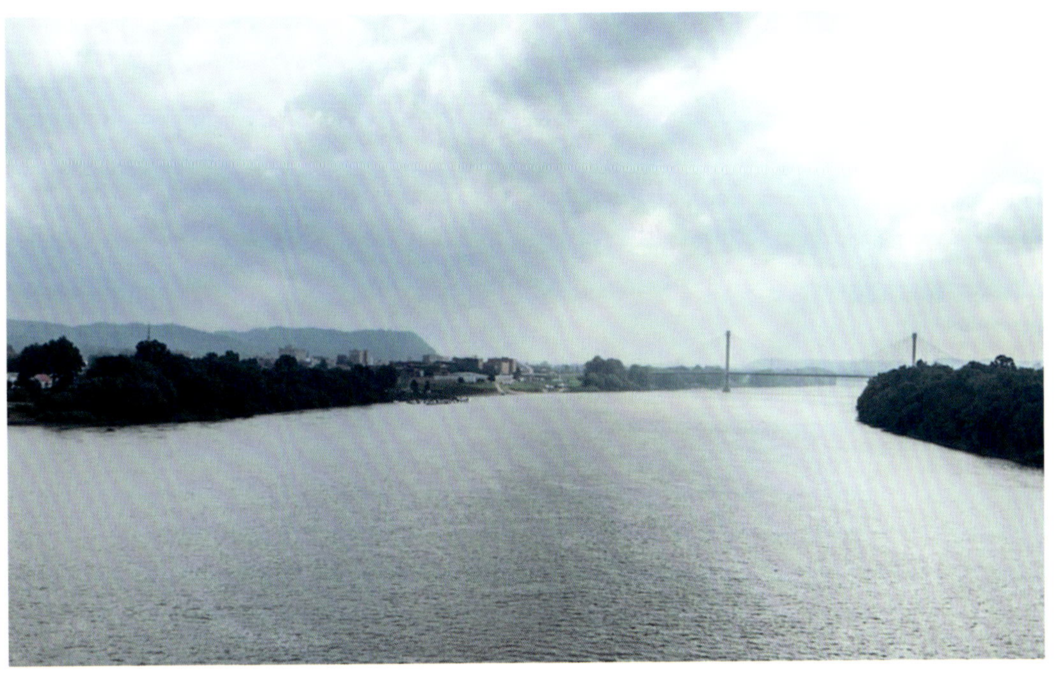

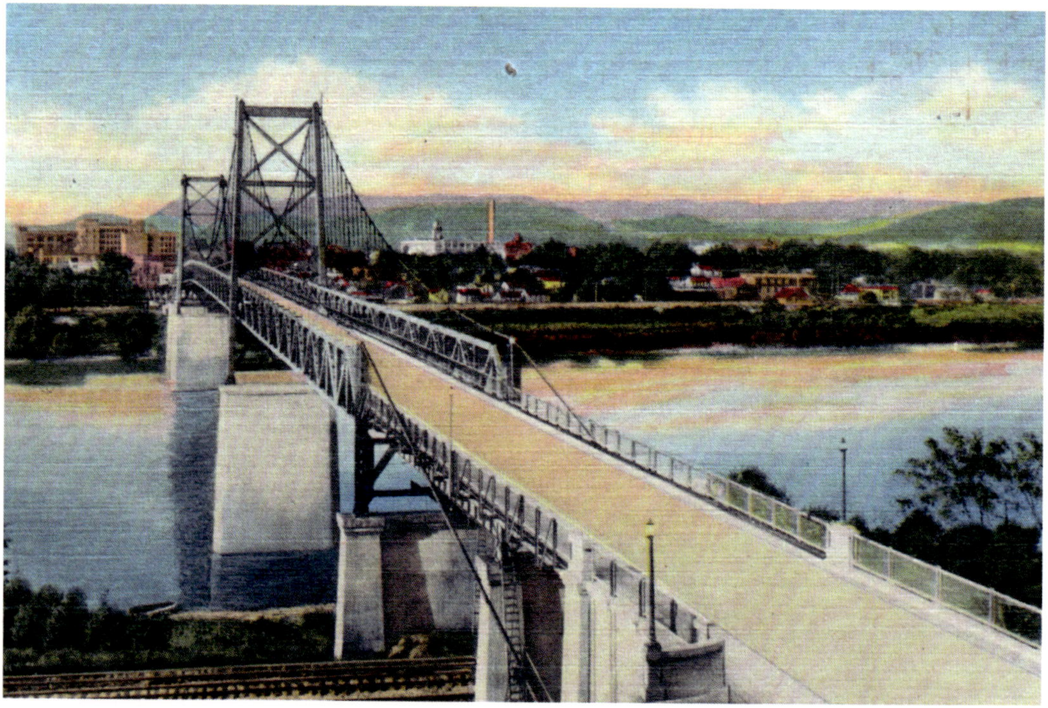

NECESSARY REPAIRS: The older U.S. Grant Bridge close for a couple of years in the late 1970s for repairs which caused a many headaches on both sides of the Ohio River. Together with the new bridge there are two other spans between Greenup County and Scioto County; the Jesse Stuart Memorial Bridge and the Carl Perkins Bridge.

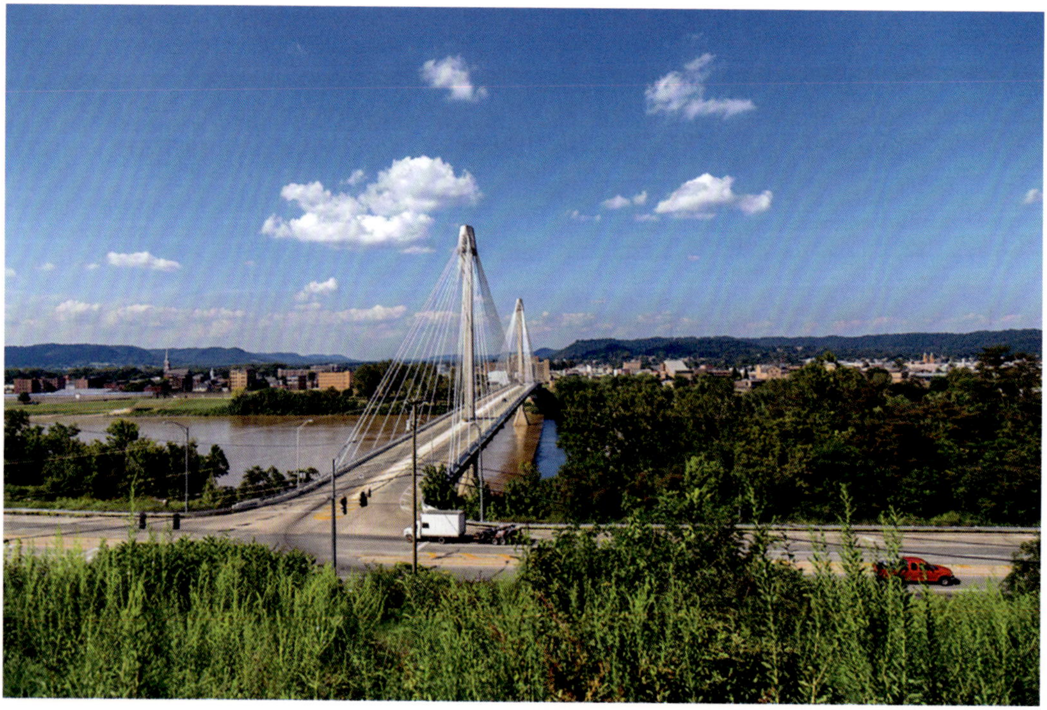

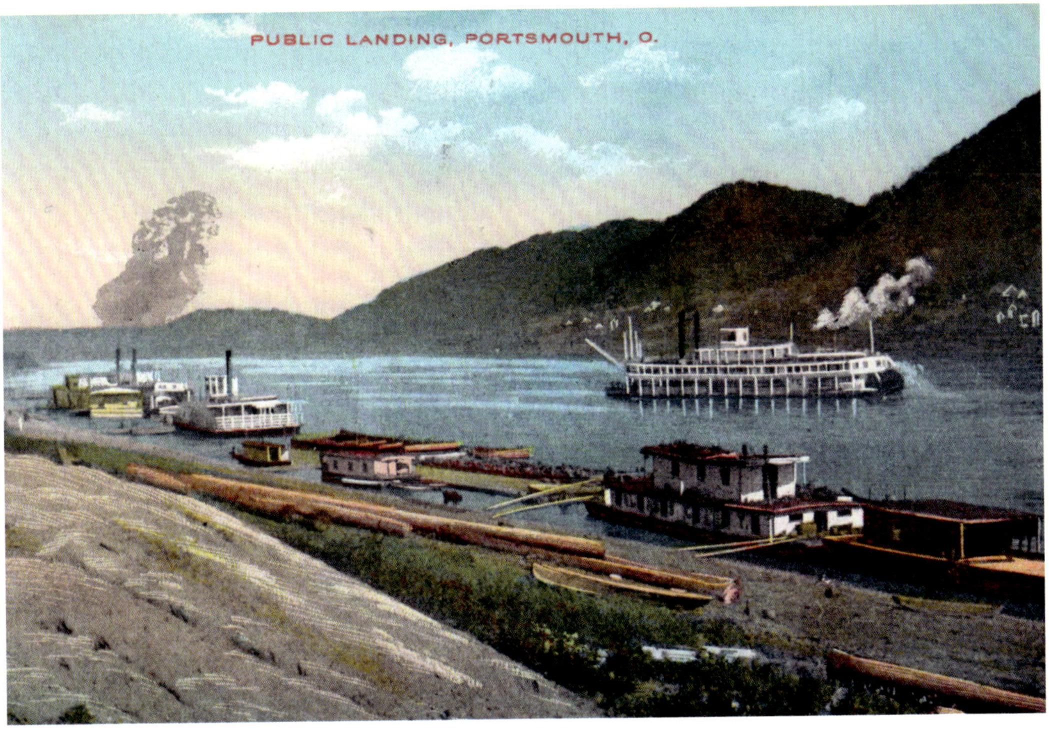

PUBLIC LANDING, PORTSMOUTH, O.

PUBLIC LANDING: From the time that French explorers began to trap for furs and occupy the area, the landing area became the point of arrival and exit for travelers. It was at this point here that village supplies were channeled in prior to the arrival of the railroads.

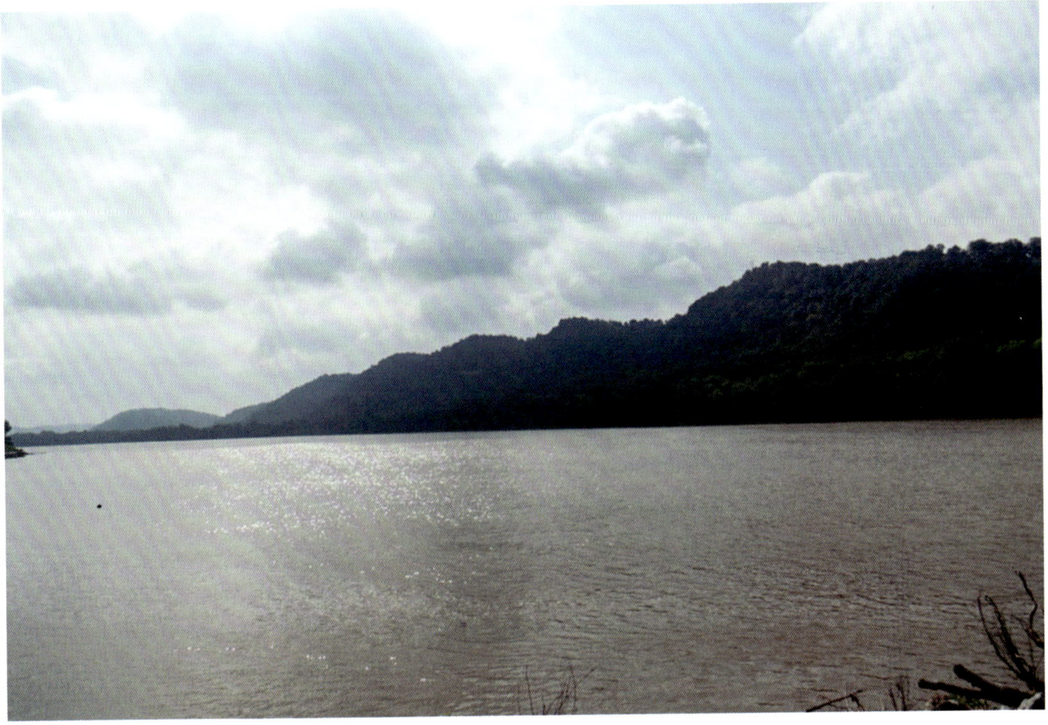

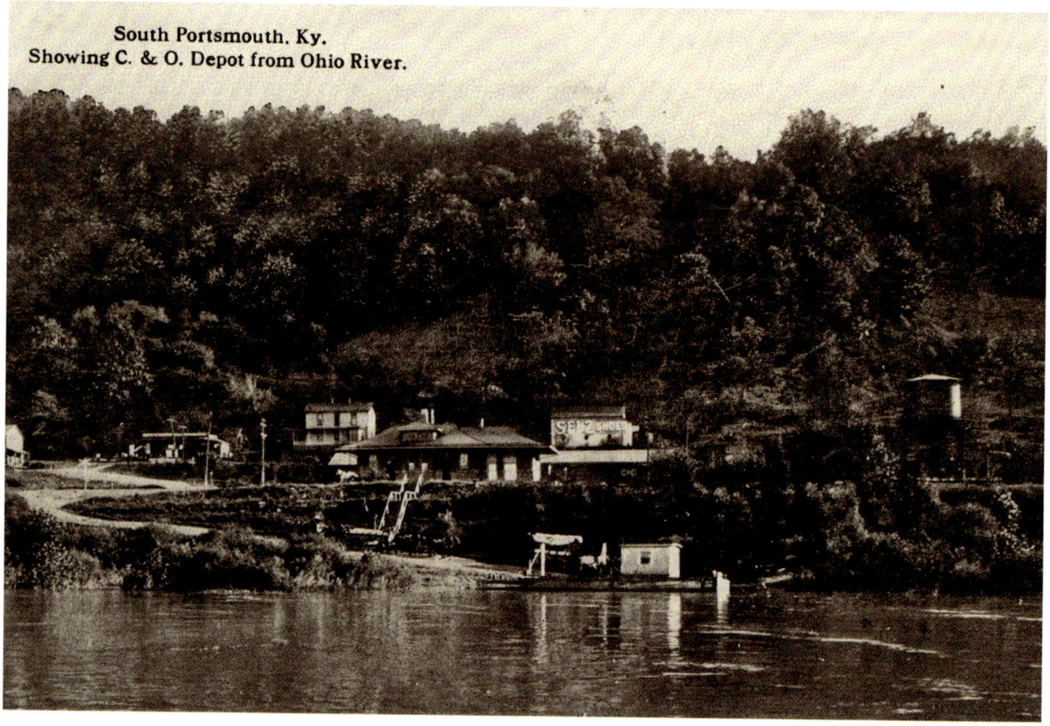

South Portsmouth, Ky.
Showing C. & O. Depot from Ohio River.

SOUTH PORTSMOUTH: Just across the Ohio River from the landing area of Portsmouth is the community of South Portsmouth, Kentucky. It is just a few miles west of the Greenup County city of South Shore. The older post photograph dates from *c.* 1915 and shows the C & O Depot, water tower, and several homes.

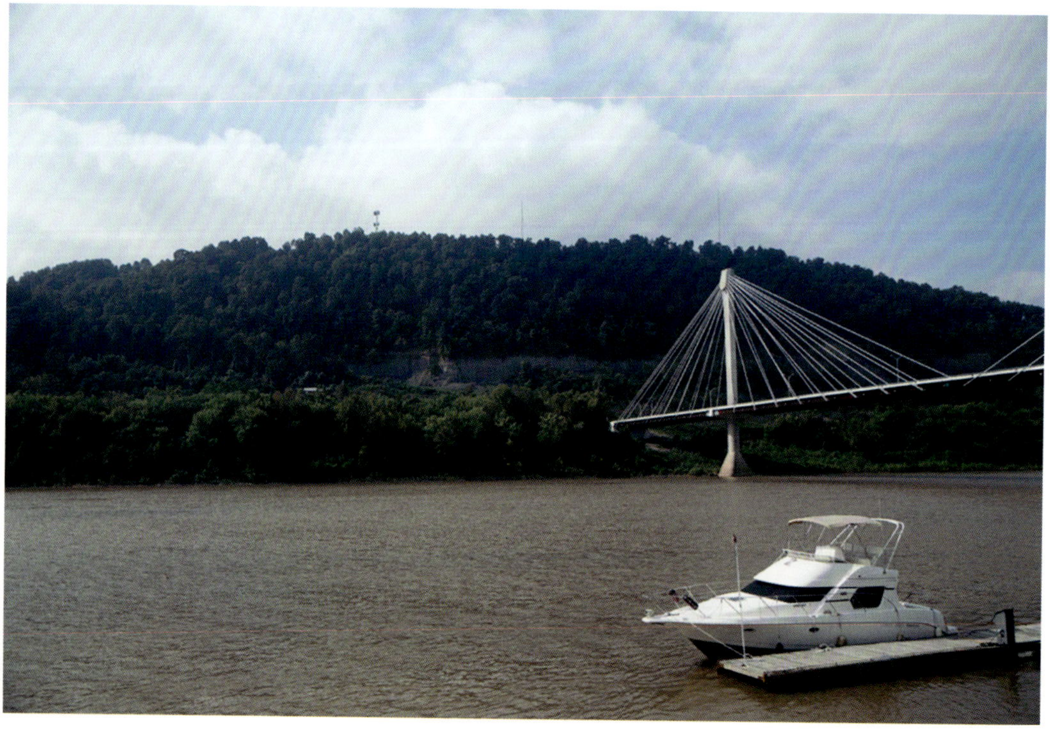

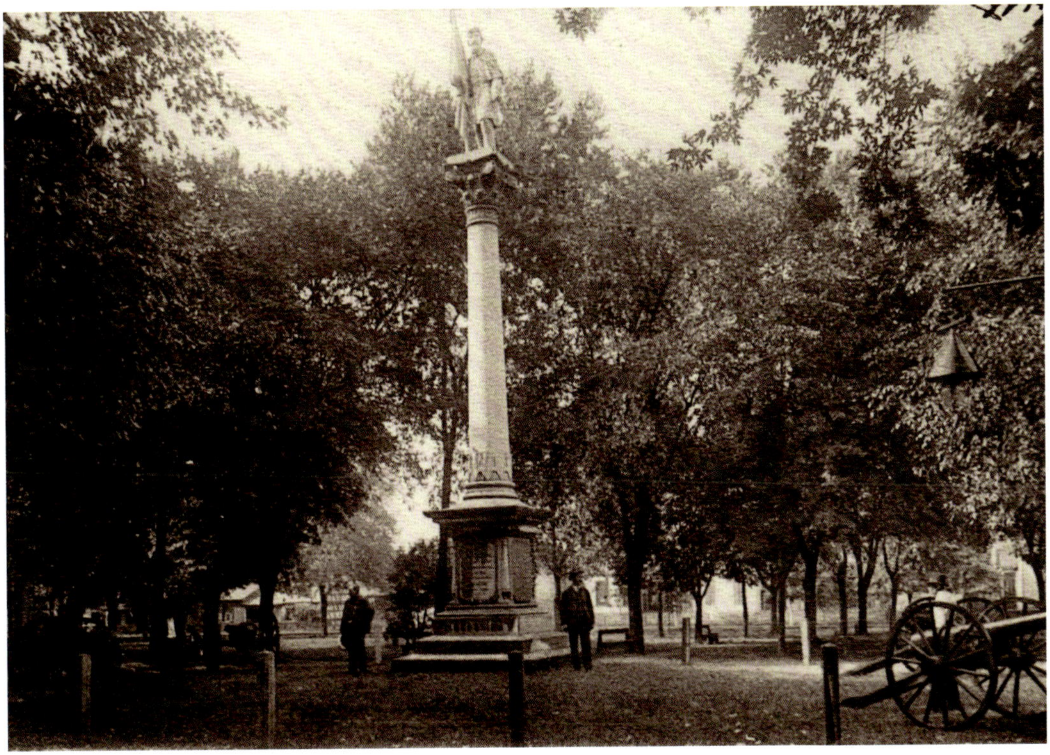

TRACY PARK: The Park, situated between Chillicothe Street and Gay Street, has been an important part of Portsmouth since the late 1870s. Many generations of citizens have enjoyed many picnics and functions over the years there below the union soldier Civil War memorial erected in 1879.

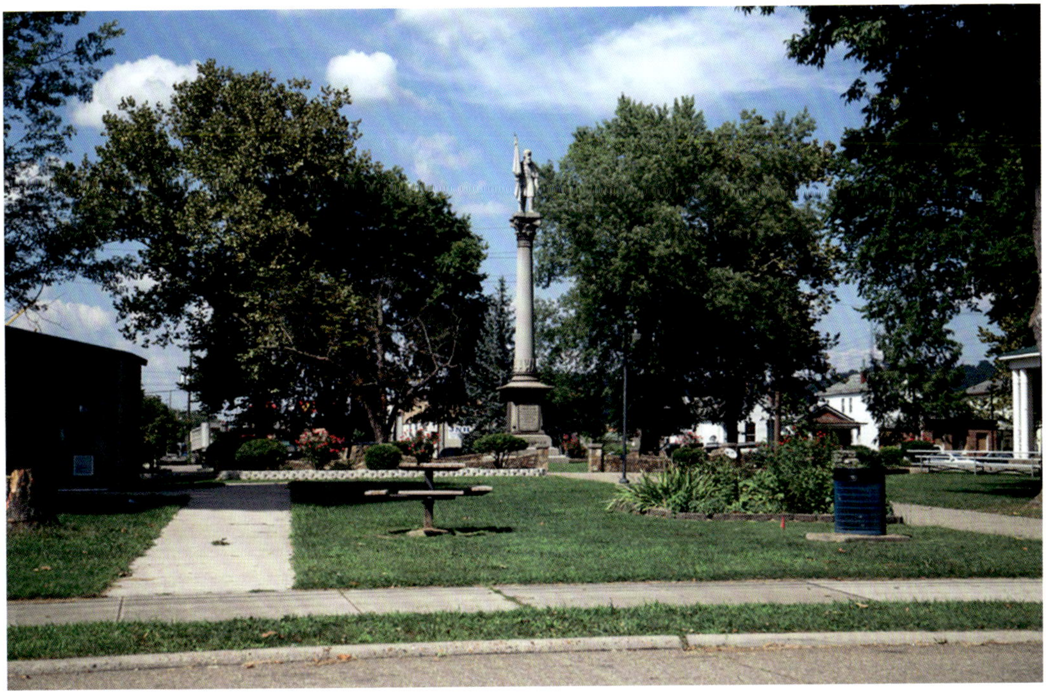

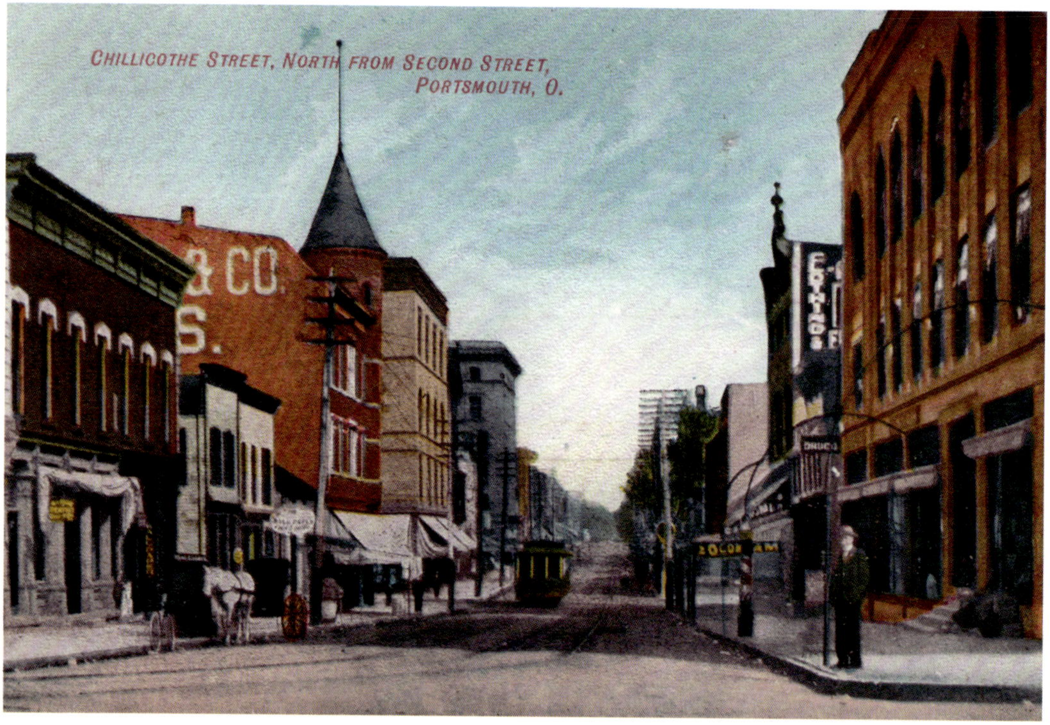

CHILLICOTHE STREET: Running from the Ohio River north through the center of Portsmouth's business district is Chillicothe Street. In the postcard which dates from the early 1900s a streetcar together with tracks running north and south from Second Street can be seen as far as the eye can see looking north.

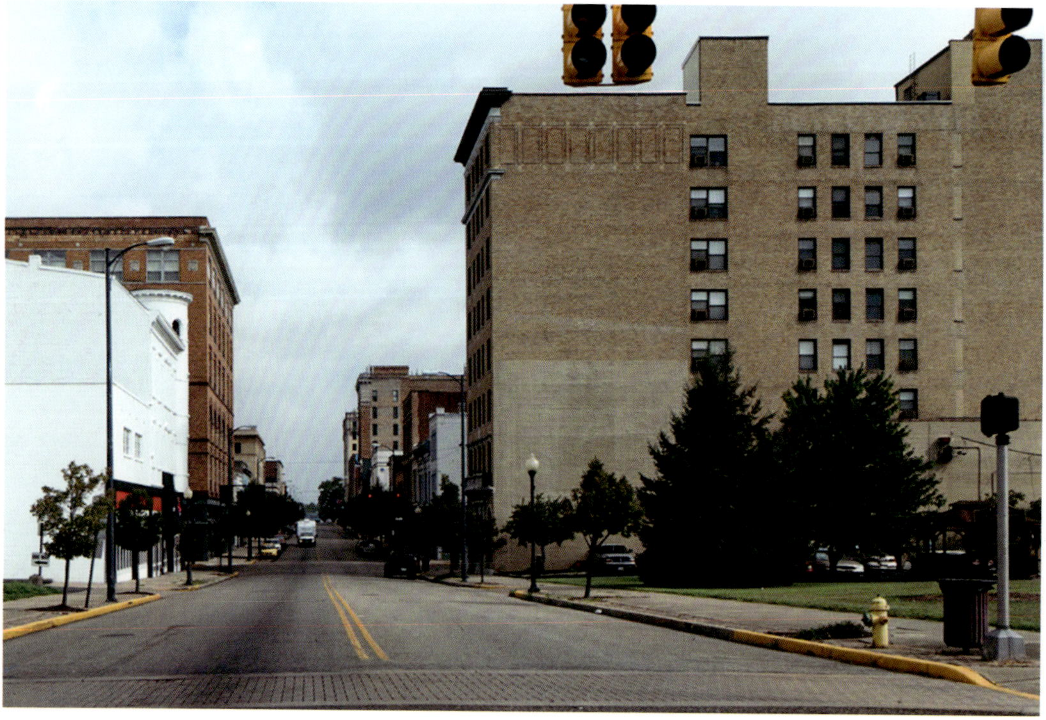

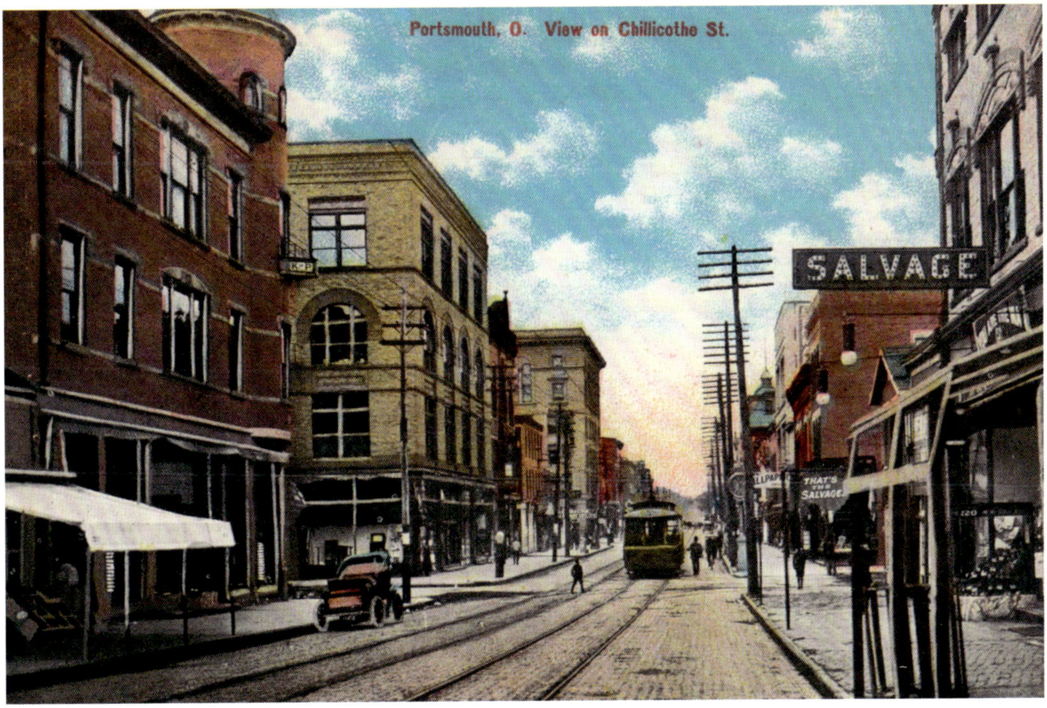

CHILLICOTHE STREET: In this color postcard from *c.* 1915, a bricked Chillicothe Street can be seen with an early automobile parked near the intersection of Third Street. The building on the northwest corner of Third Street and Chillicothe Street has had two more stories added as can be seen in the photograph below.

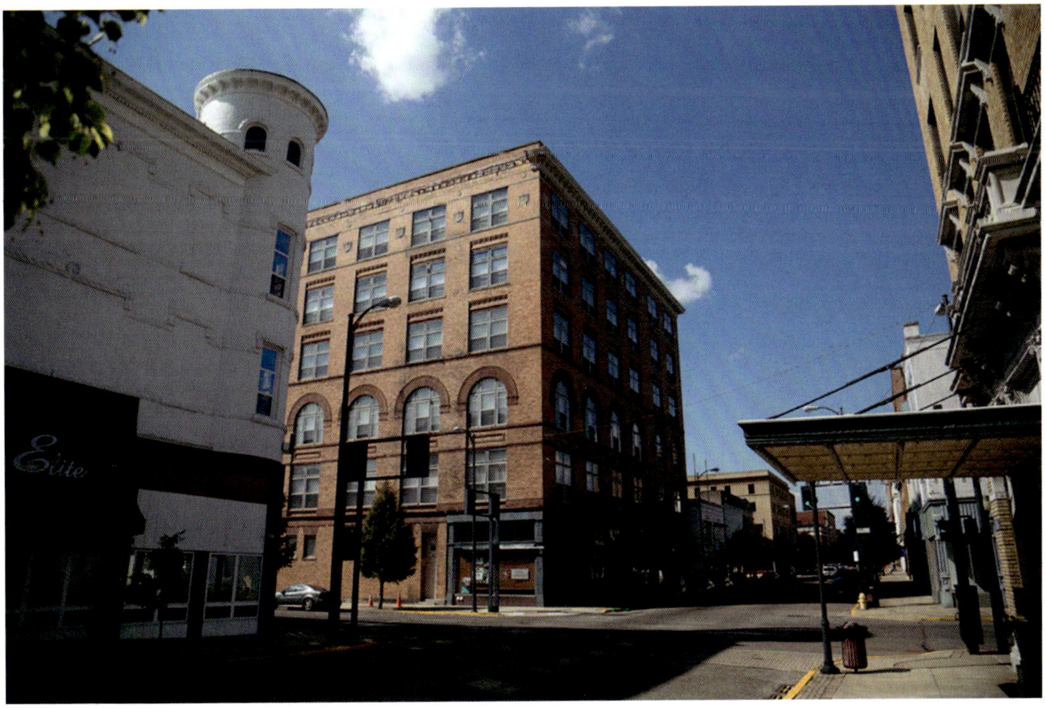

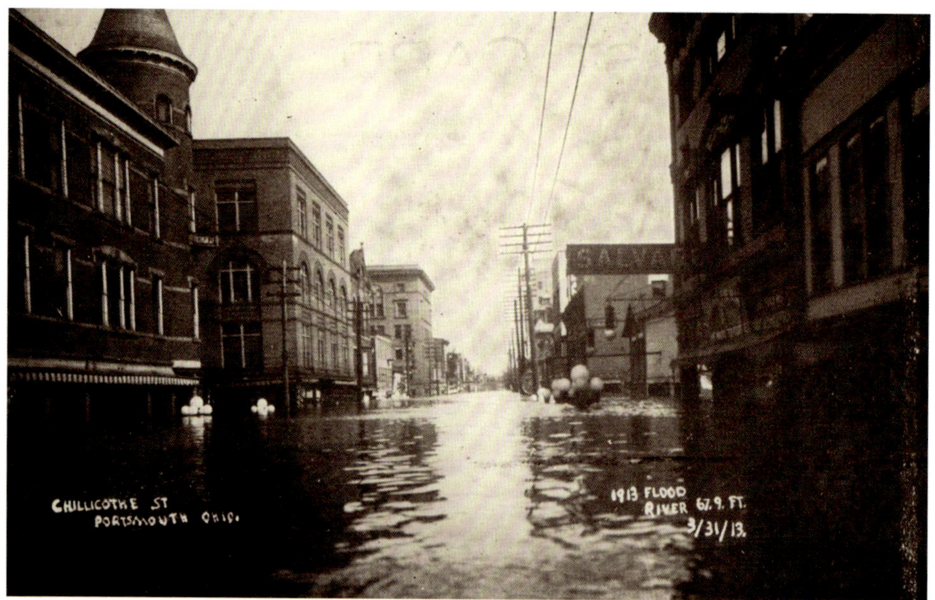


**THE FLOOD OF 1913:** Like all cities along the Ohio River, Portsmouth has been ravaged at various times throughout the city's history. On March 31st 1913 the river reached a height of 67.9 feet in Portsmouth which ruined many of the city's oldest wooden structures. This flood would pale in comparison to the great flood of 1937.

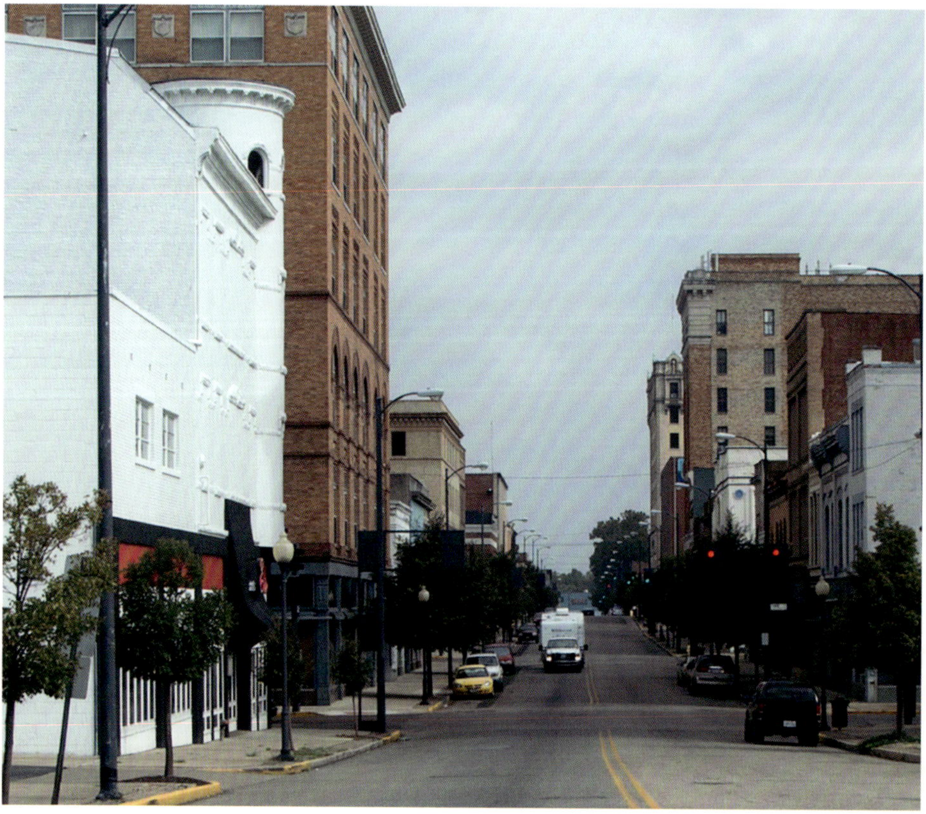

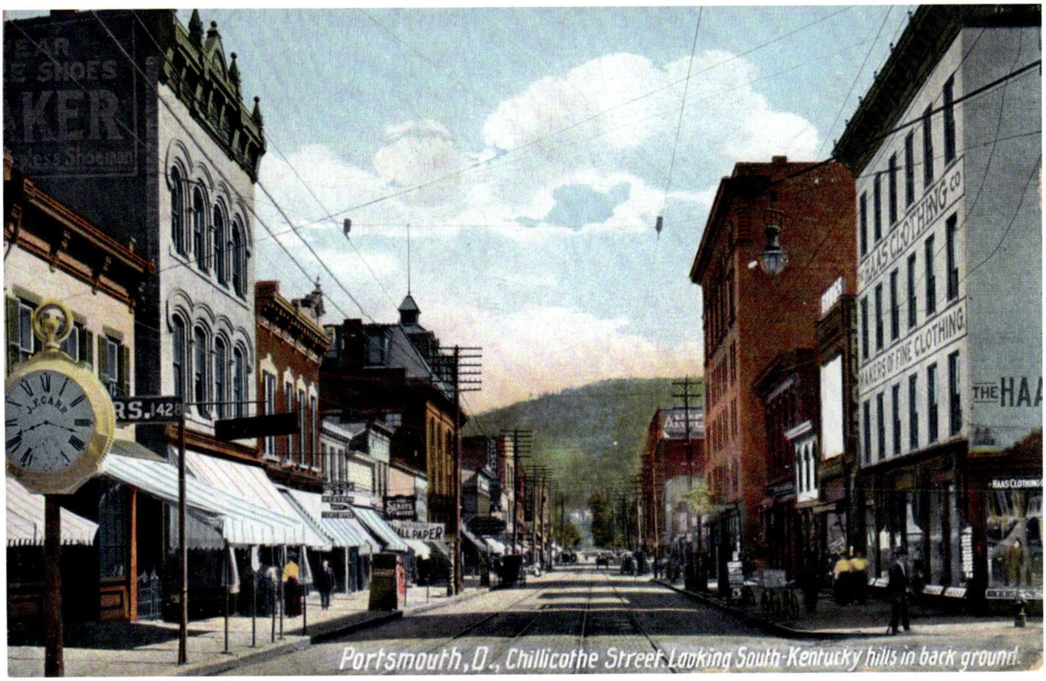

THE KENTUCKY HILLS FROM SOUTH PORTSMOUTH: The hills are visible in the distance looking south along the businesses on Chillicothe Street. This postcard from *c.* 1910 was delicately painted to match the actual color of the buildings, people, and sky.

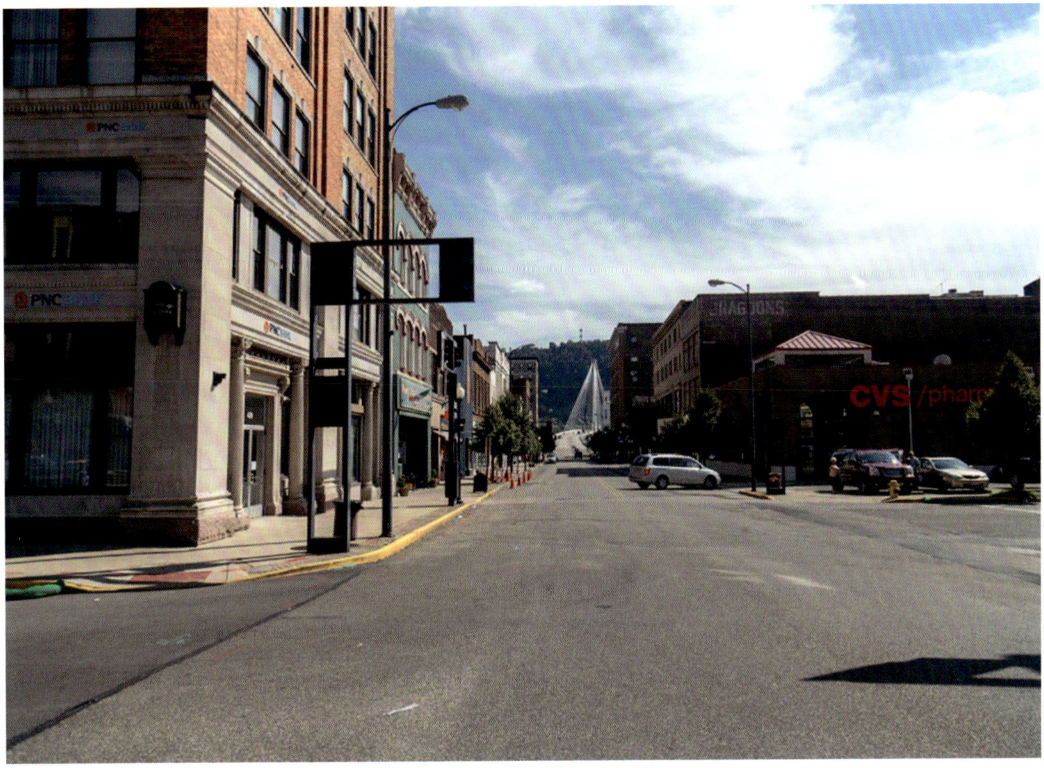

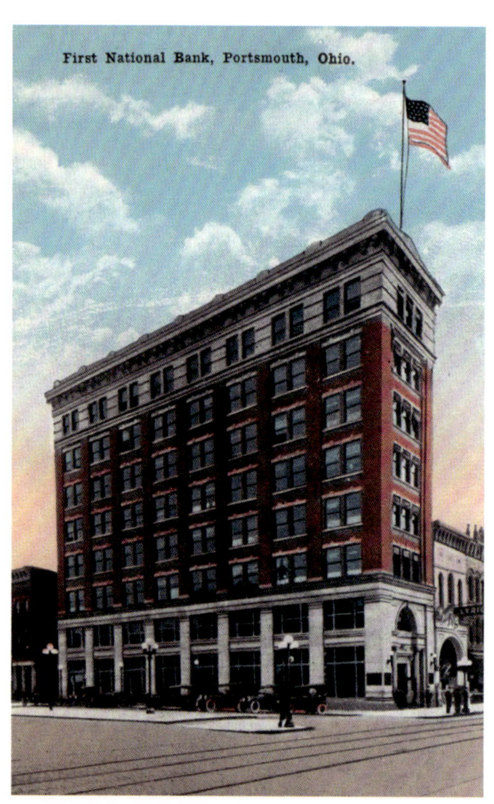


**THE FIRST NATIONAL BANK:** Portsmouth's eight story First National Bank building rises tall above all other structures in this postcard from 1925. At the time of printing this book the building is still being used as a bank by PNC Bank and continues to stand prominently in Government Square.

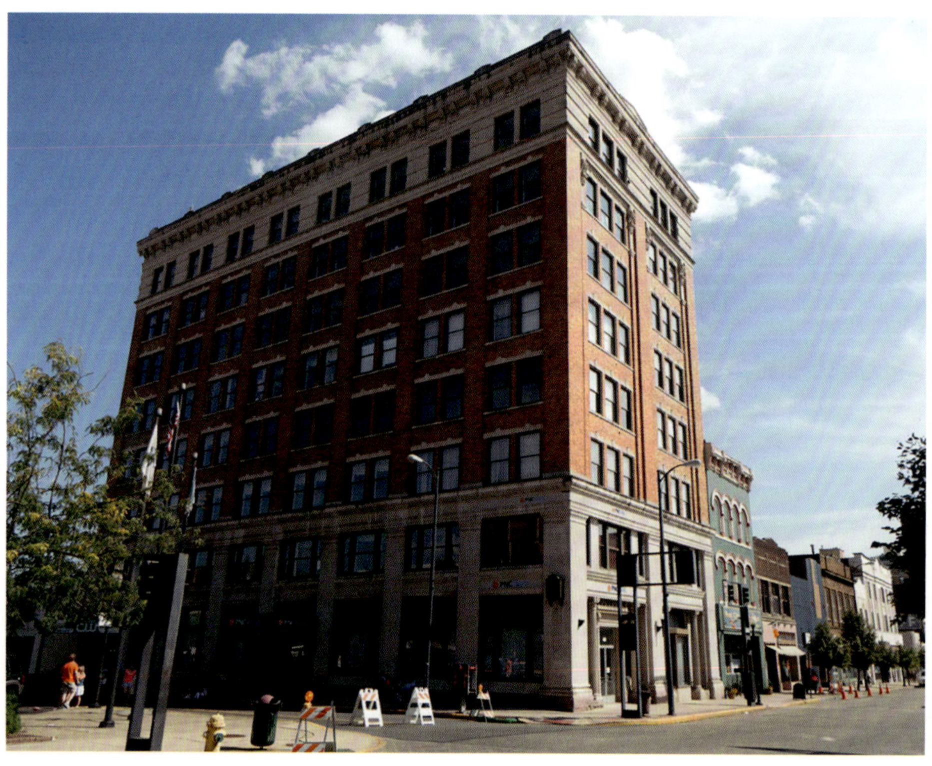

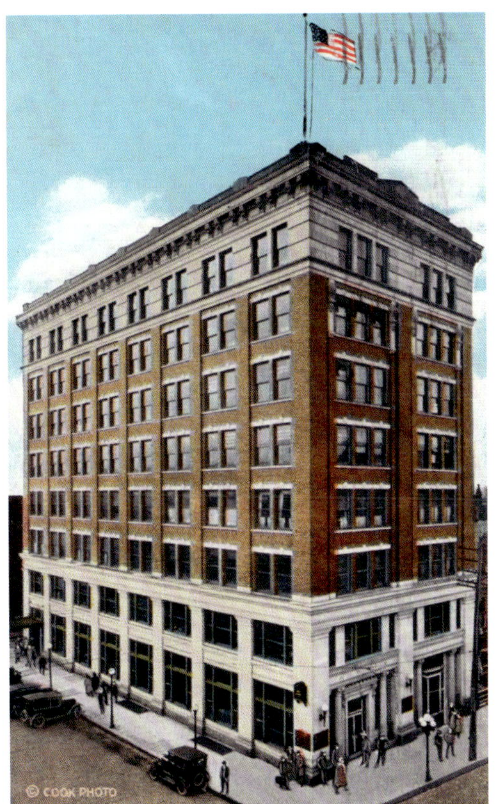


THE FIRST NATIONAL BANK: Completed in 1911 the National Bank building was right in the center of Portsmouth's business district as well as at the southern end of Government Square. A second was added to the northern side of the original building, which doubled the square footage of the structure.

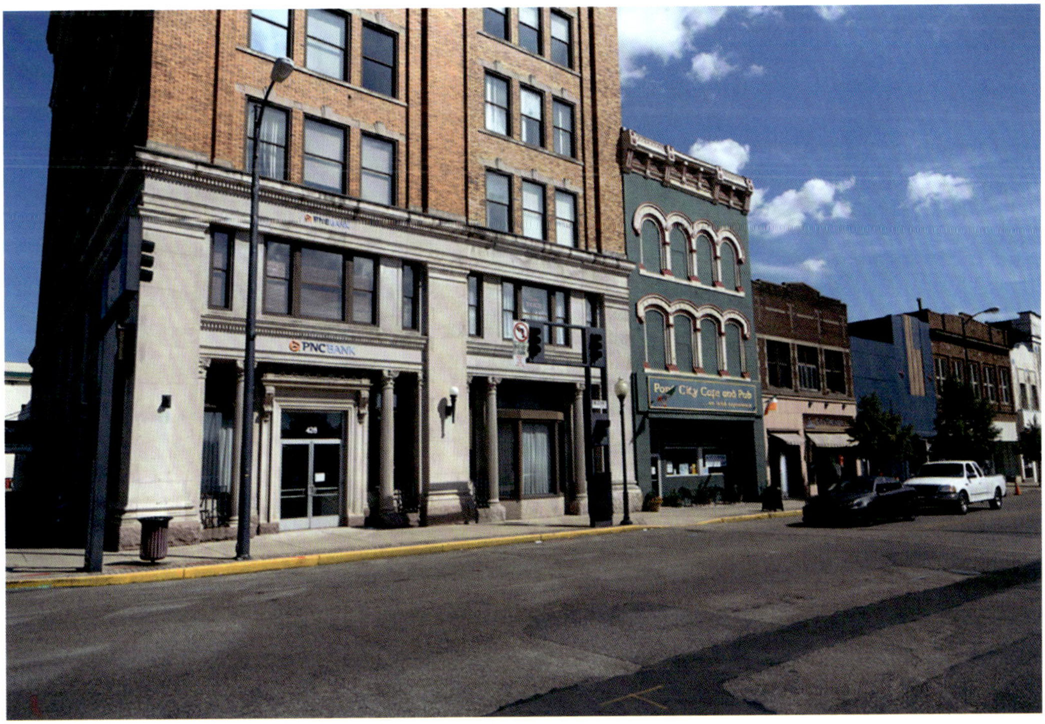

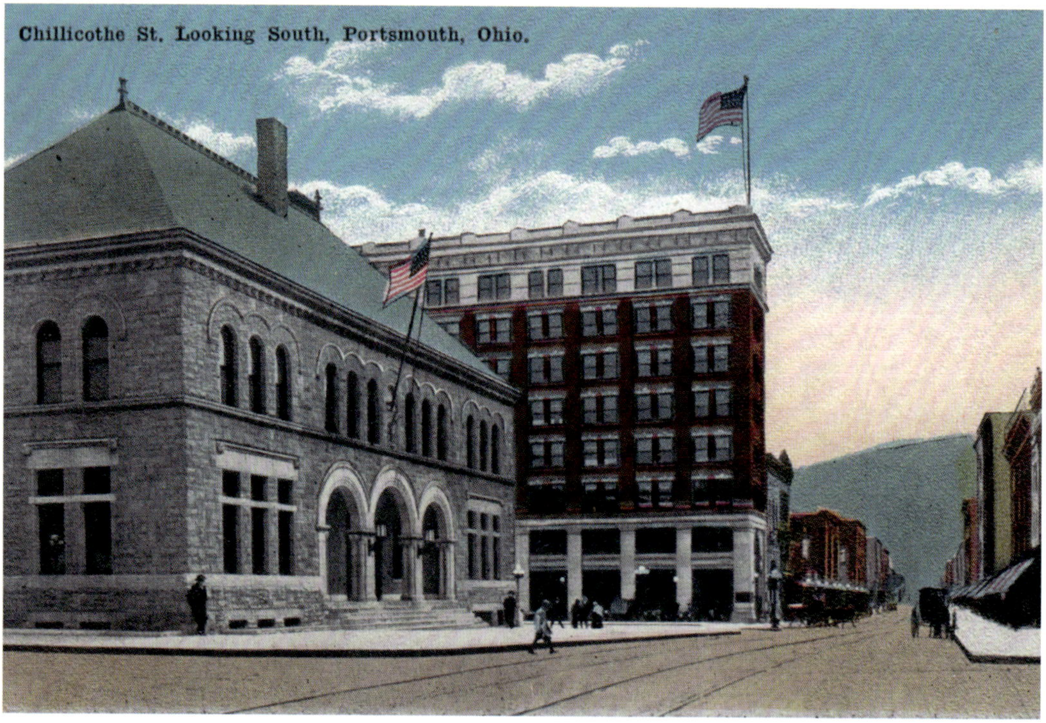

Chillicothe St. Looking South, Portsmouth, Ohio.

THE POST OFFICE: The old post office and National Bank building is seen in this color postcard from 1915 looking south toward the Kentucky hills. The post office was built from limestone quarried in Bedford, Indiana. The building was demolished and replaced in 1936.

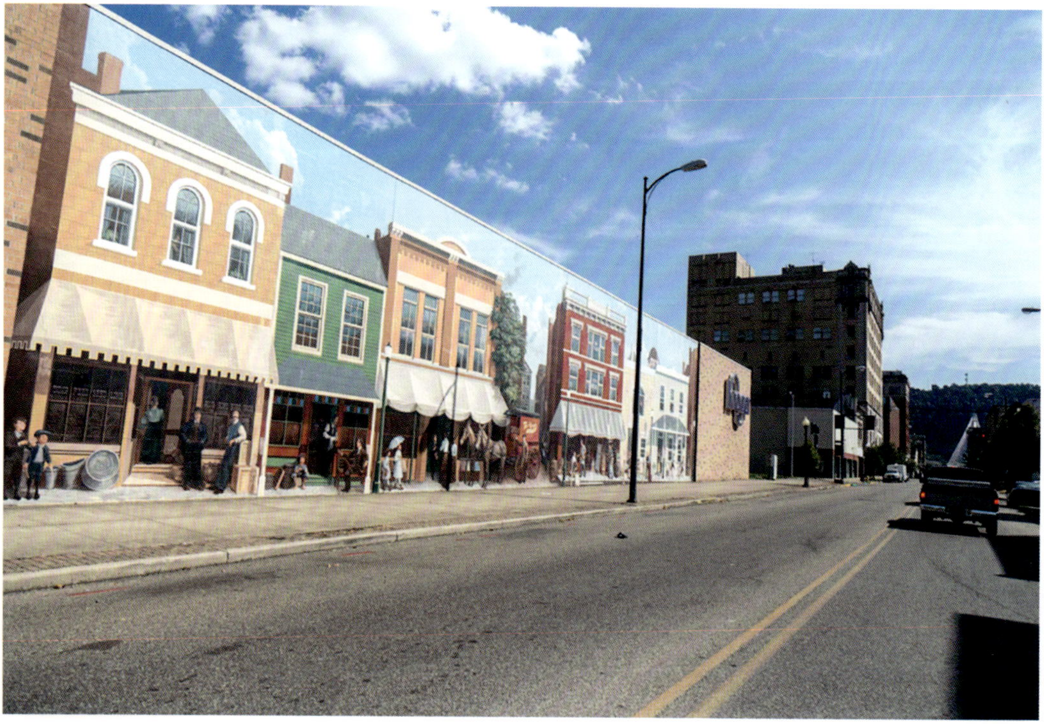

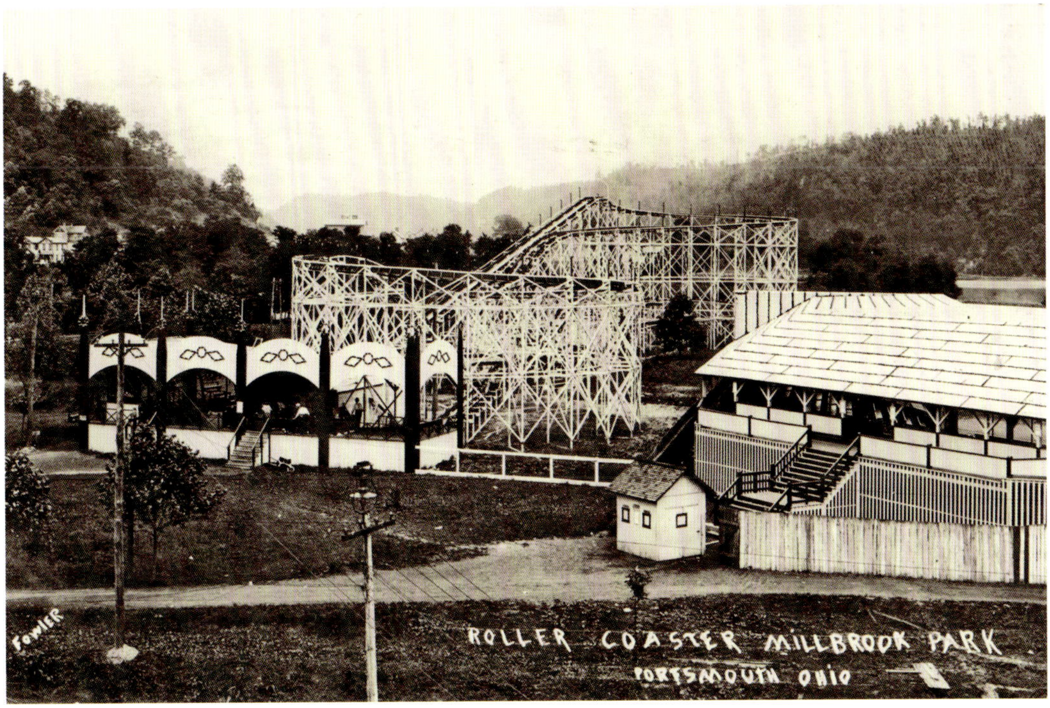

MILLBROOK PARK: The rollercoaster at Millbrook Park was an attraction that brought in many people far and wide to visit the ride and the beautiful park in New Boston. The park rivaled Camden Park in Huntington for fastest rollercoaster in the area. The 1913 and 1937 floods wiped away the rides and the park. Only a token park survives in the area.

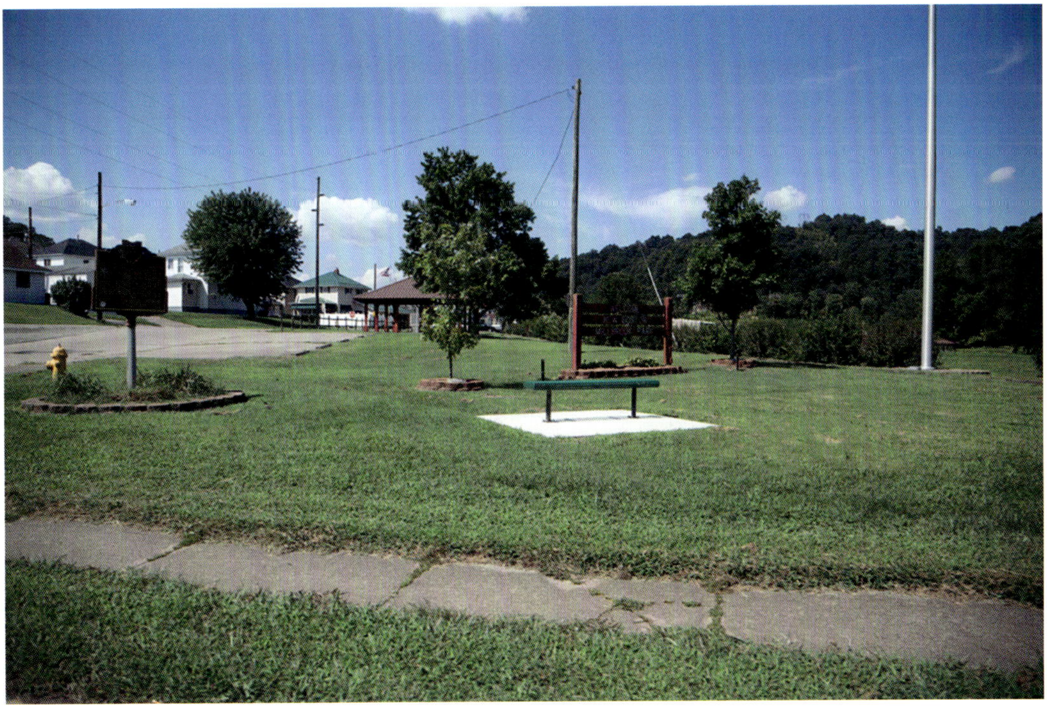

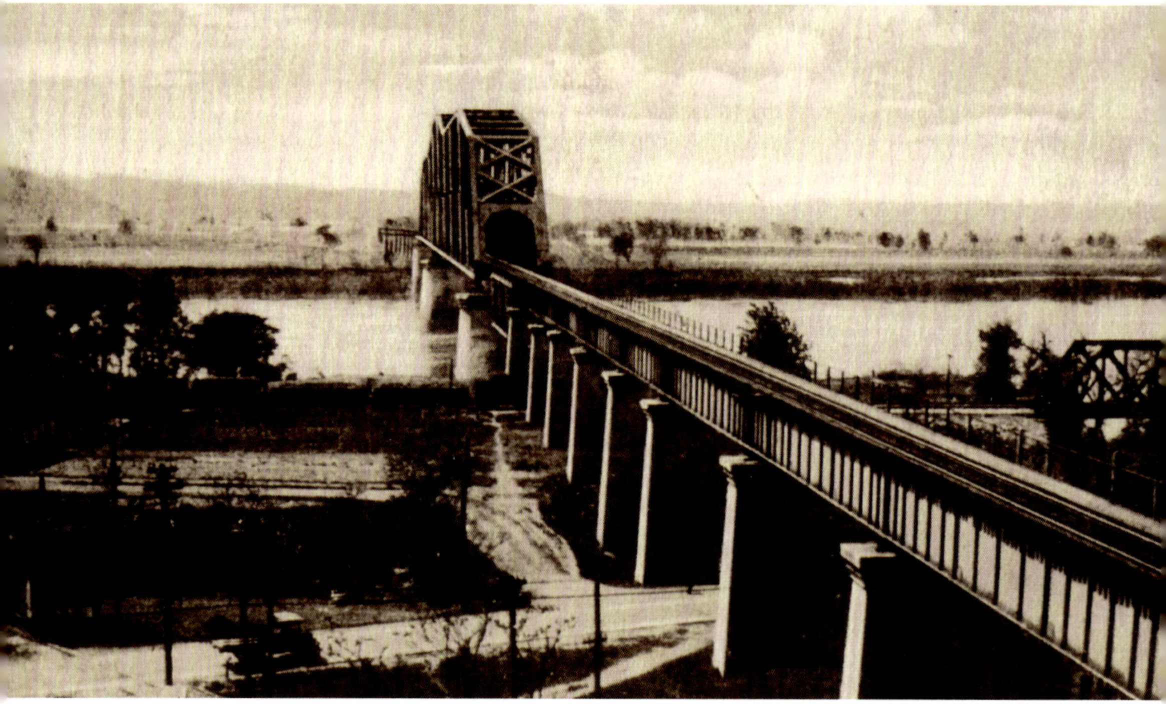

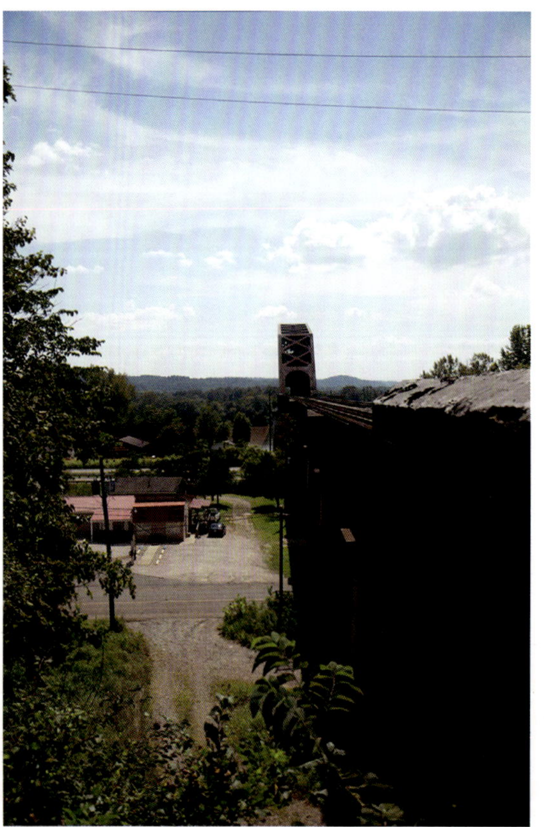

**The Sciotoville Railroad Bridge:** Built in 1917 the Sciotoville Railroad Bridge was considered an architectural marvel when completed over the Ohio River. For a number of years the bridge held the world record for the longest continuous truss bridge. Today the bridge is still in use and is a very impressive span.